Psychology for Actors

Psychology for Actors is a study of modern psychology, specifically designed for the working actor and actor-in-training, that covers discrete areas of psychological theory that actors can apply to their creative process to form and connect with characters. The book investigates many post-Stanislavsky ideas about human psychology from some of the twentieth century's most brilliant minds—from Sigmund Freud and Carl Jung to Abraham Maslow and Ken Wilber—and offers step-by-step exercises to help actors understand their characters and effectively bring them to life on stage or in front of the camera. *Psychology for Actors* also offers advice on how to cope with the stresses and strains of a highly competitive field, and provides tools for deeper self-awareness and character exploration.

Kevin Page is a seasoned professional actor/writer/theorist with a background in psychology, meditation practices, and consciousness research. He is the author of *Advanced Consciousness Training for Actors* (Routledge, 2018). For more information, please visit www.kevin page.com.

Psychology for Actors

Theories and Practices for the Acting Process

Kevin Page

Routledge
Taylor & Francis Group

NEW YORK AND LONDON

First published 2019
by Routledge
711 Third Avenue, New York, NY 10017

and by Routledge
2 Park Square, Milton Park, Abingdon, Oxon, OX14 4RN

Routledge is an imprint of the Taylor & Francis Group, an informa business

Library of Congress Cataloging-in-Publication Data
Names: Page, Kevin, 1958- author.
Title: Psychology for actors : theories and practices for the acting
    process / Kevin Page.
Description: New York, NY : Routledge, 2019. | Includes
    bibliographical references.
Identifiers: LCCN 2018014702| ISBN 9780815352259
    (hardback : alk. paper) | ISBN 9780815352266
    (paperback : alk. paper) | ISBN 9781351130950 (ebook)
Subjects: LCSH: Acting—Psychological aspects. | Psychology.
Classification: LCC PN2071.P78 P347 2019 | DDC 792.02/8019—dc23
LC record available at https://lccn.loc.gov/2018014702

ISBN: 978-0-8153-5225-9 (hbk)
ISBN: 978-0-8153-5226-6 (pbk)
ISBN: 978-1-351-13095-0 (ebk)

Typeset in Giovanni
by Swales & Willis Ltd, Exeter, Devon, UK

For my father, Dr. Monte M. Page, who both gave and saved my life.
Thanks, Daddy . . .

Contents

Acknowledgments

As with any book that endeavors to break fresh ground, *Psychology for Actors* was made stronger and more complete by the contributions of several individuals and institutions. I cannot thank them enough, but I can acknowledge their assistance and generosity in making this effort possible.

First, to my multiple mentors in both psychology and acting. I would like to thank and acknowledge, in particular, the following individuals and institutions. In no particular order: James Fadiman and Robert Frager, both, at one time or another, from the Institute of Transpersonal Psychology. Ken Wilber of the Integral Institute (and the Red Rooster Restaurant . . .). Kevin Paul Hofeditz, who first taught me movement for the stage and is now teaching me movement for academia.

My fearless editor at Routledge, Stacey Walker, and our wonderful editorial assistant, Lucia Accorsi.

Hillevi Ruumet, for guidance and editorial help with the psychology material.

Richard Feldman from the Julliard School. And the numerous master acting teachers I interviewed during 2017 that pointed out the need for a book such as this: Rhonda Blair, Jack Greenman, and Blake Hackler, all from SMU Meadows School of the Arts. Lucy Skilbeck, Director of Actor Training at the Royal Academy of Dramatic Art (RADA). Kristin Linklater, master voice teacher and author of *Freeing the Natural Voice*, as well as the Founder and Director of the Kristin Linklater Voice Centre in Orkney, Scotland. Catherine Fitzmaurice, creator of Fitzmaurice Voicework and Saul Kotzubei, who, in addition to being Catherine's son, also runs the Fitzmaurice Institute. Phillip Zarrilli, master acting teacher and cultivator of consciousness. Scott Illingworth and Mark Wing-Davey, Theatre Department Chair and Arts Professor at NYU's Tisch School of the Arts. Sharon M. Carnicke, author of *Stanislavsky in Focus: An Acting Master for the Twenty-First Century* (2nd ed., Routledge, 2009), Natsuko Ohama, and preeminent actor David Warshofsky, all from the USC School of Dramatic Arts. Barbara Marchant and Danielle Liccardo-Massood from Rutgers' Mason Gross School of the Arts. Tony McKay of Carnegie Mellon University. Melissa

Smith, Conservatory Director of the American Conservatory Theater. Josh Foldy from North Carolina School of the Arts. Peter Zazzali, Assistant Professor and Artistic Director of Kansas Repertory Theatre at the University of Kansas. R. Andrew White, Professor of Theatre at Valparaiso University. John Lutterbie and Amy Cook from Stony Brook University. Neal Utterback from Juniata College. Rick Kemp, Head of Acting and Directing at Indiana University of Pennsylvania and author of the awesome *Embodied Acting: What Neuroscience Tells Us About Performance* (Routledge, 2012).

A special thanks to the many authors, theorists, and publishers who have allowed me to quote from their copyrighted work in building my own case (parenthetical dates represent year of copyright notice):

Carnicke, S. M. (2009). *Stanislavsky in Focus: An Acting Master for the Twenty-First Century* (2nd ed.). London/New York: Routledge. Reprinted with permission of Routledge.

Erikson, E. H. (1964). *Childhood and Society* (2nd ed.). New York: W. W. Norton & Co. Reprinted with permission of W. W. Norton & Co.

Frager, R., & Fadiman, J. (2005). *Personality and Personal Growth* (6th ed.). New York: Pearson Education. Reprinted by permission of Pearson Education, Inc.

Gurung, R. A. R., Hackathorn, J., Enns, C., Frantz, S., Cacioppo, J. T., Loop, T., & Freeman, J. E. (2016). Strengthening introductory psychology: a new model for teaching the introductory course. *American Psychologist*, 71(2), 112–124. doi:10.1037/a0040012

Horney, K. (1939). *New Ways in Psychoanalysis*. New York: W. W. Norton & Co. Reprinted by permission of W. W. Norton & Co.

Jung, C. G., Excerpt(s) from *Memories, Dreams, Reflections*, translated by Richard and Clara Winston, edited by Aniela Jaffe, translation copyright © 1961, 1962, 1963 and renewed 1989, 1990, 1991 by Penguin Random House LLC. Used by permission of Pantheon Books, an imprint of the Knopf Doubleday Publishing Group, a division of Penguin Random House LLC. All rights reserved.

Jung, C. G., & Shamdasani, S. (2009). *The Red Book: Liber Novus*. New York: W.W. Norton & Co. Reprinted by permission of W. W. Norton & Co.

Maslow, A. H., & Frager, R. (1987). *Motivation and Personality* (3rd ed.). New York: Harper & Row. © 1954, 1987 by Harper & Row, Publishers, Inc.; Reprinted by permission of Pearson Education, Inc.

Maslow, A. H., & Frager, R. (1970). *Motivation and Personality* (2nd ed.). New York: Harper & Row. © 1954 by Harper & Row, Publishers, Inc., 1970 by Abraham H. Maslow; Reprinted by permission of Pearson Education, Inc.

Maslow, A. H. (1968). *Toward a Psychology of Being*. Hoboken, NJ: Wiley. Republished with permission of John Wiley & Sons, Inc., from permission conveyed through Copyright Clearance Center, Inc.

Stanislavsky, K., & Benedetti, J. (2008). *An Actor's Work: A Student's Diary*. London/New York: Routledge. Reprinted with permission of Routledge.

Urbina, S. (2014). *Essentials of Psychological Testing* (2nd ed.). Hoboken, NJ: Wiley. Republished with permission of John Wiley and Sons, Inc., from permission conveyed through Copyright Clearance Center, Inc.

Varela, F. J., Thompson, E., & Rosch, E. (2016). *The Embodied Mind: Cognitive Science and Human Experience* (rev. ed.). Cambridge, MA/London: MIT Press. Reprinted with permission of MIT Press.

Walach, H. (2013). Criticisms of transpersonal psychology and beyond: the future of transpersonal psychology. In H. L. Friedman & G. Hartelius (Eds.), *The Wiley-Blackwell Handbook of Transpersonal Psychology* (pp. 62–87). Chichester, UK: Wiley-Blackwell. Reprinted by permission of Wiley-Blackwell.

Zarrilli, P. B., & Hulton, P. (2009). *Psychophysical Acting: An Intercultural Approach After Stanislavski*. London/New York: Routledge. Reprinted with permission of Routledge.

And finally, my family, Linda, Izzy, Jolie, Joyce, Michael, and Janet, and the personal friends that have supported me (in some cases for decades), you know who you are.

Introduction

The Psychology of
an Actor

"What is my character's motivation?" While this question is perhaps a caricature of the earnest actor's quest for realistic performance, it is also a serious psychological investigation. *All* contemporary actors, whether on stage, film, or television, go to at least some lengths in exploring or making psychological choices about the characters they play. But *what* psychology do they use in making their judgments? Is it the behaviorism or Freudian psychoanalysis of the 1940s and 1950s? The "pop" psychology of the 1960s humanistic movement? Cognitive neuroscience? The personality theories of Adler, Erikson, or Jung? What about psychological types such as introvert and extrovert? Abnormal or positive psychology? Put another way, how much actual psychology does the average actor really know and use?

While nearly all actors regularly make fundamental and sometimes defining psychological decisions regarding the roles they play (even in nonrealistic dramatic forms), very rarely is psychology a formal part of an actor's education and training. Whether at the conservatory or university theater department, psychology class is simply not part of the standard training curriculum, even though working actors use it, in some form, every day!

The genesis for this book came from two separate observations I made while completing my master's degree in psychology. After a long career as a stage and screen actor, where I used some form or another of psychology every day, I had become interested in what is now generally called "positive" psychology and entered graduate school to further my studies. The kind of psychology that interested me at that time was more about healthy people and how they develop and mature than it was about pathology and mental disease. I did a lot of research on meditation and developed a theory about how meditative practice could be used as a growth tool in actor training, which I described in my first book, *Advanced Consciousness Training for Actors: Meditation Techniques for the Performing Artist* (Page, 2018). While writing that book, a couple of things occurred to me. As I stated above, while most actors would claim to "use psychology" when developing a character for performance, very rarely are actors actually *trained* in traditional forms of psychology and psychological theories. I researched that claim while interviewing the heads of several major acting conservatories, including Yale (Wilson, 2017), Julliard (Feldman, 2017), NYU (Illingworth, 2017), and others, and confirmed that a course in psychology, and particularly personality theory, which I will discuss below, was *not* a degree requirement for any major acting program that I contacted. Yet almost all of these master acting teachers acknowledged the *central importance* to the actor of a firm and fundamental understanding of human motivation and behavior.

The second thing that occurred to me as I studied both psychology and actor training simultaneously was that much of the fundamental theory that underlies traditional actor training pedagogy, which is basically the work of Constantine Stanislavsky and reactions to it, were developed based on understandings of psychology that were actually developed in the 1700s and 1800s (Bartow, 2006; Carnicke, 2009; Hodge, 2010). For, in fact, Stanislavsky was most influenced by the physiologically based psychological theories of Denis Diderot (1713–1784) and Théodule Ribot (1839–1916) from whom he borrowed the term "affective memory" (Carnicke, 2009, p. 154). From our postmodern perspective, we would consider Diderot distinctly reductionistic and almost quaintly mechanistic in his approach to the human condition, and a forefather of what would emerge in Western modern psychology in the early twentieth century as behaviorism.

As for Ribot's influence on Stanislavsky, Sharon Carnicke, author of the highly influential *Stanislavsky in Focus* (2009), explains:

While Freudian psychology took hold of the American popular imagination, Ribot gained authority in Russia. As early as 1896, Ribot had caught Russia's interest through his monograph on Schopenhauer, the German philosopher who influenced many early twentieth century Russian artists. Later, Ribot's espousal of physical methodologies (seen as sympathetic to Marxist materialism) made him acceptable in post-revolutionary Russia as well . . .

Stanislavsky's interest in psychology mirrored that of his native culture to some extent. He owned six of Ribot's books, read them voraciously and filled them with marginal notes . . . The Russian responded to the Frenchman because they both sought to define a psychophysical continuum between mind and body. By contrast, Stanislavsky seemed uninterested in Freud's work. Translated into Russian in 1910, Freud was recommended to Stanislavsky in 1911, but there is no evidence that he took the suggestion.

(Carnicke, 2009, p. 155)

The important point to this, from my perspective, is that Stanislavsky's theories were primarily, if not wholly, based on pre-Freudian psychological concepts. Certainly, in the history of modern actor training, Freud eventually got his say through the voices of the American Method acting teachers, such as Adler, Meisner, and particularly Strasberg, who adapted Stanislavsky's earlier work by focusing it through the lens of Freud's psychoanalytic theories (Bartow, 2006; Zazzali, 2016). See Chapter 1 of *Advanced Consciousness Training for Actors* (Page, 2018) for a detailed discussion of the evolution of Western actor training from its Stanislavskian origins through its global proliferation, beginning with the League of Professional Theatre Training Schools in the 1970s. However, the most important thing to note is that Freud himself made all of his contributions to Western psychology in the early decades of the twentieth century, and *there has been an awfully lot of psychology developed since Freud's day that has never been taken into account by actor trainers and theoreticians.*

That is why I wrote this book. It offers to the working professional, as well as the earnest and intelligent student of the actor's craft, a firm grounding across a number of very practical theories and models that can have a direct application in character-building and performance. It is a compendium of ideas gathered together for actors to ponder, explore, and apply to their art, and in most cases these ideas have not been specifically articulated, at least in an overt way, in the language of the actor before. Some of the theories I present will be useful in one set of circumstances but not others. Some models will work well for one individual but not another. It is up to you, the practitioner in the field, to apply what you read here and test the results in your own experience. You may want to look at this book as a toolkit of exotic wrenches whose specific uses are to be discovered through direct experimentation and trial and error. In any case, I have tried to gather together a diverse group of psychological theories and therapeutic techniques that will give a broader and more grounded perspective about our psychological life as human beings than the typical actor has access to today. So, please study as much or as little of what follows as you like. As with any good buffet, take what you want and leave the rest. But please do keep an open mind about what you learn here. The art of acting is about making interesting and compelling choices, and this book is about extending the number of choices you have available when it comes to inhabiting a role or bringing a performance to life.

There is also an ulterior application of psychology for the actor as a type of mental hygiene or "consciousness cleanser." If you consider the arc of a professional actor's career over time, there are a couple of qualities that will inevitably stand out. The first is that the profession, as a whole, is *very* competitive, and this competitive factor is *stressful* in almost every instance. After 35 years in the business of both stage and screen (and voice-overs, commercials, industrial/educational films, personal appearances, speech-making, self-marketing, etc.), I would venture to say that acting may well be one of the *most* stressful jobs in the Western world. In 2015, drawing its information from the U.S. Department of Labor, the Bureau of Labor Statistics, the Census Bureau, trade associations, and private survey firms, a research team from CareerCast.com published its annual list of *10 Most Stressful Jobs in America* (CareerCast.com, 2015), and placed professional actor at number six on that list, just after police officer and before news broadcaster and event coordinator. In such a competitive and stressful daily environment, healthy and optimal mental functioning is a necessity, not an option. It is my personal belief, again as a 35-year veteran of show business as well as a psychological researcher, that proper self-care and mental (or emotional) hygiene are important to the actor as both a competitive advantage as well as a matter of survival. If you are an emotional wreck, it is very difficult to operate at peak creative levels in the multiple domains that professional acting requires. Various forms of psychotherapy, when properly applied, can be used as personal growth tools and an inoculation for the stresses and strains on the personality, and sometimes fragile ego, of the actor. It is also sometimes just nice to have someone to talk with, that is not a part of the industry, to give us perspective on being human and alive, a perspective that can potentially be lost or distorted in between auditions, rehearsals, and the ongoing rejections that are part and parcel of the business. So, in places, I will recommend personal therapy as a way to grow and stay sane along the path of the actor. It is my view that there are two kinds of psychology, the *personal* and the *character's*, and so I will try to deal with both as part of this book.

Psychology as a Map or Model

Psychology is a very broad term that is so loosely used in postmodern times as to sometimes lose its meaning. A typical introductory textbook definition of psychology goes something like: "The scientific study of behavior and mental processes" (Myers, 2007, p. 7). I have no particular problem with this general definition, however issues start to arise when we further try to define the word "scientific" in this formulation. The term "scientific" can be used just as broadly as the term psychology, yet what someone means by "scientific study" can have a great bearing on what gets included in the field of psychology as a discipline. For some, "scientific" implies limiting the discussion entirely to what can be seen and observed by human senses and their extensions (things such as microscopes, telescopes, and outward behavior). When this narrow interpretation of science is applied to the study of psychology, it *limits* what can be studied to *external phenomena*, which of course can be significant and informative; however, it also *excludes* the entire *internal or mental realm* of meaning, purpose, emotions, beliefs, or any other item that makes up a first-person perspective on being alive and conscious. Such a psychology, which completely ignores internal experience in favor of *only* looking at external behavior, is very limited. It is essentially a psychology that does not believe in conscious experience, the very fabric of the human-being-as-actor that all performers inhabit and utilize in their craft. Indeed, there was an entire field of psychology that was very prevalent in the middle of the twentieth century that did just that, disregard all internal experience in favor of external behavior, which was called "behaviorism" (discussed in detail in Chapter 1). This was a psychology that paid no attention, nor allocated any value or meaning, to the internal emotional experience of its human "scientific subjects," oftentimes simply studying the behavior of animals and generalizing the results to include human beings. This school of psychology has mostly been discredited over the years, but the same type of "reductionism" to external, measurable behavior (including neuronal patterns in brain scans) can still be found in what is now called cognitive neuroscience and related fields. There is nothing wrong with that. Cognitive neuroscience has made some amazing discoveries about the physiology of our brains in recent years; however, when such an endeavor wholly excludes the validity of the entire internal dimension of human experience, as a psychology for use by actors, it has limited practical application.

5

I propose a slightly different view of what psychology is and how it can be used, in practical terms, by the actor. I suggest that the various "schools" of psychology can be looked at more like maps or models of consciousness than definitive, and *exclusive*, statements about existence. A map is a representation (often from a high, overview perspective) of a particular territory or area of land; in my usage, a map is equated with a psychological *theory*. A model can be thought of as a representation of a thing or object (often at a higher resolution or granularity than a map, possibly with articulatable components); in this book, a model can be thought of as a *tool*. Both a map (theory) and a model (tool) represent, at a certain level of detail, something that we can explore, experiment with, learn about, and come to know both in an abstract *as well as practical way*. Examples of psychological maps include Freud's theory of psychoanalysis and Jung's theory of psychological types, among many others. Models, or tools, include things like therapeutic techniques, such as free association or dream analysis, as well as psychological or personality tests and evaluations (discussed below). There can also be different *types* of maps and models that represent different aspects of the *same* territory or object, such as a road map and a typographical map of a region. Each type of map refers to different characteristics of the same physical territory. So, many of the psychological maps and models I will be writing about will represent various aspects or characteristics of the human internal experience so that we can explore, investigate, and learn about them in creative, abstract, and practical ways. What this means is we can use models built purely out of observable behaviors and externals, as behaviorism did, but also models that represent internal states of consciousness. In either case, regardless of its internal/external orientation, different maps and models can reveal different aspects of mental territories or functions of our psyche that may be quite useful in creating a character or expressing a role. None of these maps or models are meant to be the *only way* to envision a territory or mental construct; they are simply *different ways* to look at the inner landscape of the characters we wish to terraform inside our own experience as actors. Sometimes you need a road map, when you are going on vacation, for instance. Other times you might need a map of flood plains or the elevations of hills and valleys if you are building a highway through an undeveloped patch of land. Each map is valid, and each map has its particular use. That is how we will look at the many maps and models of psychology presented in this book; as a road atlas to our inner world, different viewpoints on the vast territory that makes up the "self" of the actor.

6

Psychological Evaluations: Pathology and Disease vs. Personality Types and Traits

As mentioned above, this book will explore a number of different psychological tools for understanding or characterizing various aspects of our personality or inner mental experiences. Many of these tools are in the form of psychological evaluations or personality tests where the participant (in some cases the actor, in some cases the actor answering on behalf of a character) answers a series of questions that reveal certain general traits or tendencies about the person/character. However, it is important to explain that there are two very general classes of these types of tests/tools.

From a practical standpoint, one class of psychological testing tools is administered by trained and licensed psychologists and is primarily concerned with diagnosing pathology or mental illness. The other general class of test is the "personality" test that in many cases purports to measure or classify the test-taker's personality traits, often bearing somewhat random or ambiguous definitions, into either binary categories (introvert/extrovert, aggressive/passive, etc.) or along a continuum ("on a scale of 1 to 10"). These tests are of various statistical quality, are often subjective and culturally biased (see the criticism in the next section), but also can provide interesting and useful models for the actor's use. In other words, you might not want to take them too seriously as realistic or accurate measures of your individual being-in-the-world (life is complex, after all); however, in the generally more simplified land of imagination in which acting and character-building takes place, they can still be very useful. So, in this book, I will look at a number of personality tests or exercises that are widely available and can be used, if applied in the proper way, as tools for the actor's character explorations.

The Multiplicity of Postmodernity

In 1985, Joseph R. Roach published his groundbreaking, and now classic, *The Player's Passion*. In it, Roach posed the idea that acting, and the theatrical event itself, down through the ages of history, has always been contextualized by the society's view of the body, through paradigmatic concepts widely held at the time, and that those physiological and (later) psychological constructs influenced, if not created, the style of theatrical presentation and interpretation during any particular historical period. In other words, theatrical expression was virtually dictated by the prevalent concepts of mind/ body embedded in the culture that produced the theatrical event. He went on to weave a convincing narrative about acting styles from the 1700s through the late twentieth century, and demonstrated how his physiological/psychological lens could be applied in broad strokes across theater history.

Roach, in essence, used the maps of human physiology and psychology, as derived from the philosophic/scientific endeavors of many eras, to chart the evolution of modern acting from its roots in Greek philosophy, through the Cartesian revolution that followed, and into the early modern era where Stanislavsky and others adopted the models of Diderot, and later Freud (in America), bringing his readers to the very brink of our now postmodern age. The important point Roach illustrates is that maps and models of the body and mind have always influenced theatrical preparation and performance. And so, I will argue in the pages that follow that in our postmodern era, with its wild profusion of all sorts of different maps now available, actors are able to make use of many different and complementary maps to build their characters into rich tapestries of expression that can include perspectives from the past as well as the present. In part, this is an ability that has been made possible by the information age. In the past, there was generally a single prevalent "official" view of how the world was understood. With the event of the information age and the postmodern era, nearly all of the maps of the past, from cultures far and wide, and a multiplicity of contemporary viewpoints, are all readily available to anyone who wishes to do a little research on the Internet. There is no longer any single view of our bodies or our psychologies. Nor is there any longer a single prescribed structure or form for the theatrical or cinematic (or digital, or devised, etc.) event. The spectrum of human existence has been fragmented through a prism of viewpoints and perspectives, changing theater, performance, and actors irrevocably along the way into rainbows of possibilities instead of a rigid set of pre-prescribed styles and forms. It is a *good* time to be an actor.

The postmodern era, in addition to its diversity of possibilities, has brought its own maps and forms into existence, including postmodern-*ism* as a philosophical lens, or map, by which we can view the world. (Postmodernism, as a coherent worldview, was not one that Roach presented or analyzed in his book, as in 1985 this movement was still emerging, its boundaries and limitations not yet clear.) Postmodernism is characterized by a "radical eclecticism . . . which accepts and criticizes at the same time" (Jencks, 1992, p. 6).

This critical voice, which can sometimes be overdone, has also been raised against the Western psychological tradition, the subject, in part, of this book, calling to attention the fact that much Western psychology was brought into being by white, European males that paid little attention or care to cross-cultural validity or impact, thereby marginalizing (or dismissing) large swathes of the non-upper-middle-class population (Pfister & Schnog, 1997, pp. 6–12). This is a fair criticism, from one perspective (the postmodern), unless it is overextended in an attempt to completely invalidate or undercut the entire psychology project, in which case I would say that it is "throwing the baby out with the bathwater," and behaving an awfully lot like postmodernism's predecessor, materialistic (modern) scientism (Wilber, 2002). So, as a theater and cinema practitioner myself, I prefer to acknowledge the postmodern critique of Western psychology, accepting and understanding the field's limitations and boundaries, while simultaneously embracing the many useful and practical aspects of psychology as a set of diverse tools and maps that have led me personally to certain previously undiscovered terrains of performance. Like I said: it's a *good* time to be an actor!

Theater practitioner and theorist Phillip B. Zarrilli, in *Psychophysical Acting* (2009), seems to make a similar point when he explains:

9

The psychologically whole character was no longer central to many types of theatre after the 1960s . . . What the actor or performer does on stage at the start of the twenty-first century ranges from playing a psychologically realist character to the sequential playing of multiple roles or personae to the enactment of tasks or entry into images without any character implications.

(Zarrilli & Hulton, 2009, p. 7)

Zarrilli goes even further:

However important psychology has been to shaping the dramaturgy of realist and naturalist plays from the late nineteenth century through the twentieth centuries, conventional realist approaches to acting and/or textural analysis may be inadequate or even inappropriate to the realization of the dramaturgy and acting tasks that constitute an actor's performance score in a post-dramatic text or performance. I argue here that the "psychological" is no longer—if it ever was—a paradigm with sufficient explanatory and/or practical power and flexibility to fully inform the complexities of the work of the contemporary actor . . .

The psychological is not to be rejected, but considered as one of several conceptual paradigms that can tactically inform certain specific aspects of the work of the actor as and when appropriate.

(Zarrilli & Hulton, 2009, pp. 7–8)

I wholly agree with Zarrilli's analysis and position. My only critique is in what may be the overestimation of the "post-dramatic" movement and its supplanting of the "realist and naturalist" style of performance as the working professional actor's bread-and-butter work, particularly in the cultural West. In my experience, I would argue that realistic and naturalistic performance is still a major portion of what a professional actor is asked to do, even if the psychology of those realistic characters has changed and become more diverse; all the more reason to understand *multiple* psychological approaches. Ironically, most actors, particularly in the large university conservatories, are not being trained in any specific detail about the schools of, or possible uses for, Western psychology, as if they are merely expected to understand these subtleties by intuition (Feldman, 2017; Marchant, 2017; Warshofsky, 2017; Wilson, 2017).

Regardless of whether certain schools of thought I am about to present may have gone out of fashion, or the postmodern critique may find some of their bases dubious, or even if they may not be applicable to every performance challenge in the "post-dramatic" world, someone needed to provide a text that presented these basic post-Diderot psychological concepts in a way that could be understood by actors so that, when appropriate, these tools would be available to the skilled hand. Lack of knowledge is little excuse when the lights come up and the actor stands revealed before an audience. Every actor I have ever known, at least all the good ones, always wanted to be *more* prepared rather than less, even if it was a matter of pre-performative training rather than intellectual analysis; they all wanted tools and maps to make their journeys more adventurous and artistically profitable. So, in that spirit, I have tried to include in this book material that is both practical and useful for application on the stage or in front of the camera. How adroit you become at their application is up to you.

What Is Here and What Is Not

The purpose of this book is essentially threefold: to teach twentieth-century psychology to actors; to give actors tools to become self-aware and self-developed in order to become better artists and workers in a highly stressful field; and to extend the actor's capacity for active and psychologically sound character/text analysis.

To those ends, I present a number of exercises throughout the book, based on various theorists' maps and models of the psyche, that I believe can ultimately become useful tools in the working actor's toolbox. In general, these exercises begin with personal exploration, followed by suggestions of various ways the same exercises might be repeated with regard to building or deepening a certain character. What I don't do is give explicit examples, utilizing these tools, of an analysis of an existing or classical text. For a very worthy example of this type of exercise, see Robert Blumenfeld's book *Tools and Techniques of Character Interpretation* (2006). The reasons for my particular approach are twofold. First, all of the exercises in this book, to one degree or another, are *experiential*; they are intended to unfold in your own immediate consciousness as an experience, not as a purely analytical exercise. Therefore, even though they may appear as predominately introspective (some have called this quality "navel-gazing"), I argue that they are actually quite active and, when properly executed, involve a full engagement of the personality and the spirit. If I am right in this, it should head off any argument by the actor training purist that what I have proposed here will somehow entrap the actor "in their head" and send them spiraling into a disembodied vortex of intellectual remove. That is the farthest thing from my intention.

So, please consider, when evaluating the proposed exercises in this book, that they are meant to be *done* and not merely described. You will find, in your own experience, whether they are useful to you and whether they lead to deeper connections and actionable understandings of your character *or not*. You certainly won't need my written descriptions to make that judgment. If, however, I were to fill this book with examples of how I have conceived of the outcomes of this work from my own, singular perspective, I fear I would be doing your homework for you, and the value of what I have proposed would be diminished by my own demonstrations.

Make no mistake: this stuff is *active*, not passive, and whatever outcomes proceed will be wholly individual, rendering the opinions of the author about what *should* happen as moot. Therefore, I

11

have left many questions about how I have personally applied this work over the years intentionally unanswered in the hopes that the answers you find for yourself will be much more valuable than what I might conjure for you. I will perhaps address more explicit ideas of how these techniques might be applied in traditional scene analysis in a later volume, but here I offer the applied work as a tool for self-transformation and growth rather than a codified system for analyzing a script.

The Multi-Perspectival Actor

Often, scientists (as well as psychologists) have been guilty of "totalizing" their particular perspective of the world. In other words, they sometimes decide that their chosen map or model is the *only* valid perspective or viewpoint on the human condition.

Actors tend to be different. They often will look for alternative explanations, varieties of motivating factors, unique and novel solutions to the psychological problems of their characters. In other words, actors are generally interested in taking *multiple perspectives* on their character's inner lives and outwardly expressed behavior, as might be suggested by the postmodern view introduced in a previous section. This book is intended to provide additional tools for this "multi-perspectival" orientation. The important point to make for the actor is that many of the psychological maps and models we will be looking at are presented as if they were the *only* correct or viable solution or answer to a problem. However, the most effective way to use these theories and practices is as if any one of them, or even a combination of several, might provide different-but-not-exclusive insights into the character-building process. Think of this material as different faucets of a finely cut jewel or prism; each aspect makes the light shimmer in a uniquely beautiful way (like a diamond)!

One could say that the actor's job is *innately* multi-perspectival in that when we act, we are almost always asked to take a different (and sometimes unique) perspective for each different character or performance we create. So, open-mindedness and the flexibility to take multiple perspectives is not only a useful quality for the actor to have, but a requirement for success! Therefore, take these practices as *interchangeable* tools; learn them, digest them, build some discernment around which might work best when, but foremost remain open to multiple interpretations of the psychological ground of the characters you inhabit. I assure you, equipped with the multivariant tools you

12

will find in the following chapters, you will be better equipped to make challenging, insightful, inspired, and creative choices about the art that you bring forth into the world.

References

Bartow, A. (2006). *Training of the American Actor*. New York: Theatre Communications Group.

Blumenfeld, R. (2006). *Tools and Techniques of Character Interpretation: A Handbook of Psychology for Actors, Writers, and Directors*. Montclair, NJ: Limelight Editions.

CareerCast.com (2015). *The Most Stressful Jobs of 2015*. Retrieved from www.careercast.com/jobs-rated/most-stressful-jobs-2015.

Carnicke, S. M. (2009). *Stanislavsky in Focus: An Acting Master for the Twenty-First Century* (2nd ed.). London/New York: Routledge.

Feldman, R. (2017). *Interview: Richard Feldman, the Julliard School*. Interviewer: K. Page, May 16.

Hodge, A. (2010). *Actor Training* (2nd ed.). London/New York: Routledge.

Illingworth, S. (2017) *Interview: Scott Illingworth, NYU*. Interviewer: K. Page, May 10.

Jencks, C. (1992). *The Post-Modern Reader*. London/New York: Academy Editions/St. Martin's Press.

Marchant, B. (2017). *Interview: Barbara Marchant, Rutgers*. Interviewer: K. Page, April 27.

Myers, D. G. (2007). *Psychology* (8th ed.). New York: Worth Publishers.

Page, K. (2018). *Advanced Consciousness Training for Actors: Meditation Techniques for the Performing Artist*. New York: Routledge.

Pfister, J., & Schnog, N. (1997). *Inventing the Psychological: Toward a Cultural History of Emotional Life in America*. New Haven, CT: Yale University Press.

Roach, J. R. (1993). *The Player's Passion: Studies in the Science of Acting*. Ann Arbor, MI: University of Michigan Press.

Warshofsky, D. (2017). *Interview: David Warshofsky, USC*. Interviewer: K. Page, May 2.

Wilber, K. (2002). *Boomeritis: A Novel That Will Set You Free*. Boston, MA/New York: Shambhala/Random House.

13

Wilson, W. (2017). *Interview: Walton Wilson, Yale School of Drama.* Interviewer: K. Page, April 27.

Zarrilli, P. B., & Hulton, P. (2009). *Psychophysical Acting: An Intercultural Approach After Stanislavski.* London/New York: Routledge.

Zazzali, P. (2016). *Acting in the Academy: The History of Professional Actor Training in US Higher Education.* London/New York: Routledge.

14

CHAPTER 1

A Very Brief History of Psychology in the West

Psychology, as an interest in understanding and describing the internal human experience, has been around for as long as recorded human history, maybe longer when you consider ancient shamanic practices and religious rituals dating back more than 50,000 years. However, as a discipline in modern Western culture, psychology really began in the mid-nineteenth century and has been on an exponential growth path ever since.

15

My first map of psychology, then, will be at the "world atlas" scale, looking down, as it were, from 50,000 feet upon the entire history of the field in the broadest of strokes to give us a context for some of the finer-grained maps and models we will explore later. This general history lesson will be of interest to some students and not to others. If you are purely concerned with applications of psychology to the actor's craft, feel free to skip ahead and come back here when you become more intrigued with how this whole thing came about. However, for the rest, this is where our story begins.

The Antecedents of Psychology: Buddha and the Greeks to Descartes and the Scientific Method

In sixth-century India, an enlightened sage called the Buddha evolved the idea from his personal ruminations during meditation practice that sensations and perceptions together become ideas in a human's consciousness. The Buddha's ideas about human consciousness and psychology would not become widely available in Western culture until the 1950s and 1960s when translations of Eastern esoteric texts finally arrived in America (Page, 2007). Similarly, around the same time in China, the philosopher Confucius pondered the notions of thought and learning in the human experience. But the real questioning and conversation about the nature and meaning of human consciousness, particularly in what would become Western psychology, began in the fifth and fourth centuries BCE between a small number of deeply ponderous Grecian philosophers.

Hippocrates (460–377 BC), popularly known as the Father of Medicine, disagreed with the contemporary notion of his day that diseases were caused by the maleficent work of gods and demons, and instead put forward the idea that diseases, both physical and mental, could be attributed to natural causes. In his time, this was revolutionary. He created a theory of "humors," or bodily fluids, based on the four-elements idea attributed to Empedocles (495–430 BC) that all matter was made up of earth, air, fire, and water held together in various combinations by the forces of either love or strife. Hippocrates held that health and sound thinking could be attributed to a proper balance of humoral fluid, and that sickness and even mental disorders were caused by an imbalance of humors in the body. These ideas led to the widespread practice of bloodletting over many centuries that were not discontinued until early in the modern era (Greenspan, 2006, pp. 80–91).

A contemporary of Hippocrates, Democritus (460–362 BC), also known as the "laughing philosopher," came up with the concept that matter was constructed of invisible particles called "atoms." In his view, things or objects in the world would imprint their own image on the atoms of the air and would then travel to the eye of the human observer. From this, he extrapolated that humans can have no real way of knowing anything, in a final sense, about the world around them because they must rely on their individual perceptions of this interaction of atoms, and it is impossible to tell if, or how much, people's perceptions might vary from one another. His famous quote, "We know nothing for certain, but only the changes produced in our body by the forces that impinge upon it," places him in agreement with other philosophers of his time, such as his friend and sophist Protagoras (485–411 BC), who believed every person's perspective of reality was relative to their own senses. This view is a denial of "objective truth," and has been a source of debate and contention in both philosophy and later psychology from the fifth century BC until modern times (Hunt, 1993, pp. 15–17).

Socrates (469–399 BC), among many other things, made a direct impact on the field that would become psychology by contradicting the above-stated idea of reality's relativity. According to writer Morton Hunt:

[Socrates] held that the existence of innate knowledge, revealed by the dialectic method of instruction, proves that we possess an immortal soul, an entity that can exist apart from the brain and body. With this, the vague mythical notions of soul that had long existed in Greek and related cultures assumed a new significance and specificity. Soul is mind but is separable from the body; mind does not cease to be at death.

On this ground would be built Platonic and, later, Christian dualism: the division of the world into mind and matter, reality and appearance, ideas and objects, reason and sense perception, the first half of each pair regarded not only as more real than but as morally superior to the second.

(Hunt, 1993, pp. 21–22)

17

This argument for a dualistic view of the world would survive and influence Western thinking down to this day. Most notably, the idea of the monological spirit gazing "out" at the world of objects, and otherwise free to act upon these objects (including other human beings) at will, would be extended and elaborated upon at the birth of the modern era by the French philosopher René Descartes (1596–1650). Descartes' dualism, also known as the Cartesian split, was radical and became the basis for modern scientific thinking. By the beginning of the twentieth century, particularly in the West, the only widely available alternative views to the scientific paradigm were the traditional religions, mostly Christianity and Judaism, whose fundamental philosophies were based on ancient mythological tales and superstition. In fact, much of the scientific worldview, based on Descartes' dualism, was in acrimonious *reaction* to the traditional religions and their historically totalitarian and repressive regimes, which more and more often were being effectively undermined by rational, scientific arguments, leaving few other options available other than to pick a side and join the feud. By the mid-twentieth century, the chasm that existed between these two worldviews, the scientific and religious, would become wide and deep.

Birth of the Modern Psychology Project: Mimicking "Science"

Most college textbooks on modern psychology hold that psychology was born as an independent field of experimental inquiry in 1879, when Wilhelm Wundt (1832–1920) founded the first laboratory dedicated exclusively to psychological research at Leipzig University, Germany. It is also believed that Wundt was the first person to refer to himself formally as a psychologist (Carlson, 2010, p. 18). Around the same time, in 1875, a Harvard professor of physiology, William James (1842–1910), who had visited Wundt's laboratory, started doing laboratory experiments of his own and making demonstrations to his students in the classroom. However, as the laboratory was not used, at that time, for original research, it remains a matter of opinion as to whom actually founded the "first" laboratory for scientifically studying the human psyche. Later, James would go on to publish a two-volume treatise, *The Principles of Psychology* (1890), which would become one of the most influential early texts of the field in the West. More on James shortly.

An alternative view is that modern psychology began with a little-known figure, Franz Brentano. Brentano was a professor of philosophy as well as a Catholic priest. In 1866, he had argued that philosophy's method needed to become more scientific and experimental, a new view at the time, and the basic argument that would become embedded in the field of scientific psychology in the coming years. Brentano's influence over the emergence of psychology as a discrete field of inquiry, however, will never fully be known. His dealings with the church on the issue of papal infallibility led to his resignation as a priest, and his marriage to a Jewish woman created a scandal that forced him to resign his position at the University of Vienna, which he was never able to reclaim. While various figures who would contribute mightily to the nascent field of psychology were influenced by his lectures, including Freud, Husserl, and Stumpf, his own contributions remained mostly incomplete and unpublished due to his lack of academic appointment (Walach, 2013, pp. 64–65).

Wundt's laboratory at Leipzig primarily focused on reaction time experiments that aimed to discover the differences between a subject's perception and interpretation of stimuli. He believed that consciousness was made up of a series of discrete elements that in turn could be studied. Wundt and his students developed a strict form of introspection, observing one's own perceptions and feelings in relation to stimulus events, such as the clicking of a metronome or flashing of an image, and then reporting them as "objectively" as possible (Hunt, 1993, pp. 134–137). His insistence that the elements of consciousness be explored scientifically is one of the reasons he has been widely christened "the father of experimental psychology." He called his 1874 book *The Principles of Physiological Psychology* "an attempt to mark out [psychology] as a new domain of science" (Fancher, 1979, p. 126). In 1881, he established the first academic journal to be exclusively dedicated to publishing research on psychological topics.

Wundt considered himself a serious scientist and his passion was to establish the new field of psychology in the mold of physics or chemistry. Wundt did not believe that "mind" existed apart from the body. He thought that conscious phenomena were purely based on neural events occurring in the brain (Lowry, 1971, p. 105). One interesting example of Wundt's intense desire that his work be perceived as "scientific" occurred in 1877 when a Leipzig physics professor, Johann Karl Zöllner, became interested in the performances of an American medium, Henry Slade. Zöllner had developed a theory about a fourth "spiritual" dimension that he felt should be included in the study of physics and that Slade's performances might help prove his theory. Another man, Hermann Ulrici, wrote about Zöllner's study of Slade and concluded that spiritism was of the utmost importance to science, and in the process mentioned Wundt in his article. Wundt was furious at the public mention of his name in this context, and felt that any association of the new nascent field of psychology he was formulating with such things as potentially fraudulent mediumistic performances was a direct threat to the field's academic standing. From that point on, Wundt believed that any association of psychology with parapsychological phenomena was to be avoided at all costs. Later, he included clear warnings in his published writings that stated his position in no uncertain terms (Walach, 2013, p. 65).

Wundt was known as a dogmatic and pedantic professor who would deliver long lectures without glancing at his notes. He was often characterized as authoritarian. His student, and the American champion of his theories, Edward Titchener (1867–1927) called him "humorless, indefatigable, and aggressive." William James wrote, "he's a professor—a being whose duty is to know everything, and have his own opinion about everything, connected with his [specialty]" (Hunt, 1993, pp. 133–134). Perhaps Wundt shared a similar sentiment for James when commenting on James' 1890 masterwork *The Principles of Psychology*; he said, "It is literature, it is beautiful, but it is not psychology" (Bjork, 1983, p. 12).

Another American, G. Stanley Hall (1846–1924), had studied briefly with Wundt before returning to America, and in 1883 established the first acknowledged psychology research laboratory in the United States at Johns Hopkins University. Hall, who would become a major figure in American psychology, would go on to found the first American psychological journal and play an active role in the formation of the American Psychological Association (APA) and act as its first president.

Titchener, who studied directly with Wundt for two years in the early 1890s, took his ideas back to the United States and popularized them under the term "structuralism." He set up his own psychology laboratory at Cornell University where he focused on identifying the basic elements of consciousness. In 1896, he published a textbook entitled *An Outline of Psychology*, in which he listed more than 44,000 individual qualities of conscious experience (Schultz & Schultz, 1987). However, the influence of structuralism on the rapidly broadening field of psychology faded after Titchener and Wundt's deaths in the 1920s primarily due to the difficulties of introspection as its primary tool of investigation. Simply put, introspective observations, regardless of how much effort the subjects put into trying to be objective, tend to be erratic, subjective, and not reproducible. All of these qualities tended to undermine the "scientific nature" of the structuralist's approach, and so after its initial burst of popularity and its impact on the birth of the field it simply faded away after the passing of its founders.

William James was a contemporary of Wundt's, developing his own ideas at the same time as the German professor, and liked to joke that "the first lecture on psychology I ever heard [was] the first I ever gave" (Perry, 1996, p. 228). As a counterpoint to Wundt and Titchener's structuralism, James developed a different view of understanding and studying consciousness called "functionalism." To James, the important aspect of consciousness was not its discrete elements viewed from a static position in time, but how those components worked together to allow people to function in real-world situations. He envisioned consciousness as a dynamic process or stream and was the first to introduce the concept of a "stream of consciousness" into the terminology of psychology (James, 1890).

James had been heavily influenced by the publication of Darwin's theory of evolution and had come to believe that ways of thinking and behaving that were functional to man's survival were mental traits that would be "naturally selected" and reinforced by evolution, and those thinking patterns and behaviors that were less useful would lead to extinction.

Although James was considered of seminal influence in the burgeoning field, his influence began to wane, and he eventually fell out of fashion altogether as psychology first blossomed and then exploded during the twentieth century; and the volatile fuel mix for that explosion, in both America and across Europe, was made up of two components: Freudian psychoanalysis and behaviorism.

The First Force in the West: Freud vs. Jung

Sigmund Freud (1856–1939) was a Viennese medical student around the same time Wundt was beginning his researches into reaction timing at Leipzig University. He was born to a Jewish family, and thus his professional options in Viennese culture at that time, which was quite anti-Semitic, were limited to either law or medicine. He chose medicine, even though the practicalities of practice he found personally repellent, and entered medical school at the University of Vienna in 1873. There, he met a well-known physiology professor, Ernest Brücke (1819–1892), who influenced his interests toward physiological psychology. The older man by nearly 40 years, Brücke came to be a mentor to the young Freud, and Freud became a dedicated researcher in Brücke's laboratory until his graduation in 1881. At the time, Freud wanted to continue as a professional researcher in physiology, but Brücke discouraged him from that path as a research career in that day required personal financial wealth, which Freud did not possess. Freud's early practice was in neurology and brain disorders. He had chosen the specialty as a way to make enough money to marry and start a family (Hunt, 1993, pp. 169–171).

Freud had befriended another older doctor and physiologist who he had met through Brücke named Josef Breuer (1842–1925), and began discussing various clinical cases with him in 1882. Breuer often treated patients with hysterical disorders and shared with the young Freud several therapeutic techniques he had tried with his patients. It was through Breuer that Freud was first introduced to the nascent practice of medical hypnotism, which was mostly frowned upon in Viennese medical circles at the time. Later, Freud would study briefly with Jean-Martin Charcot (1825–1893), a renowned neuropathologist and a skilled hypnotist himself. Charcot was credited with discovering the phenomenon of hysteria, and treated the syndrome as a progressive and irreversible inherited disease.

By 1886, Freud had opened his own private practice specializing in neurological and brain disorders, and had married his longtime fiancée Martha Bernays (1861–1951). At first, his practice was slow, and he was helped by referrals of hysteria patients by his friend Breuer. For several years, he used hypnotherapy with his patients, trying to get them to remember traumatic events that had first brought on their symptoms. However, his results were unpredictable, providing relief for some and leaving others unchanged. Eventually, he and Breuer worked out their own theory of hysteria that, in contrast to Charcot's purely physiological views, was based on psychology. According to historian Morton Hunt:

> [Freud and Breuer] concluded that "hysterics suffer from reminiscences"—memories of emotionally painful experiences—that have somehow been excluded from consciousness. As long as such memories remain forgotten, the emotion associated with them is "strangulated" or bottled-up and converted into physical energy, taking the form of a physical symptom. When the memory is recovered through hypnosis, the emotion can be felt and expressed, and the symptom disappears.

> (Hunt, 1993, p. 174)

In 1893, the two published a paper together on their findings. Sometime later in 1889, Freud was applying these techniques of hypnosis and posthypnotic suggestion to a patient with whom he was having some temporary but erratic success. During the course of the woman's treatment, he discovered almost by accident that if he let the patient talk freely without much interruption, she was more likely to uncover the base causes of her hysterical symptoms than when directed by prompts or questions. This event, with a patient he eventually called "Frau Emmy" in his later writings, led him to discover a critical foundational technique in what would become the psychoanalysis process: *free association*. And with that, Freud had made his first step toward developing psychoanalytic theory, which would both challenge and revolutionize the field of psychology for the next 50 years.

By 1896, Freud had begun using the term "psychoanalysis," and by 1900 he had developed the basic structure of what was to become his "talking cure" (a term first used by one of Breuer's patients around 1882). The elements of his model by that time consisted of a patient lying on a couch in a relaxed position, the therapist telling the patient that free association would yield useful information about their problems, the patient agreeing to speak freely their thoughts aloud without any form of censorship at all, and then the therapist tracking the sorts

22

of unconscious associations that came out of the patient's memories and ideas as they rambled.

Over time, Freud added to his theories. These additions included ideas such as dream interpretation. Unlike many others of his day who felt dreams were either meaningless or symptoms of physiological disturbance during sleep, such as indigestion, Freud began to see the dream life of his patients as a repository for painful and otherwise repressed feelings that became more obvious in dream imagery than in the patient's waking life, where they were likely to deny the feelings or unconsciously repress them.

Between 1897 and 1900, Freud subjected himself to a brutally honest self-directed psychoanalysis. He had himself experienced what could only be described as neurotic symptoms for many years, which included fear of travel, obsessive worries about money and potential heart attack, and an excessive fear of death. And so, the physician set out to heal himself. Freud had developed another friendship with an ear, nose, and throat doctor who also shared an interest in psychology, Wilhelm Fliess (1858–1928). During his period of self-analysis, Freud wrote often to Fliess as a confidant and sounding board. In the end, Freud attributed his self-analysis with helping significantly to relieve his symptoms, as well as giving him a number of key insights into the psychotherapeutic process that would come out in his formal work in coming years.

23

One such theory to arise out of Freud's work on himself later became his famous "Oedipus complex." Earlier, in 1896, he had written a controversial paper on what became known as his "seduction theory." From work with his patients, he had come to the conclusion that much of what caused neurotic disorders was the result of childhood sexual abuse by adults. That theory, at the time, was received skeptically and with much hard criticism. For one thing, Freud's paper would seem to imply that sexual abuse, particularly of daughters by fathers, was not only widespread, but endemic. As a result of this early position, Freud felt personally abhorred and professionally isolated. However, during his self-analysis, Freud revised this theory to propose that while sexual abuse no doubt did exist even in the puritanical society of that day, many neurotics were actually projecting their own feelings of childhood sexuality onto experiences or "false memories" of events that never actually occurred.

Other ideas that came forth from both his work with clinical patients and his self-analysis included the concept of the dynamic unconscious and a tripartite model of the mind: preconscious, conscious, and the unconscious, which Freud felt made a much greater impact on conscious life than any of his predecessors. The unconscious mind, held Freud, was a highly active center of primitive drives and repressed wishes that generated immense pressure on the conscious mind, thus motivating and determining behavior in ways that could otherwise not be explained. He also proposed the idea of primary and secondary processes of thinking. He argued that the urges for satisfaction and infantile fulfillment located in the unconscious mind are primarily urges that demand fulfillment but are by their very nature unacceptable to people living in a modern society. If all people were merely to yield to primary process thinking, there would be nothing but rape, murder, and chaos in the world. And so, the moderating forces of the conscious "ego" mind are secondary processes, such as thinking, knowing, and problem-solving mental activities that help the person control and fulfill the primitive desires in socially acceptable and civilized ways.

He also proposed the "pleasure principle," which in his conception meant that the fulfilling or sating of primary process desires is a fundamental motivating factor in human behavior. While the unconscious is driven by the pleasure principle constantly seeking fulfillment, the conscious mind is governed by the "reality principle" and seeks to fulfill the desires of the unconscious mind, but in ways that are appropriate (and hopefully non-criminal) to society's norms. In this case, much of conscious thought and behavior is actually controlled by the unconscious desire for pleasure, or at least the release of pressure from such pent-up desires.

In 1909, Freud and his then protégé Carl Gustav Jung (1875–1961), (pronounced 'yůŋ) were invited to lecture at Clark University in Massachusetts by university president G. Stanley Hall. The conference was in celebration of the university's twentieth anniversary of becoming the second graduate program in psychology in the United States. Freud's lectures were mostly well received by the audience, although some attendees were appalled, which included William James, among others. By the time Freud returned home to Europe, his reputation had been considerably broadened and his fame, particularly in America, assured.

By 1910, he had fully formulated his ideas about childhood sexuality, and their potent influence on the conscious mind by unconscious primary process thinking, and gave his theory the title "Oedipus complex." This idea was essentially that in childhood, sexual primary process thinking toward a parent, usually of the opposite sex, creates a great deal of tension and anxiety within the personality that is either resolved by maturing into commonplace roles of adult behavior, or when left unsuccessfully resolved can turn into pernicious and painful adult neurosis.

Freud also contributed the notions of repression, projection, and defenses; the terms rationalization, denial, displacement, sublimation, and reaction formation; as well as "ego," "id," and "superego." All of these ideas and terms have come to be adopted, or reacted against, by professional psychologists in the West and are at least cursorily understood by most educated laypeople in our culture. Freud's impact has not only been wide and pervasive, but it is also unprecedented. Because of his vast influence, Freud is, to this day, considered one of the most important thinkers and contributors to Western culture that has ever lived.

It is important to note that even though Freud introduced an entire world of inner experience to the field of psychology, he always viewed himself as a scientist and a dedicated determinist. He believed staunchly "that every mental event has its cause, and that free will is only an illusion" (Hunt, 1993, p. 185). According to Harald Walach:

Freud [was] stimulated by Brentano's teaching. But Freud was also fighting for scientific recognition, and he knew that being associated with quackery and esotericism would be the death of psychoanalysis. So he made a scientific vow: no dealings with spiritual issues, please, in order to not endanger the still fragile flower of psychoanalysis. And psychoanalysis, true to its master's heritage, steered clear from the muddy waters of religion and transpersonal experiences.

(Walach, 2013, p. 65)

Freud considered himself a lifelong atheist and is famous for characterizing any religious or spiritual sentiments as repressed, infantile sexuality. Freud's irreligiosity and forceful attacks on anything with a spiritual tenor would ultimately contribute to his alienation and separation from one of the more important relationships of his life, his one-time protégé and heir apparent (by Freud's own declaration) Carl Jung (Jung & Jaffé, 1989, p. 157).

The foregoing sketch of Freud's biography and contributions is, of course, incomplete and significantly abbreviated. Freud's story is widely available from many other authors and with many other interpretations. The important point I am trying to establish is that Freud, as a pioneer, had *opened up the realm of the unconscious to psychology* in a way that far transcended the physiological psychology of his day and the simplistic dimensions of the structuralists and functionalists who preceded him. Freud's work and ideas were controversial from the start, and in many ways remain so today, but they also overflowed the boundaries of the field to influence the beliefs and understandings of the general public in a way that no other map of psychology, at least to that time, ever had. Perhaps Freud's greatest contribution in his own time was to offer an alternative view to a force that had rapidly arisen to dominate modern psychology near the turn of the twentieth century, particularly in the academy, called behaviorism.

But before we turn to behaviorism, let us first explore another figure who was to have a substantial impact on the world of psychology. Carl G. Jung, as noted above, was a contemporary of Freud. In ways similar to Freud's relationship with Breuer and later Fliess, Jung as a younger man had become a follower, friend, and protégé of the older Freud.

As a young medical doctor specializing in psychiatry at the Burghölzli Hospital in Zürich, Switzerland, Jung was assigned to work with neurotic and psychotic patients. Around 1900, at the age of 25, Jung was first exposed to Freud's ideas about repression and the unconscious when he read *The Interpretation of Dreams* (1913). At the time, Jung himself admits that the concepts were over his head, but three years later, when he returned to the book with more clinical experience under his belt, he found it very helpful in understanding certain of his patients' symptoms (Jung & Jaffé, 1989, pp. 146–147). In 1903, Freud's theories were still not accepted in medical circles, and were only spoken of in the corridors at medical congresses, not the main floor. As Jung, at the time, was focusing on an academic career, the very thought that his work was in agreement with Freud's "was far from pleasant" (Jung & Jaffé, 1989, p. 148). But by 1906, Jung felt compelled to write an article that supported Freud's work. This is how Jung described the reaction to that article in his autobiography, *Memories, Dreams, Reflections*:

In response to this article, two German professors wrote to me, warning that if I remained on Freud's side and continued to defend him, I would be endangering my academic career. I replied: "If what Freud says is the truth, I am with him. I don't give a damn for a career if it has to be based on the premise of restricting research and concealing the truth." And I went on defending Freud and his ideas.

(Jung & Jaffé, 1989, p. 148)

In 1907, Jung sent a copy of his own book *The Psychology of Dementia Praecox* (Jung, Peterson, & Brill, 1909) to Freud and was invited by him to Vienna for a personal visit. They met for the first time in March of 1907 and talked nearly nonstop for 13 hours. During that conversation, the two men discovered they had much in common. But they also had differences. Jung was much impressed with Freud's sexual theory, but when he tried to voice his own reservations the older man rebuked him several times, saying that Jung merely lacked the clinical experience to understand. This aspect of Freud's personality would trouble Jung throughout what became their stormy relationship until that relationship finally ended in acrimony six years later in 1913. Again, Jung speaks:

Above all, Freud's attitude toward the spirit seemed to me highly questionable. Wherever, in a person or in a work of art, an expression of spirituality (in the intellectual, not the supernatural sense) came to light, he suspected it, and insinuated that it was repressed sexuality. Anything that could not be directly interpreted as sexuality he referred to as "psychosexuality." I protested that this hypothesis, carried to its logical conclusion, would lead to an annihilating judgement upon culture. Culture would then appear as a mere farce, the morbid consequence of repressed sexuality. "Yes," he assented, "so it is, and that is just a curse of fate against which we are powerless to contend."

(Jung & Jaffé, 1989, pp. 149–150)

Freud's attitude of both hyper-emphasizing sexuality in human nature and assiduously denying any possible alternative explanations for spiritual experience became the key issues that ultimately led to the end of the two men's relationship. At one point, as late as 1909, Freud had viewed Jung as his direct successor and the future standard-bearer for his cherished psychoanalytic theory. But the issue of spirituality and Freud's dogmatic belief that almost all of human behavior could by understood in relationship to frustrated or repressed sexual urges finally opened a chasm between the two that was never to heal.

In many ways, this extended feud between the two men, one who was a scientific materialist and believed that consciousness could ultimately be reduced to an epiphenomenon of physiological processes and fundamental base drives, and the other with a much more liberal view of phenomenology and the spiritual dimension of human existence, became an analogy for the ideological war that was waged, and still rages, in the field of psychology as a whole. This fundamental schism of perspectives is at the heart of what drove both the humanistic and transpersonal revolutions in psychology nearly three-quarters of a century later (discussed below).

In 1913, Jung and Freud finally had their public break over *Psychology of the Unconscious*, a book that Jung had published in which he stated clearly his ideas that differed from Freud's. The consequences of this break were dire for Jung and temporarily disrupted his career and status.

As had Freud before him, Jung set out on a radical program of self-analysis that eventually led to the birth of many of his most singular theories, including the existence of a collective unconscious, the "anima" and "animus," the integration of the personality, and *active imagination* as a therapeutic technique (which we will explore as a tool for actors in Chapter 3).

Jung began keeping detailed journals of his own imaginings and fantasies. It appears he kept this material mostly separated from his dream journals (Jung & Shamdasani, 2009, p. 200). This process started with a few very powerful visions, which later seemed to foretell World War I in Europe, that initially made him question his own sanity. From approximately December of 1913 for a period of nearly 16 years, Jung would regularly evoke mental fantasies in his waking state and then carefully make notes of the experience as if he were making notes on a patient or an experiment.

Jung had come to believe in the importance of a "personal mythology," which he had realized that he himself had lost. According to historian and Jung scholar Sonu Shamdasani, "In studying his fantasies, Jung realized that he was studying the myth-creating function of the mind" (Jung & Shamdasani, 2009, p. 199). He called the black leather-bound notebooks in which he was documenting his experiences "my most difficult experiment." And as he filled each and started another, he also began to draw and paint various images that came to him in this work. Eventually, he purchased a large folio-style red leather-bound book of blank pages in which he began to carefully transcribe in calligraphic style the contents of the various notebooks and to make comments on the content of the fantasies themselves so that in one regard, he was recording his uncensored fantasies, and in another he was making a psychological commentary on the content. The production of this book he eventually titled *The Red Book: Liber Novus* (Jung & Shamdasani, 2009).

In his 1961 autobiography *Memories, Dreams, Reflections,* published in the same year as his death, Jung described the process he was undergoing, which he would later name "active imagination," and how it had unfolded in him:

An incessant stream of fantasies had been released, and I
did my best not to lose my head but to find some way to
understand these strange things. I stood helpless before
an alien world; everything in it seemed difficult and
incomprehensible. I was living in a constant state of tension;
often I felt as if gigantic blocks of stone were tumbling down
upon me . . . from the beginning there was no doubt in my
mind that I must find the meaning of what I was experiencing
in these fantasies . . .

I was frequently so wrought up that I had to do certain yoga
exercises in order to hold my emotions in check. But since it
was my purpose to know what was going on within myself,
I would do these exercises only until I had calmed myself
enough to resume my work with the unconscious . . . As a
result of my experiment I learned how helpful it can be, from
the therapeutic point of view, to find the particular images
which lie behind emotions.

(Jung & Jaffé, 1989, pp. 176–177)

And so, Jung's work in trying to understand his own unconscious became a kind of obsession for him. In April of 1914, he resigned his position as the president of the International Psychoanalytical Association and as a lecturer at the University of Zurich. However, in most of his worldly affairs he stayed connected and active, never indicating the turmoil of his inner psychological life. In July of that year, the Zurich Psychoanalytic Society voted to leave the International Psychoanalytical Association and rename itself the Association for Analytical Psychology, and Jung remained an active member. He also maintained a full schedule of psychiatric consultations with patients during this time. When World War I broke out, Jung performed his military service and family obligations without interruption and mentioned to almost no one what he was doing in the process of self-analysis. He kept his professional and personal lives almost completely segregated from the emotional upheavals of his "most difficult experiment." However, over the years of its writing, ideas that first appeared in *The Red Book* began to find their way into his formal lectures and writings.

Near the end of 1929 or early 1930, Jung completed his work on *Libra Novus*, leaving the transcription incomplete and breaking off his writing literally in mid-sentence. Shamdasani summarizes Jung's experiences with *The Red Book* and its meaning and impact on his theoretical work as follows:

> Out of his experiences, he developed new conceptions of the aims and methods of psychotherapy. Since its inception at the end of the nineteenth century, modern psychotherapy had been primarily concerned with the treatment of functional nervous disorders, or neuroses, as they came to be known. From the time of the First World War onward, Jung reformulated the practice of psychotherapy. No longer solely preoccupied with the treatment of psychopathology, it *became a practice to enable the higher development of the individual* through fostering the individuation process. This was to have far-reaching consequences not only for the development of analytical psychology but also for psychotherapy as a whole.
>
> (Jung & Shamdasani, 2009, p. 215, emphasis added)

In Jung and Freud's fundamental disagreements, like the Greeks before them, we can see the conflict between worldviews, one mechanistic and reductive and the other more open to the transcendent aspects of being. However, there was one other form of psychology that would come to the fore in the early twentieth century, particularly in America's academic institutions, that would first become a dominant, crushing force and then spur the birth of the humanistic reaction to it, and that psychology was called behaviorism.

The Second Force: Power of Reduction

While behaviorism had several antecedents, it is generally agreed that the field was founded by John B. Watson (1878–1958) in 1913 when he published his first article in *Psychological Review*. Following is the introductory statement from that article:

Psychology as the behaviorist views it is a purely objective
experimental branch of natural science. Its theoretical goal is
the prediction and control of behavior. Introspection forms no
essential part of its methods, nor is the scientific value of its data
dependent upon the readiness with which they lend themselves
to interpretation in terms of consciousness. The behaviorist, in
his efforts to get a unitary scheme of animal response, recognizes
no dividing line between man and brute. The behavior of man,
with all of its refinement and complexity, forms only a part of the
behaviorist's total scheme of investigation.

(Watson, 1948, p. 457)

From many accounts, Watson was a flamboyant, self-promoting,
"gifted huckster" (Hunt, 1993, p. 253), who sold himself and the idea
of behaviorism to the entire field of psychology that was, at that time,
floundering for direction. He was teased in grammar school by his
classmates, but as he grew into a strikingly handsome young man
with a firm jaw and dark hair his outward confidence grew. In pursuing both his degrees, undergraduate and Ph.D., he corresponded
directly with the presidents of the schools where he wished to study
and made his case for admission. The strategy appears to have worked
as he was admitted to both institutions, including the University of
Chicago where, after completing his Ph.D. in psychology, he was
offered an assistantship to stay on. Eventually, after several promo-
tions in Chicago, he was offered the chair of the psychology department at Johns Hopkins University in Baltimore, Maryland.

Watson's criticism of the general field of psychology boiled down
to one of method. He was strongly against the idea of introspection, which was used as a primary tool of investigation by both the
structuralists and functionalists of the time, and remains a key tool
for the actor today. While pioneers such as Wundt, James, and even
Freud were highly concerned with creating a field that could be
"taken seriously" as a scientific endeavor, they still relied heavily on
the concept of consciousness and introspection, and Watson took
serious exception to that:

I do not wish unduly to criticize psychology. It has failed
signally, I believe, during the fifty-odd years of its existence as
an experimental discipline to make its place in the world as an
undisputed natural science. Psychology, as it is generally thought

31

of, has something esoteric in its methods. If you fail to reproduce my findings, it is not due to some fault in your apparatus or in the control of your stimulus, but it is due to the fact that your introspection is untrained. The attack is made upon the observer and not upon the experimental setting. In physics and in chemistry the attack is made upon the experimental conditions. The apparatus was not sensitive enough, impure chemicals were used, etc. In these sciences a better technique will give reproducible results. Psychology is otherwise.

(Watson, 1948, p. 461)

His attacks on the state of the field in 1913 were vicious and unrelenting. He called for nothing less than the literal and total exclusion of all inner experience from study or consideration by psychology, if it were to be a science within the strict terms that he now dictated:

The time seems to have come when psychology must discard all reference to consciousness; when it need no longer delude itself into thinking that it is making mental states the object of observation. We have become so enmeshed in speculative questions concerning the elements of mind, the nature of conscious content (for example, imageless thought, attitudes, and Bewusseinslage, etc.) that I, as an experimental student, feel that something is wrong with our premises and the types of problems which develop from them. There is no longer any guarantee that we all mean the same thing when we use the terms now current in psychology.

(Watson, 1948, p. 461)

In Watson's personal life, he could be charming in social situations, and often seemed to seek out relationships with the most influential people to whom he had access, but was often uncomfortable in discussing personal feelings or emotions. He was described as "emotionally cold" (Hunt, 1993, p. 253). Looked at from a psychoanalytic perspective, Watson's passionate distaste for emotion and the inner experiences of human consciousness might have been construed as a gigantic reaction formation toward the entire dimension of emotionality and an attempt to destroy the basic legitimacy of feelings as a personal defense mechanism. However, regardless of his motivations, the arguments he put forth for limiting the scope of psychological investigation to only observable behaviors eventually took hold, particularly within the university environment in the United States.

By 1915, John Watson was voted president of the American Psychological Association, where he used his presidential address in 1916 to further his arguments for using animal subjects in place of humans for psychological experiments. Much of this argument was drawn from the work of a Russian physiologist, who had a very low opinion of psychology as a field of study, named Ivan Pavlov (1849–1936).

Pavlov had been a Russian seminary student who had forsaken the religious views of his father, and the seminary school that he attended, for a more modern scientific and mechanistic view of the world after reading Charles Darwin's *On the Origin of Species* (1859). He struggled financially for many years in the Russian academic system of the time until 1890 when he received an appointment as an assistant professor of pharmacology at the Military Medical Academy in St. Petersburg (Todes, 2014, pp. 111–113). At St. Petersburg, he organized a research institute and began the experiments that would eventually make him world-famous.

Pavlov was interested in the digestive systems of dogs. He would implant devices in the dogs' stomachs to monitor digestive fluids. For his work, he won a Nobel Prize and became a full member of the Academy of Sciences. Near the turn of the twentieth century, he noticed some irregularities in the secretion of gastric juices and saliva when the dogs would see or hear their feeders before food was actually delivered. At first, this discrepancy annoyed him, but eventually he began to study the phenomenon, always considering it a physiological response and not a psychological one. Throughout his adult life, Pavlov was a strict scientific materialist, and found the ideas prevalent in the psychology of his day both esoteric and overly subjective (Hunt, 1993, pp. 249–250). He developed the ideas of conditioned responses and reflexes, and believed that there was a neurological connection between the nerves in the spine and the lower brain. He developed a detailed theory that fit his findings, although much of it was later disproved. However, in 1908, Pavlov's work was discovered by a pair of American psychologists in a German medical journal, which they then translated and summarized in an article for *Psychological Bulletin* (Yerkes & Morgulis, 1909). And so it was that in 1916, Watson picked up Pavlov's ideas around conditioning, and even though he had only the vaguest understanding of them at the time, appended them to his own behaviorist approach,

33

where conditioning would later become a basic key component of almost all behaviorist theory (Hunt, 1993, p. 253).

By 1920, behaviorist ideology and methods had found a firm foothold in American academic psychology departments and the general public began to pick up the ideas too. For the next 40 years, behaviorism nearly dominated all academic psychology, squeezing out funding and course time for virtually any other kind of study in the field. Animal research came to the fore, and in many situations was preferred to human research.

Ironically, just as behaviorism was making its meteoric rise in universities across the United States, its founder, John Watson, found himself embroiled in a sex-related scandal that would see the sudden and dramatic end of his academic career. While working on an experiment in infant learning and conditioning, Watson became romantically involved with a student, which his wife, Mary Ickes Watson, later discovered. Watson had a history of extramarital affairs, but this situation was particularly galling to Mary, and ended in a high-profile divorce and Watson's forced resignation from his position at Johns Hopkins. He never returned to academia. Although he wrote several books in the decade following the scandal, he was forced to start a second career where he used his reputation in psychology, and his skills at self-promotion, to become a successful advertising executive at Madison Avenue ad agency J. Walter Thompson (Hunt, 1993, pp. 258–260).

The Third and Fourth Forces in American Psychology

After World War II, American culture exploded into the modern age of technology and unprecedented prosperity. There was a sheltered optimism in the air. New products were coming into the marketplace almost daily that promised convenience and a new freedom from the drudgery of common tasks. A growing middle class was accompanied by the rise of megacorporations and a belief that American ingenuity could conquer almost any challenge. Scientific progress across a myriad of endeavors, from automation to chemistry, transportation to medicine, even the conquest of space, became a culturally embedded expectation and an inevitability by consensus. And in this atmosphere of ever-evolving progress and growth came a faith in psychology and psychotherapy as a new scientific "medicine for the mind" that could help average citizens to predictably solve their personal problems and

34

readily adjust to the complexities of the new and constantly shifting world around them (Grogan, 2013, pp. 4–9).

The popular imagination of Americans in particular had been captured by the stereotyped image of the bearded psychoanalyst (à la Sigmund Freud) sitting by a couch taking notes while a reclining patient recounted their dreams and memories from childhood. In 1957, *Life* magazine published a five-part series entitled "The Age of Psychology in the US" (Havemann, 1957) that extolled the idea that "the science of human behavior permeates our whole way of life—at work, in love, in sickness and in health."

By the 1950s, academic psychology was nearly completely controlled by behaviorism, particularly in the United States, where funding for research and academic appointments was almost exclusively doled out to subscribers of the behavioristic view and withheld from researchers who would take a different approach (DeCarvalho, 1991, p. 7). As an example, the cofounder of both humanistic and transpersonal psychology, Abraham Maslow (1908–1970), took nine years to achieve associate professor status at Brooklyn College where he began his career as an academic, and while he continued to publish prolifically through the 1940s and 1950s, the quality and reach of the journals that would accept his work declined precipitously (Grogan, 2013, p. 61).

The humanistic movement was first, and in some ways foremost, a protest movement against the monolithic backdrop of these two dominant schools: reductionistic behaviorism and Freudian psychoanalysis (DeCarvalho, 1991, pp. 1–2). In the 1940s and 1950s, a small group of psychologists, who included Abraham Maslow, Carl Rogers, Rollo May, Clark Moustakas, Charlotte Bühler, James Bugental, Sidney Jourard, and Anthony Sutich became disillusioned and frustrated by the limited opportunities afforded them to publish their work. Very much in the minority at the time, this group of individuals was interested in more of a person-centered approach to psychology and psychotherapy, which was actively resisted by the "mainstream" psychological institutions, including the American Psychological Association, which controlled many of the top journals in the field. Maslow, in particular, was interested in including interior states of consciousness and personal, subjective motivations in the formal study of psychology, which was generally verboten during this period of behavioristic and Freudian dominance. Once again, as it had during the time of the Greeks and again after Descartes, psychology had become contentious and fragmented along the division between external, observable, "scientific fact," and the internal world of subjective experience. On the whole, the group who would become known as humanistic psychologists acknowledged the many useful truths that had been discovered by both of the earlier forces and wanted to *add* observations from the internal dimensions of experience to create a more holistic map of humanity and its cultures.

Maslow was the firstborn of a Jewish family from Brooklyn, New York. He had struggled in school until he discovered psychology in college at the University of Wisconsin—Madison, where he became a promising researcher and a dedicated behaviorist in the 1930s. He did research on primates and dogs and published papers with his graduate advisor and mentor Harry Harlow (Maslow & Harlow, 1932a, 1932b). However, when he completed his Ph.D. in 1934, at the height of the Depression era, he found it extremely difficult to find a job, finally landing a position as a tutor at Brooklyn College, a position below instructor. The pay was poor, and it was not a prestigious institution, but it was a tenure-track position and it allowed him and his wife, Bertha, to stay in New York near where they had both grown up.

Maslow's early research was on the sexual and dominance behaviors in animals, but eventually he began to extend his theories to human beings, running some of the earliest research on human sexuality in the United States. This eventually led him into deeper studies of human motivation that transformed his interests and personal views from strict behaviorism to a much more liberal "humanistic" outlook. Even though he was recognized as brilliant by many, he suffered professional isolation and even anti-Semitic bigotry from some of his colleagues in academia. In 1951, it seemed his fortunes had turned when he was offered the chair of the psychology department at the newly launched Brandeis University in Massachusetts. In 1954, he published the now classic book *Motivation and Personality* (Maslow, 1954), where he posited a theory of human motivation based on a model of needs fulfillment, now called "Maslow's hierarchy of needs," which would make him world-famous. Yet even with the recognition that certain of his books and articles brought him, he still found it difficult to get his ideas published in the better psychology journals of his day. Out of frustration, he began to assemble a mailing list of like-minded academics and psychotherapists, as well as interested intellectuals from other allied fields, that could mail their writings to each other when no other publication outlet would print their work.

Early in 1949, while staying in California to recover from a health problem, Maslow was introduced to a Palo Alto-based psychotherapist named Anthony "Tony" Sutich. Sutich was a unique man. Disabled in his teens by a severe case of juvenile arthritis, he spent his entire adult life confined to a customized rolling gurney bed with limited use of his hands and arms. Sutich made his living as a licensed psychotherapist and had experienced some of the same types of resistance by publishers as Maslow had. The two men forged a strong, if unlikely, friendship that would ultimately change the face of Western psychology as it had been known up until that time. All through the 1950s, the two men corresponded by mail and commiserated about the conservative and reductive environment of the psychology field. At the peak of behaviorism's dominance of U.S. academic psychology, and encouraged by Maslow, Sutich launched a journal and an association for alternative views that he ultimately called "humanistic psychology." The first issue of the *Journal of Humanistic Psychology* was published in the Spring of 1961 and represented a nascent turning point in the overall field of psychological study.

In 1964, at Old Saybrook, Connecticut, the first humanistic psychology invitational conference was held, an historic gathering that did much to establish the character of the new movement. Attendees included psychologists, among whom were Gordon Allport, J. F. T. Bugental, Charlotte Bühler, Abraham Maslow, Rollo May, Gardner Murphy, Henry Murray, and Carl Rogers, as well as humanists from other disciplines, such as Jacques Barzun, Rene Dubos, and Floyd Matson. The conferees questioned why the two dominant versions of psychology, behaviorism and psychoanalysis (or depth psychology), did not deal with human beings as uniquely human, nor with many of the real problems of human life. They agreed that if psychology were to become more than a narrow academic discipline limited by the biases of behaviorism, and if it were to study human attributes such as values and self-consciousness that the depth psychologists had chosen to de-emphasize, their "third force" would have to offer a fuller concept and experience of what it meant to be human (Hara, 2014).

Most of all, as it was conceived by its academic and psychotherapist founders, humanistic psychology was a psychology of growth, of human experience more than outward behavior, and of healthy functioning rather than psychopathology and mental disease. The early humanistic psychologists were interested in what could make us healthier rather than ill. They were interested in understanding the psychological characteristics of the best and most developed of human beings, instead of basing their theories on the mentally disturbed or clinically neurotic as Freud and many of his contemporaries had done. Humanistic psychology aspired to reinject the notion of subjectivity and the value of individuality back into the psychological conversation, something they felt had been totally lost under the weight of Freud and the controlling domination of behaviorism. They were interested in using psychology to answer important human questions about value and meaning, as well as improving society with their efforts. Humanistic psychology, in its origins, was intended to be a utopian view in counterpoint to the darker, deterministic dystopia that they felt the first two forces in psychology had envisioned and brought forth.

The birth of humanistic psychology coincided with a larger cultural shift in America that combined criticism for the Vietnam War and traditional cultural institutions, a rising youth culture, the influx of translations of Eastern esoteric and philosophical literature, the "New Age" spirituality movement, and the rise of feminist and civil rights movements that all coalesced into the popular "hippy" counterculture and the human potential movement (Grogan, 2013) and marked the overall beginnings of what is now known as postmodernism (Jencks, 1992).

As humanistic psychology took hold, suddenly alternative voices to the first two forces began to be heard, and heard loudly, both in academia and in the public domain. Carl Rogers promoted his ideas of "client-based" therapy and "unconditional positive regard" in the therapeutic encounter, and Maslow's hierarchy of needs entered the popular lexicon, rocketing its creator to international fame. Closely allied existential psychology, which had mostly started in Europe, became popularized in the United States by the writings of such authors and psychologists as Rollo May and Viktor Frankl. Group therapy and encounter sessions became a widespread fad through such high-profile movements as Gestalt therapy and Erhard Seminars Training (EST). Humanistic psychology cofounder Abraham Maslow met the owners of a new growth center launching near Big Sur, California, called the Esalen Institute, in the early 1960s. The Esalen Institute would grow to be the premier center for the human growth and potential movement, and a major force in popularizing both humanistic psychology and the psychotherapeutic culture that proliferated though much of the American middle and upper middle class mainstream beginning in the 1970s. Humanistic practices began to emphasize the experiential over the theoretical and intellectual. Psychology and psychotherapy, which only a few years earlier had been the exclusive domain of expert academics and trained physicians, suddenly became democratized and widely available, as well as *extremely popular*.

38

This wild and uncontrolled explosion of growth atop the cultural wave of the 1960s, however, had a downside that quickly overtook and then subsumed the original impulses of the humanistic psychology movement. As the movement proliferated, bodywork, "encounter" groups, and weekend "growth seminars" became a main feature, often to the exclusion of the more theoretical and intellectually grounded ideas of the humanistic psychologists who had founded the field. By the mid-1960s, Esalen was sponsoring hundreds of seminars per year, many of which were academically rigorous or represented alternative but practical explorations of the human condition. However, both visitors and the resident staff at Esalen were also experimenting with activities that went well outside of the norm or that had little empirical legitimacy at the time, including alternating heat and cold while hyperventilating, heat and cold while fasting, trance states, extended silence, rebirth rituals, death rituals, nursing bottles for adults, inhaling CO_2, confessional games, induced emotional outbursts, adults playing doctor, social nudity, fantasy trips, wrestling, dancing, and intensive group encounter sessions where confrontation and humiliation were often used as "therapeutic tools."

Two of the ways that humanistic psychology proliferated throughout the culture were through the university system and an explosion in "self-help" literature, which today represents a multibillion-dollar industry.

As the 1970s wore on, many of the original psychologists who had played founding roles in the humanistic movement became vocal critics of the direction the field seemed to be taking as it was led by the sheer force of the popular human potential movement. In 1975, humanistic psychology hit its peak when its annual convention, held in Estes Park, Colorado, was attended by an estimated 2,500 people. The program, while it included many intellectual and theoretical sessions, was predominated (at least according to attendance numbers) by a series of sensational, experiential workshops that included an EST presentation by that organization's founder, Werner Erhard, who some had referred to as the "Henry Ford of human potential," and a group led by parapsychologist Stanley Krippner, who, along with a group of followers, tried to make telepathic contact with a receiving group in Bogotá, Colombia, "through their connection to the earth" (Grogan, 2013, p. 298). Rollo May, who by this time had distanced himself from the movement because of his discomfort over emotion-centric therapies and bodywork, which he felt were essentially promoting anti-intellectualism, criticized humanistic psychology and its public activities as a "circus," and stated that the movement had been "formed by scholars" but "taken over by hippies" (Grogan, 2013, pp. 285–286).

In 1976 and 1977, AHP convention attendance declined to around 2,000 participants, and by 1980 it was down to 1,000. In the 1980s, a new conservative wave began to sweep over the American cultural landscape, and the influence, and many of the more extravagant and sensational practices that humanistic psychology had spawned, began to recede into history.

Perhaps the final significance of humanistic psychology, particularly for the theatrical profession, is in its introduction and popularization of bodywork techniques. Many of the theories around voice and movement work for theater training still in use today, including that of Kristin Linklater, Catherine Fitzmaurice, and Moshe Feldenkrais, were influenced by the experiential and bodywork aspects of the human potential movement, which had been inspired by humanistic psychology (Feldenkrais, 1977; Fitzmaurice, 2017; Linklater, 2017).

Interestingly, before his untimely death from a heart attack in 1970, Abraham Maslow went on to formulate, along with Tony Sutich, yet another "force" in psychology that became known as *transpersonal psychology*. As early as 1966, both Maslow and Sutich were having their doubts about the rapidly evolving landscape of the humanistic psychology movement they had helped to create. Like some of their cofounders, they found the overemphasis on experiential practices, group process, and the general anti-intellectualism troubling. Their original intention in founding the field was to expand the explorations of human psychology in both empirical and hermeneutic ways to include inner experience as a legitimate area of study, but not to exclude the empirical; their fundamental interest had been in *augmenting* the first two forces of psychology, not ignoring them. To reduce everything to merely felt experience and "feelings in the moment" was tantamount to the same move the scientific reductionists of behaviorism had attempted from the opposite direction. Furthermore, while Maslow's personal studies had surrounded the positive aspects of the human personality and what he had coined "self-actualization," the successful fulfillment of a human's potential across their entire developmental life cycle, he felt that the larger wave of humanistic techniques and practices were focusing too much on the individual self, and perhaps causing narcissism rather than an integration of the personality and self-actualization. In many ways, even though he was a revered leader of the humanistic movement, he still felt his work was being misunderstood and misinterpreted as a framework for overindulgence and even infantile behavior.

To his dying day, Maslow viewed himself as a scientific thinker who had taken umbrage with the methods of the established institutions of psychology that he wished to reform and improve. But the wildness and often regressive behavior that seemed to be justified if not downright encouraged by the emerging humanistic movement seemed, to Maslow at least, too far in the opposite direction; the protest had gotten out of hand, the revolution was devolving rather than evolving psychology itself. Much like Rollo May, Maslow had the growing feeling that the humanistic movement had somehow been hijacked by those who preferred to indulge their personal experiences rather than to attempt a deeper understanding and evolution of the human psyche.

One of Maslow's chief areas of investigation had been what he called "peak experiences." Peak experiences were considered the highest and best moments of a healthy, and usually mature, human being's conscious life. Maslow described them as "rare, exciting, oceanic, deeply moving, exhilarating, elevating experiences that generate an advanced form of perceiving reality, and are even mystic and magical in their affect upon the experimenter" (cited in Corsini, Auerbach, & Anastasi, 1998, p. 21). In many ways, a peak experience, as Maslow viewed it, is a secularized term for spiritual, religious, or enlightenment experience. Maslow described such experiences in different ways, particularly in his later work, but they usually included qualities or combinations of qualities such as: a loss of awareness of time and space; a sense of "oneness" with something greater than the individual self; free of dissociation or inner conflict; the feeling of using all capacities and capabilities at their highest potential; being without inhibition, fear, doubt, and self-criticism; naturally flowing behavior that is not constrained by conformity; complete mindfulness of the present moment without influence of past or expected future experiences; and a possible identification with the entire universe as not separate from the self (often called "unity consciousness" or "enlightenment"). For his studies of peak experiences, he interviewed what he considered to be exceptional and especially emotionally mature people, surveyed college-aged students, acquired descriptions of such experiences from people who wrote to him after reading his work, and conducted a deep literature review of material about mysticism, religion, art, creativity, and love (Maslow, 1968). Maslow came to believe that most traditional religions were actually founded based on these types of peak spiritual experiences by individuals (the saint, prophet, or savior figure) that were then interpreted, or in many cases misinterpreted, by the followers that came afterward, which often codified into

41

dogma what the founding figure had tried to describe. In antiquity, these experiences had been interpreted as supernatural events, but in modern times could be seen (and studied) as natural evolutions of human beings moving into maturity and full, optimal functioning or self-actualization (Maslow, 1968, pp. 71–102).

Yet Maslow and Sutich, who was just as interested in the psychological aspects of mystical and spiritual experience as Maslow, which they came to call the higher or farther reaches of human nature, found they had a problem. The rational and empirically oriented psychologists who formed the core of the humanistic movement, as well as the swelling ranks of the public entering the human potential movement, were as consistently resistant and dismissive of most subject matters that had any kind of tie to the labels "religion" or "spirituality" as were the hardcore scientific reductionists who made up much of traditional academic psychology and Freudian psychoanalytic practice. Religion and spirituality were verboten subjects of study and even discussion for most members of all three camps.

As a result of this limitation, and in many cases flat-out denial of mystical or spiritual subject matter as legitimate topics for psychological study, Maslow and Sutich, along with a number of other psychologists who had become prominent in the humanistic movement, formed yet another journal and association to provide a publishing outlet and research platform for peak experiences and other phenomena that was otherwise outside of the purview of the first three forces of psychology. As early as 1967, just five years after the formal launch of the *Journal of Humanistic Psychology*, Sutich was working on a draft of a definition for the new field that characterized it as a "fourth force" in psychology and included a list of potential areas of investigation. The list of subject matters was intentionally long and inclusive, containing items such as states of being, becoming, self-actualization, expression and actualization of meta-needs (individual and "species-wide"), ultimate values, self-transcendence, unitive consciousness, peak experiences, ecstasy, mystical experience, awe, wonder, ultimate meaning, transformation of the self, spirit, species-wide transformation, oneness, cosmic awareness, maximal sensory responsiveness, realization, and expression of transpersonal and transcendental potentialities, and related concepts, experiences, and activities (Sutich, 1976, p. 13).

In 1969, just one year before Maslow's death, the same month as the first moon landing took place, the first issue of the *Journal of Transpersonal Psychology* was released. The history of the transpersonal psychology movement was just as volatile, although for mostly different reasons, as the humanistic movement had been in the previous decade. Transpersonal psychology provided a platform for the first serious studies of religious and spiritual experience, something that had previously been completely ignored by mainstream Western psychology and science in general. Practices such as yoga and meditation suddenly became subjects of scientific investigation (Goleman, 1971, 1988; Kabat-Zinn & University of Massachusetts Medical Center/Worcester Stress Reduction Clinic, 1990; Page, 2007; Ram, 1970; Shapiro & Walsh, 1984; Tart, 1971; Timmons & Kamiya, 1970). Eastern gurus were invited by transpersonal psychologists to teach topics such as Buddhist and Hindu concepts of the human mind, furthering an influx of translations of Eastern philosophical and mystical literature that had never been available to Western scholars before (Trungpa & Gimian, 2003). Transpersonal psychologists began to study altered states of consciousness from intensive meditative states to the effects of drugs such as LSD (Grof, 1972, 2006; Harman, Kamiya, Krippner, Pahnke, & Tart, 1969; Tart, 1969, 1975; Wilber, Engler, & Brown, 1986). Transpersonal psychologists began to investigate the nature and effects of spiritual pathologies in the context of the psychotherapeutic setting and creating new therapies to help people suffering from spiritually oriented and non-ordinary psychological disturbances (Grof, 1973; Scotton, Chinen, & Battista, 1996; Vaughan, 1986, 1995). In the 1990s, membership in the Association for Transpersonal Psychology reached nearly 4,000 and there were courses on spiritual and transpersonal psychology being taught at mainstream universities, as well as a number of private institutes who offered both master's and Ph.D. level degrees (Moss, 1999; Page, 2006). However, after the passing of Maslow in the early days of the movement, and Tony Sutich just a few years later in 1976, and exponential growth that brought a similar sort of fragmentation and disarray as humanistic psychology had suffered from, the movement seemed to lose steam and focus after the new millennium and contract in influence and broader appeal (Page, 2011).

43

In the final analysis, both humanistic and transpersonal psychologies have faded from the academic scene from which they were born and are often little remembered or even known in the popular culture today. However, both movements left behind important contributions, including theories (maps) and techniques (models) that can be of great use to the actor, and we will explore a number of these later in the book. Both fields still exist today through their associations and respective academic journals (Sutich, 1961, 1969), but their activities have been much reduced in scale from their heydays in the 1960s and 1970s.

The Cognitive and Postmodern Turns

Another response to the oppressive dominance of behaviorism in American psychology through the 1950s took the form of what would eventually be called "the cognitive turn." By the early 1960s, a handful of psychologists were rejecting behaviorism's narrow mandate and reintroducing an interest in the core elements of human consciousness, much as William James had done at the beginning of the century. This new breed of psychologist began to explore the phenomenon of human cognition. "Cognition comprises mental processes such as perceiving, thinking, remembering, evaluating, planning, and organizing" (Frager & Fadiman, 2005, p. 272).

In 1958, psychologist Allen Newell and computer scientist Herbert A. Simon proposed the idea that the human mind was essentially an information-processing system, much like an electronic computer, and behavior was analogous to a program running on a computer that would interact with, evaluate, and respond to the various data inputs it received through the system (such as the sense organs). These two colleagues created rudimentary artificial intelligence (AI) computer programs that were intended to solve problems of logic, in a way they claimed was similar to the functions of the human mind. Their work gave the emerging cognitivists a new model of mind to work with that eventually became a revolution in psychology eclipsing, and surviving, the humanistic and transpersonal movements that arose around the same time.

Along with the rise of the computer model of cognition were several advances in other fields that would fuel the cognitive revolution. Physiological neuroscience developed microelectrodes and other technologies that could observe neural events in the brain, and scientists began to relate these to mental processes. Information theory began to account for the capabilities and limitations of human communication. Anthropologists completed more comprehensive cross-cultural studies and to identify traits they believed to be truly universal. Psycholinguists started to understand more fully how humans acquire and manipulate the complex symbols of language (Hunt, 1993, p. 513). These developments and others began to cross-fertilize with psychology to displace what had become the stagnant movement of behaviorism in American academia and replace it with a multidisciplinary movement that blossomed under the general umbrella of "cognitive science" (Gardner, 1985, pp. 36–37).

Researchers Francisco J. Varela, Evan Thompson, and Eleanor Rosch, in their now classic book *The Embodied Mind* (1991), advanced the field of cognitive psychology even further when they proposed a model of cognition that was "enactive" rather than simply based on computer information-processing, which had become a problematic idea early on when it was criticized as being too limited and not taking into account the internal experience of consciousness and the more complex processes of phenomena such as insight, sometimes called the "aha moment" (Frager & Fadiman, 2005, p. 274). Varela et al. suggested that *enactment* was an open-ended, self-modifying process where:

Cognition is not the representation of a pregiven world by a pregiven mind but is rather the enactment of a world and a mind on the basis of a history of the various actions that a being in the world performs.

(Varela et al., 1991, p. 9)

In other words, cognition, internal experience, and environment interact with and modify each other, meaning that mind affects brain and brain affects the states of the mind *reciprocally*. This viewpoint essentially, once again, attempts to marry internal experience with the external, purely physical structures (such as brain physiology), which is the same conflict that humanistic psychology was trying to resolve with behaviorism, and which goes back to Descartes and the Greek philosophers discussed at the beginning of this book. This notion of *embodied cognition*, which is now a strong thread in psychological theory, has also become popular with many acting theorists (Blair, 2008; Blair & Cook, 2016; Kemp, 2012; Lutterbie, 2011; Zarrilli, Daboo, & Loukes, 2013).

Another important theorist who expanded cognitive psychology is Albert Bandura, who formulated social learning theory (later renamed the social cognitive theory) and the theoretical construct of self-efficacy. Social cognitive theory looks at how people learn by observing others. In the behaviorist paradigm, all behavior was thought to be reinforced through experience. However, Bandura demonstrated that there was much learning that took place purely by observation and imitation. Self-efficacy is the belief in one's capabilities to organize and execute the courses of action required to manage prospective situations; in other words, a person's belief in themselves to be capable of taking action.

Bandura, somewhat like Varela discussed above, also believed that our behavior had effects on our own cognitive processes, as well as

45

being influenced by, and having influence on, social factors in our environment so that humans and society were *reciprocally determining*. So, to Bandura, people contribute to their own motivations, behaviors, and development within a social context of reciprocally interacting influences (Frager & Fadiman, 2005, p. 276).

One of the most important influences that cognitive psychology has had is on the world of psychotherapy and its more popular relation, "self-help" literature. In the 1960s, psychoanalyst Aaron T. Beck had the realization that often his patients seemed to have a stream of thoughts in their minds that were self-monitoring and often self-critical, and seemed to arise automatically without much relation to the content of the therapeutic situation. From what Beck discovered about these automatic thought streams, he created a new approach to therapy where he helped his patients first become aware of their automatic, and oftentimes distorted, thought patterns and then take responsibility for changing the thoughts, in the process reducing much of their negativity and commensurately reducing the impact of their symptoms. Beck's approach, which eventually became known as cognitive behavioral therapy (CBT), had a revolutionary impact on the psychotherapy industry that was growing into a massive cultural movement by that time (see a discussion of the growth of the "therapy culture" in the previous section). Traditional psychoanalysis had come under criticism for low success rates and long, sometimes indefinite treatment windows. In contrast, CBT tended to focus more on individual problems and empowering the patients to take control of their own healing by making them aware of their negative automatic thinking patterns and then educating them on ways to change those patterns themselves. Patients who had otherwise seemed to languor in traditional psychotherapy often responded well to CBT, and *responded more quickly*. As therapy became more mainstream, and insurance companies were asked more often to pay for therapy, the speed and specificity of the CBT approach became more attractive and more prevalent.

This direct approach to self-awareness and individual empowerment to change also had a great impact on the self-help industry for books, workshops, etc., which, along with the rise of CBT and other similar therapy approaches, grew into a multibillion-dollar industry. Many very popular self-help books, covering such diverse topics as assertiveness, self-esteem, anger issues, depression, marriage and relationships, or simply feeling good, have been based on the work of cognitive therapists influenced by Beck and cognitive psychology (Frager & Fadiman, 2005, p. 284).

The postmodern turn in psychology of the last 20 years or so has been a turn away from the self as a subject of psychology altogether. From the postmodern view, there is no "self" for psychology to study and understand, only an ongoing series of culturally created identities, or personas, that are ever-shifting and non-permanent. I cannot speak to the veracity of this position as a map or model of reality, but I can say that it is an interesting definition of the *actor's reality* from within the world of the character. For indeed, from the actor's perspective during the moment of performance, there is no hard and concrete self of the character; there is merely a constructed self that will live a few moments while the audience is there, or the cameras are rolling, and then slip away into the next role or challenge that presents itself, ever-shifting, always constructed, non-permanent to the core. So, it would seem that the postmodern view, at least as described above, might best define the approach of this book. The various schools or movements in Western psychology described above, along with the more detailed discussions to follow, all constitute construction tools for building detailed, perspective-bound personas for the explicit purpose of presentation to an audience who is forever embedded in a social context created mostly by language and structures of power that always lie in the background, mostly unconscious to all participants. So, *who* are the actors and *who* are the audience members? In many ways, actors have always been postmodernists with the form's embedded necessity to take multiple and diverse perspectives at every turn. You could even say that every act of performance is a postmodern gesture where the actor merely replaces the typical political/feminist/eco/diversity paradigm of the postmodern "movement" with the given circumstances of the playwright, thereby selecting an orienting context before the fun begins.

While much of mainstream psychology may not yet have fully acquiesced to the notion of the "death of the self," as postmodernism might suggest, it has certainly diversified its own menu of acceptable worldviews from the days when behaviorism and psychoanalysis held full sway. Today, approximately 13,000 instructors in the United States teach an Introduction to Psychology course at least once a year (Gurung et al., 2016). "Intro to Psych" is the second most popular college course in the nation, second only to English Composition, and is completed by 60% of college students who have earned 10 or more college credits (Adelman, 2004). This statistic seems ironic given that very few college-trained actors receive any formal psychological training at all. In 2016, the American Psychological Association (APA) published recommendations for standardizing the teaching of

Intro to Psych courses in the American university system. The APA is the world's largest professional organization for psychologists, with more than 117,500 members (APA, 2017). Their recommendations included teaching the intro course to integrate:

(a) scientific foundations, (b) 5 major domains or pillars of knowledge (biological, cognitive, developmental, social and personality, and mental and physical health), and (c) cross-cutting themes relevant to all domains (cultural and social diversity, ethics, variations in human functioning, and applications) . . .

No longer a collection of independent topic areas based on historical or administrative distinctions, psychology in the 21st century has become an integrative multilevel science. . . . An integrative approach conceptualizes the science of mind and behavior as different levels of organization (e.g., biological, cognitive, and social), with each contributing to our understanding of human behavior.

(Gurung et al., 2016, pp. 112–113)

48

In order to organize a standard for the delivery of Intro to Psych courses, the researchers defined five major "pillars" that include these various traditional and emerging topic areas:

Pillar 1: Biological (e.g., Neuroscience, Sensation, Consciousness)

Pillar 2: Cognitive (e.g., Cognition, Memory, Perception, Intelligence)

Pillar 3: Development (e.g., Learning, Life Span Development, Language)

Pillar 4: Social and Personality (e.g., Social, Personality, Emotion, Multicultural, Gender, Motivation)

Pillar 5: Mental and Physical Health (e.g., Abnormal, Health, Therapies)

(Gurung et al., 2016, p. 118)

For the purposes of this book, and the practical application of psychology by actors, we will concentrate primarily on material found in pillars 3 and 4. While there are some very interesting things going on in the neuro, biological, and cognitive sciences, as well as the mental health field in general, we are primarily interested in maps and models that can be immediately and directly adapted to the task of character creation and performance, and those types of maps and models have traditionally been built by social and personality theorists. Perhaps in a later volume we will explore in more detail the uses and applications of these other approaches to human psychology and mental functioning.

References

Adelman, C. (2004). *The Empirical Curriculum: Changes in Postsecondary Course-Taking, 1972–2000*. Washington, DC: U.S. Department of Education.

APA (2017). *Advertise with APA*. Retrieved from www.apa.org/ads/index.aspx.

Bjork, D. W. (1983). *The Compromised Scientist: William James in the Development of American Psychology*. New York: Columbia University Press.

Blair, R. (2008). *The Actor, Image, and Action: Acting and Cognitive Neuroscience*. London/New York: Routledge.

Blair, R., & Cook, A. (2016). *Theatre, Performance and Cognition: Languages, Bodies and Ecologies*. London: Bloomsbury Methuen Drama.

Carlson, N. R. (2010). *Psychology: The Science of Behavior* (7th ed.). Boston, MA: Allyn & Bacon.

Corsini, R. J., Auerbach, A. J., & Anastasi, A. (1998). *Concise Encyclopedia of Psychology* (2nd ed.). New York: J. Wiley.

Darwin, C. (1859). *On the Origin of Species by Means of Natural Selection*. London: J. Murray.

DeCarvalho, R. J. (1991a). *The Founders of Humanistic Psychology*. New York: Praeger.

Fancher, R. E. (1979). *Pioneers of Psychology*. New York: Norton.

Feldenkrais, M. (1977). *Awareness Through Movement: Health Exercises for Personal Growth* (illustrated ed.). New York: Harper & Row.

Fitzmaurice, C. (2017). *Interview: Catherine Fitzmaurice*. Interviewer: K. Page, June 10.

Frager, R., & Fadiman, J. (2005). *Personality and Personal Growth* (6th ed.). Upper Saddle River, NJ: Pearson Prentice Hall.

Freud, S. (1913). *The Interpretation of Dreams* (3rd ed.). New York: Macmillan.

Gardner, H. (1985). *The Mind's New Science: A History of the Cognitive Revolution*. New York: Basic Books.

Goleman, D. (1971). Meditation as a meta-therapy: hypotheses toward a proposed fifth state of consciousness. *Journal of Transpersonal Psychology*, 3(1), 1–25.

Goleman, D. (1988). *The Meditative Mind: The Varieties of Meditative Experience*. Los Angeles, CA/New York: J.P. Tarcher/St. Martin's Press.

Greenspan, R. E. (2006). *Medicine: Perspectives in History and Art*. Alexandria, VA: Ponteverde Press.

Grof, S. (1972). Varieties of transpersonal experiences: observations from LSD psychotherapy. *Journal of Transpersonal Psychology*, 4(1), 45–80.

Grof, S. (1973). Theoretical and empirical basis of transpersonal psychology and psychotherapy: observations from LSD research. *Journal of Transpersonal Psychology*, 5(1), 15–53.

Grof, S. (2006). *When the Impossible Happens: Adventures in Non-Ordinary Realities*. Boulder, CO: Sounds True.

Grogan, J. (2013). *Encountering America: Humanistic Psychology, Sixties Culture, & the Shaping of the Modern Self*. New York: Harper Perennial.

Gurung, R. A. R., Hackathorn, J., Enns, C., Frantz, S., Cacioppo, J. T., Loop, T., & Freeman, J. E. (2016). Strengthening introductory psychology: a new model for teaching the introductory course. *American Psychologist*, 71(2), 112–124. doi:10.1037/a0040012

Hara, M. O. (2014). *What is Humanistic Psychology?* Retrieved from www.ahpweb.org/about/what-is-humanistic-psychology.html.

Harman, W. W., Kamiya, J., Krippner, S., Pahnke, W., & Tart, C. T. (1969). *A New Science: Altered States of Consciousness* [sound recording]. S.l.: Big Sur Recordings.

Havemann, E. (1957). The age of psychology in the US. *Life*, 42, January 7.

Hunt, M. M. (1993). *The Story of Psychology*. New York: Doubleday.

James, W. (1890). *The Principles of Psychology*. New York: H. Holt & Company.

Jencks, C. (1992). *The Post-Modern Reader*. London/New York: Academy Editions/St. Martin's Press.

Jung, C. G., & Hinkle, B. M. (1916). *Psychology of the Unconscious: A Study of the Transformations and Symbolisms of the Libido—A Contribution to the History of the Evolution of Thought*. New York: Moffat, Yard & Co.

Jung, C. G., & Jaffé, A. (1989). *Memories, Dreams, Reflections* (rev. ed.). New York: Vintage Books.

50

Jung, C. G., Peterson, F., & Brill, A. A. (1909). *The Psychology of Dementia Praecox*. New York: The Journal of Nervous and Mental Disease Publishing Company.

Jung, C. G., & Shamdasani, S. (2009). *The Red Book: Liber Novus*. New York: W. W. Norton & Co.

Kabat-Zinn, J., & University of Massachusetts Medical Center/Worcester Stress Reduction Clinic (1990). *Full Catastrophe Living: Using the Wisdom of Your Body and Mind to Face Stress, Pain, and Illness*. New York: Delacorte Press.

Kemp, R. (2012). *Embodied Acting: What Neuroscience Tells Us About Performance*. London/New York: Routledge.

Linklater, K. (2017). *Interview: Kristin Linklater*. Interviewer: K. Page, June 20.

Lowry, R. (1971). *The Evolution of Psychological Theory: 1650 to the Present*. Chicago, IL: Aldine · Atherton.

Lutterbie, J. H. (2011). *Toward a General Theory of Acting: Cognitive Science and Performance*. New York: Palgrave Macmillan.

Maslow, A. H. (1954). *Motivation and Personality*. New York: Harper.

Maslow, A. H. (1968b). *Toward a Psychology of Being* (2nd ed.). Princeton, NJ: Van Nostrand.

Maslow, A., & Harlow, H. (1932a). Comparative behavior of primates II. *Journal of Comparative Psychology*, 14(1), 97–107.

Maslow, A., & Harlow, H. (1932b). Delayed reaction tests on primates at Bronx Park Zoo. *Journal of Comparative Psychology*, 14, 97–101.

Moss, D. (1999). *Humanistic and Transpersonal Psychology: A Historical and Biographical Sourcebook*. Westport, CT: Greenwood Press.

Page, K. (Writer) & Page, K. (Director) (2006). *Transpersonal Conversations: James Fadiman, Ph.D.* Transpersonal Media.

Page, K. (Writer) (2007). *Science of the Soul: The Story of Transpersonal Psychology*. Transpersonal Media.

Page, K. (Writer) (2011). *Science of the Soul: Expanded Edition 2011*. Transpersonal Media.

Perry, R. B. (1996). *The Thought and Character of William James* (new paperback ed.). Nashville, TN: Vanderbilt University Press.

Ram, D. (1970). *Yoga of Daily Life* [sound recording]. S.l.: Big Sur Recordings.

Schultz, D. P., & Schultz, S. E. (1987). *A History of Modern Psychology* (4th ed.). San Diego, CA: Harcourt Brace Jovanovich.

Scotton, B. W., Chinen, A. B., & Battista, J. R. (1996). *Textbook of Transpersonal Psychiatry and Psychology*. New York: Basic Books.

Shapiro, D. H., & Walsh, R. N. (1984). *Meditation: Classic and Contemporary Perspectives*. New York: Aldine.

Sutich, A. J. (1976). The emergence of the transpersonal orientation: a personal account. *Journal of Transpersonal Psychology*, 8(1), 5–19.

Sutich, E. A. (1961). Journal of Humanistic Psychology. *Journal of Humanistic Psychology*, 1(2): 1–114.

Sutich, E. A. (1969). Journal of Transpersonal Psychology. *Journal of Transpersonal Psychology*, 1(2), 1–114.

Tart, C. T. (1969). *Altered States of Consciousness: A Book of Readings*. New York: Wiley.

Tart, C. T. (1971). A psychologist's experience with transcendental meditation. *Journal of Transpersonal Psychology*, 3(1), 135–140.

Tart, C. T. (1975). *Transpersonal Psychologies*. London: Routledge & Kegan Paul.

Timmons, B., & Kamiya, J. (1970). The psychology and physiology of meditation and related phenomena: a bibliography. *Journal of Transpersonal Psychology*, 2(1), 41–59.

Titchener, E. B. (1896). *An Outline of Psychology*. New York/London: The Macmillan Company.

Todes, D. P. (2014). *Ivan Pavlov: A Russian Life in Science*. Oxford: Oxford University Press.

Trungpa, C. G., & Gimian, C. R. (2003). *The Collected Works of Chögyam Trungpa*. Boston, MA/London: Shambhala.

Varela, F. J., Thompson, E., & Rosch, E. (1991). *The Embodied Mind: Cognitive Science and Human Experience*. Cambridge, MA: MIT Press.

Vaughan, F. E. (1986). *The Inward Arc: Healing and Wholeness in Psychotherapy and Spirituality*. Boston, MA/New York: New Science Library/ Random House.

Vaughan, F. E. (1995). *Shadows of the Sacred: Seeing Through Spiritual Illusions*. Wheaton, IL: Quest Books.

Walach, H. (2013). Criticisms of transpersonal psychology and beyond: the future of transpersonal psychology. In H. L. Friedman & G. Hartelius (Eds.), *The Wiley-Blackwell Handbook of Transpersonal Psychology* (pp. 62–87). Chichester, UK: Wiley-Blackwell.

Watson, J. B. (1948). Psychology as the behaviorist views it, 1913. In W. Dennis (Ed.), *Readings in the History of Psychology* (pp. 457–471). New York: Appleton-Century-Crofts.

Wilber, K., Engler, J., & Brown, D. P. (1986). *Transformations of Consciousness: Conventional and Contemplative Perspectives on Development.* Boston, MA/New York: New Science Library/Random House.

Yerkes, R. M., & Morgulis, S. (1909). The method of Pavlov in animal psychology. *Psychological Bulletin, 6,* 257–273.

Zarrilli, P. B., Daboo, J., & Loukes, R. (2013). *Acting: Psychophysical Phenomenon and Process.* Hampshire, UK: Palgrave Macmillan.

Two Freuds

Free Association and the Defense Mechanisms

Sigmund Freud, as briefly profiled in the previous chapter, was one of the most influential thinkers of modern, and by extension postmodern, times. His theories took the rudimentary and physiologically based explorations of Western psychology prior to his time and added multiple dimensions to the ways we (still) look at the human mind and our experience (Frick, 1991, p. 8). While he did not create the concept of the "unconscious," he was the first to introduce it into the realm of psychology and build a vast map of the psyche that included a *dynamic interaction* between preconscious, conscious, and unconscious elements. For Freud, the conscious mind contained anything the individual was aware of at any given moment. Preconsciousness, on the other hand, is the easily accessible part of the unconscious mind, where the contents can be made readily conscious by an act of directed will. Preconsciousness is basically the memory storage area for the conscious mind; facts about the self and past experience that can be drawn into consciousness are the contents of the preconscious mind. The unconscious mind, in Freud's theory, is the storehouse for basic instincts that are never directly available to the conscious mind, and also repressed or censored thoughts and memories. This tripartite model of mind was one of Freud's major innovations in psychology and the basis for most of his theories that followed.

For Freud, the unconscious is populated by primal drives or impulses based almost exclusively on sex and aggression. He felt that these two fundamental instincts were the unconscious drivers of almost all human behavior.

54

The Id, Ego, and Superego

Freud also came up with a three-part model of the personality, consisting of the "id," the "ego," and the "superego." According to psychology scholars Robert Frager and James Fadiman (2005), Freud's words in German were simply: "it," "I," and "above I," but due to faulty and obscure translations into English we now have the somewhat ambiguous terms id, ego, and superego. The id houses all of the primitive urges and drives that come along with being human, and the raw desire to satisfy those drives at any cost without the slightest concern for others or the constructs of society. Freud called the id's drives "primary process" thinking. The id is modified, or controlled, by the ego, whose job it is to manage the desires of the id and relations with "the outside" world through "secondary process" thinking. The ego is essentially in charge of fulfilling the desires of the ego in society, as well as preserving the integrity and sanity of the personality. The ego strives for self-preservation; becomes aware of external circumstances, and then either avoids pain, adapts to the situation, or attempts to alter the external circumstances to make them safer and more comfortable; deals with internal impulses by either controlling them, putting off satisfaction until a more appropriate time, or suppressing them altogether; and generally seeks to pursue pleasure and avoid pain while in service to the id drives. The ego is the id's coping mechanism with the external world and a civilizing influence that makes modern societies possible. In Freud's model, without the ego to control the id's base desires, there would be nothing but constant rape, murder, and robbery in the world. The superego acts as a judge and censor for the thoughts and actions of the ego structure. The superego contains the moral codes and standards of conduct enculturated into the individual by the society in which it lives, and inhibits the personality to act in "socially acceptable" ways. The superego can act in both conscious and unconscious ways. In the conscious realm, the superego acts as the "conscience," which makes judgments about behavior and inhibits actions through the process of guilt. In the unconscious realm, the superego's inhibitory activities can be seen through compulsions and moral aversions. According to Freud, the id is completely unconscious, and the ego and superego are only partly unconscious.

Psychoanalysis, then, is:

The therapeutic method that Freud developed, [which] has a primary goal to strengthen the ego, to make it independent of the

55

overly strict concerns of the superego, and to increase its capacity to become aware of and control material formerly repressed or hidden in the id.

(Frager & Fadiman, 2005, p. 25)

It is important to note that even though there have been many other models of the human psyche proposed since Freud first emerged, (a) many of the theories that followed Freud utilized at least some of his formulations in their own construction; and (b) prior to Freud, models of the psyche were much more rudimentary and ill-defined, and character was considered fixed and static by physiological causes and heredity. Freud's concept of a *dynamic* and evolving personality with multiple dimensions nearly single-handedly brought the Victorian age into the modern era, and people prior to Freud (including characters you may be asked to play if they are in an historical context prior to the twentieth century) did not have a concept of the unconscious or its influence on consciousness as we do now. As Roach pointed out, the prevailing models of consciousness at any given point in history deeply influence how audiences and actors interpret the theatrical experience, and this includes the playwrights who create the stories (and characters) to be depicted. As an example, many of Shakespeare's characters are motivated by forces outside of themselves or "passions" arising in their bodies from the various "humors" that were thought to flow through living beings before science understood the circulation of blood or Freud had introduced the concept of the unconscious into psychology (Roach, 1993, p. 65). Therefore, in a very real sense, many of Shakespeare's characters may not be motivated by the same kinds of psychological concerns that we have today because of Freud and those who came after him. Another example of Freud's influence on acting, as touched upon in the introduction to this book, was the reinterpretation of Stanislavsky's work, which as you will recall relied mostly on Diderot and Ribot for its psychological underpinnings, through the lens of Freud by American Method purveyors, particularly Lee Strasberg (Carnicke, 2009, pp. 63–64).

Stages of Psychosexual Development

Freud also contributed a model of psychosexual development to the literature of psychology that still influences, in part, how we view individual development today. Freud believed that every child was born with a libidinal (sexual) drive, and that as they developed through the various stages of early childhood the focus of satisfaction of that drive would shift to various body parts, which he called *erogenous zones*. For instance, during breastfeeding, the infant receives satisfaction through the mouth; thus, in Freud's model, this is called the "oral stage."

Following is a brief outline of Freud's various stages of childhood psychosexual development from Wikipedia (2017b):

The first stage of psychosexual development is the oral stage, spanning from birth until the age of one year, wherein the infant's mouth is the focus of libidinal gratification derived from the pleasure of feeding at the mother's breast, and from the oral exploration of his or her environment, i.e. the tendency to place objects in the mouth. The id dominates, because neither the ego nor the super ego is yet fully developed, and, since the infant has no personality (identity), every action is based upon the pleasure principle. Nonetheless, the infantile ego is forming during the oral stage; two factors contribute to its formation: (i) in developing a body image, he or she is discrete from the external world, e.g. the child understands pain when it is applied to his or her body, thus identifying the physical boundaries between body and environment; (ii) experiencing delayed gratification leads to understanding that specific behaviors satisfy some needs, e.g. crying gratifies certain needs (Leach, 1997).

The second stage of psychosexual development is the anal stage, spanning from the age of eighteen months to three years, wherein the infant's erogenous zone changes from the mouth (the upper digestive tract) to the anus (the lower digestive tract), while the ego formation continues. Toilet training is the child's key anal-stage experience, occurring at about the age of two years, and results in conflict between the id (demanding immediate gratification) and the ego (demanding delayed gratification) in eliminating bodily wastes, and handling related activities (e.g. manipulating excrement, coping with parental demands). The style of parenting influences the resolution of the id–ego conflict, which can be either gradual and psychologically uneventful, or which can be sudden and psychologically traumatic.

57

The third stage of psychosexual development is the phallic stage, spanning the ages of three to six years, wherein the child's genitalia are his or her primary erogenous zone. It is in this third infantile development stage that children become aware of their bodies, the bodies of other children, and the bodies of their parents; they gratify physical curiosity by undressing and exploring each other and their genitals, and so learn the physical (sexual) differences between "male" and "female" and the gender differences between "boy" and "girl."

The fourth stage of psychosexual development is the latency stage that spans from the age of six years until puberty, wherein the child consolidates the character habits he or she developed in the three, earlier stages of psychologic and sexual development. . . . The instinctual drives of the id are inaccessible to the Ego, because his or her defense mechanisms repressed them during the phallic stage. Hence, because said drives are latent (hidden) and gratification is delayed—unlike during the preceding oral, anal, and phallic stages—the child must derive the pleasure of gratification from secondary process-thinking that directs the libidinal drives towards external activities, such as schooling, friendships, hobbies, etc.

The fifth stage of psychosexual development is the genital stage that spans puberty through adult life, and thus represents most of a person's life; its purpose is the psychological detachment and independence from the parents. The genital stage affords the person the ability to confront and resolve his or her remaining psychosexual childhood conflicts. As in the phallic stage, the genital stage is centered upon the genitalia, but the sexuality is consensual and adult, rather than solitary and infantile. The psychological difference between the phallic and genital stages is that the ego is established in the latter; the person's concern shifts from primary-drive gratification (instinct) to applying secondary process-thinking to gratify desire symbolically and intellectually by means of friendships, a love relationship, family and adult responsibilities.

Freud felt that frustration of, or a failure to, successfully develop through the various psychosexual stages he identified could lead to anxiety and fixation, which ultimately might be expressed as an adult *neurosis*, neurosis being a functional mental disorder involving chronic distress, but neither delusions nor hallucinations as in psychosis. Anxiety, in Freud's view, was the main cause of adult neurosis. Anxiety is caused by a perceived or foreseen increase in tension (from unfulfilled primary needs) or displeasure, and can develop from either real or imagined sources when a threat to some part of the body or psyche is too great to be ignored or mastered (Frager & Fadiman, 2005, p. 30). Loss of a desired object, loss of love, loss of identity or self-respect, and loss of love for the self or guilt over past behavior can all be causes for anxiety. Anxiety is dealt with in two basic ways. The first is to deal directly with the problem or threat by overcoming the obstacle, either by confrontation or escape, and resolving the issue or otherwise coming to terms with its consequences. The second possible approach to anxiety is through *ego defenses* that serve to distort or deny the problem or threat itself. The ego essentially protects the personality by falsifying the nature of the threat in some way. Oftentimes called "defense mechanisms," these psychological maneuverings can be exhibited by both healthy and unhealthy individuals as responses to life circumstances. The way in which people utilize defense mechanisms can either lead to successfully dealing with psychological problems, or repetitive and maladaptive, or even self-destructive, behavior that if not resolved becomes a long-term neurosis.

One of Freud's more controversial concepts was the Oedipus complex (Freud & Brill, 1915; Nagera, 1969). During the phallic stage of development, children become aware of their genitals and the differences between male and female. This interest, Freud maintained, leads the child toward an attraction to the parent of the opposite sex. For young boys, they begin to have sexual desires for the mother, which, in a symbolic way, makes the father figure a rival for the child in their quest for their mother's attention and affection. At the same time, the boy also values the affections of the father, who is seen as both powerful and dangerous (as a rival), and so the child is thrown into irreconcilable conflict (assuming there is a nuclear family context). The accompanying anxiety caused by this internal and unresolvable conflict is generally surmounted by the superego repressing the feelings and even the awareness of the conflict from the conscious mind. Freud thought that a similar psychological conflict arose for girl children, but that it had slightly different features and was possibly less intense for girls than it was for boys.

Freud's Oedipus complex was perhaps one of his most criticized theories, particularly from the feminist perspective (Pfister & Schnog, 1997, p. 7); however, as a psychological tool for actors, it raises some important questions that can be enormously useful during the character development process. For instance, does the character have repressed sexual desires or hidden feelings that may express themselves unconsciously? What is the character's relationship with her parents? Is that relationship the same as it was in childhood? Or has it changed (and how)? If the character has a spouse or love relationship, is the partner similar to one of the character's parents? If so, which one (and in what ways)? What are the character's sexual fantasies toward other characters in the story, etc.?

Psychoanalysis and Free Association

In Freud's traditional psychoanalytic therapy, the patient, or "analysand," lies on a couch facing away from the analyst. The analyst attempts to remain as neutral as possible, in terms of interactions with the patient, so that the patient can introspect as fully as possible without influence. Once the patient has relaxed on the couch or chair, they are encouraged to narrate whatever thoughts come into their head without censoring or altering the content in any way. This technique is called *free association*, and is one of Freud's foundational discoveries (the history of which is discussed in more detail in Chapter 1). The basic idea is that as the process continues over time, more and more repressed (hidden) psychic material will be revealed in the monologue of the analysand, providing the analyst with material to bring to the attention of the analysand, thus making the previously unconscious material conscious. From the Freudian analyst's perspective, the vast majority of the material revealed will relate back to the patient's childhood psychosexual development, and upon becoming conscious will become resolvable.

Traditional psychoanalysis, as described above, has long since fallen out of favor with the Western psychotherapeutic community, and while it may often be foundational in some respects to postmodern techniques, it is rarely used in its "pure" form (Hale, 1995, pp. 300–301). However, Freud's technique of free association can be very useful to the actor in ways that Freud himself probably never imagined or envisioned. We will look at practical applications of free association for the actor in a section below.

Another entry into the material of the individual unconscious that Freud pioneered was work with dreams. Until Freud's time, dreams (in the medical community from whence Freud arose) were considered either irrelevant, nonsensical, or functions of disturbed physiological, particularly digestive, systems. Freud came to believe that dreams were purposeful and that they represented a vehicle for the personality's wish fulfillment system that compensated for certain limitations during waking life. While Freud made some generalizations about certain kinds of dreams, he held that the most important aspects of dreamwork with psychoanalytic patients was in the analysand's own associations with the dream images (Freud & Brill, 1915). While Freud's work with dreams marks an important contribution to the literature of psychology, we will concentrate more explicitly on the dreamwork theories of Freud's colleague Carl Jung in a later chapter.

One of the other tasks of the analyst during psychotherapy is to penetrate or circumvent the patient's resistances or defense mechanisms that prevent the unconscious material from being exposed. While Freud himself originally proposed the concept of the defense mechanisms and their functions, it was his youngest daughter, Anna Freud (1895–1982), who further developed her father's work on defenses and the use of psychotherapy with children and non-neurotics who were going through difficult times in their lives.

Anna Freud: Defenses and Developmental Lines

Anna Freud was the only one of Freud's six children to follow in her father's footsteps into psychiatry. When she was 23, Anna entered analysis with her father, a relationship that Freud strictly forbade in his colleagues and student psychoanalysts. Anna became a noted psychoanalyst in her own right and focused much of her career on the psychoanalysis of children, as well as making significant contributions to what would become known as "ego psychology," an extension of her father's tripartite model of the personality that focused more on ego structure and function than on analysis of repressed childhood memories (Blumenfeld, 2006, p. 71).

Anna focused on the ego's unconscious defenses and introduced many important theoretical and clinical considerations into the field. In *The Ego and the Mechanisms of Defense* (1936), she argued that the ego was predisposed to supervise, regulate, and oppose the id through a variety of defense mechanisms. She described these defenses and linked them to the stages of psychosexual development. She went on to identify and elucidate various psychopathological formations in which the defense mechanisms played a prominent role. Clinically, Anna felt that the psychoanalyst's attention should always be on the defense mechanisms of the ego, which could be observed in the patient's free associations. The analyst needed to stay focused on the details of what the patient said in order to identify, label, and probe the defenses as they arose during therapy. For Anna Freud, interpretation of repressed content was less important than understanding the ego's methods for keeping things out of consciousness (Wikipedia, 2017a).

Following is a brief description of some of the major defense mechanisms that Anna Freud documented and explored.

Repression is considered one of the primary ego defense mechanisms. Repression is the unconsciousness act of purposeful or motivated forgetting, where a potentially painful or anxiety-provoking mental event is pushed out of (or repressed from) consciousness. As Sigmund Freud put it, "The essence of repression lies simply in turning something away, and keeping it at a distance, from the consciousness" (Freud & Brill, 1915, p. 147). The problem with repressed material, at least in the psychoanalytic model, is that the unsated desire or other type of traumatic material being repressed tends to resurface as neurotic symptoms, compulsions, slips of the tongue, and the like. It is always an interesting exercise for the actor to question what a character might be repressing from consciousness and investigate how that material might be expressing itself in the character's behavior or scripted speech. Often, an important part of psychotherapy is the bringing into consciousness repressed material in order to relieve the psychic pressure and reduce neurotic symptoms.

Denial is another primary ego defense mechanism that might be considered a subcategory of repression. Denial is the act of distorting, altering, or explaining away facts to avoid a confrontation or threat to the ego. As a psychological defense, denial tends to distort reality and create "false memories" of circumstances that never actually occurred in the service of avoiding a perceived or unconscious conflict. Denial can be a powerful and often irrational defense that can seem absurd to the objective observer who is not caught up in the denier's emotional frame or situation. Denial essentially represses the awareness of a threat or changes its interpretation so as to negate the legitimacy of the threat or undercut its danger. Denial in a theatrical character can often provide ironic insight or comic relief for an audience.

Rationalization is the defense of justifying negative behavior with seemingly laudatory motives. In other words, a person will make an excuse or rational argument about the basis or reason for an unacceptable behavior or action in order to make the action appear acceptable to themselves (or others). Rationalization is a way of disguising motives in order to make actions seem morally acceptable.

As with many of the ego defense mechanisms, rationalization tends to function as an unconscious response to things that the ego has a hard time accepting or dealing with.

A *reaction formation* is an emotional reaction or attitudinal position, oftentimes exaggerated, that is counter to or diametrically opposed to the actual underlying desire or feelings. The person engaged in a reaction formation has repressed some unacceptable emotion, yearning, or belief, and in order to keep it out of awareness, or defend against the unacceptable feelings, takes a strong opposing position. A potent and somewhat common example of a reaction formation might be the highly moralistic crusader who condemns sexual activity (particularly in others) that is secretly subject to strong sexual compulsions and acting out behaviors of their own. The moralistic and critical judgment of others' behavior is a reaction formation defending against such feelings in the self. The reaction formation can be a highly interesting defense mechanism to explore in relationship to certain characters, particularly as this defense often leads to overexaggerated responses that can be both dramatic and comedic, depending on the given circumstances of the particular dramaturgy.

Projection is the defense of placing or attributing one's own feelings, qualities, or intentions onto someone or something else. In the case of projection, the individual displaces their own internal feelings onto the external environment, thus shifting responsibility for the unacceptable material from "self" to "other." Projection is characterized by a strong sense that whatever is evil/depraved/sinful/perverse, etc. is "out there" or the quality of "someone else," while simultaneously denying the possibility that the individual might have the very same feelings or attributes.

Isolation separates an anxiety-provoking aspect of the personality or consciousness from the rest of the personality and expresses it in a manner detached from emotion. When isolating a particular part of the personality, the individual might discuss it in a highly detached, rational tone with little emotional affect. Sigmund Freud felt that the prototype, or "healthy" version, of isolation was traditional "rational thinking," where in common practice the speaker tries to detach the subject matter from emotional overtones and stick with measurable or objective facts. However, when this cool rationality bleeds over into the emotional realm, preventing the ego from confronting anxiety-producing situations or relationships, it becomes an often unconscious defense mechanism.

Regression is the falling back to an earlier developmental stage or even childlike mode of expression in order to avoid what is perceived

63

as an overwhelming or unacceptable situation. As a defense, it is a way of avoiding anxiety by abandoning realistic, rational thinking in favor of a mental posture that might have removed or avoided such anxiety in the past. In traditional Western psychological dramas, regression by a character has often been used as a device to indicate a losing touch with reality or even a slide into insanity.

Sublimation, for Freud, was the repression of sexual and aggressive urges and the redirection of the libidinal energy into other, more cultur-ally acceptable forms, such as artistic, intellectual, or other endeavors. Sublimation is like the dams and levees that control the flow of water along a river, redirecting the water in service of the society who built them, instead of leaving the town or village in the river's path to the chaotic and unpredictable whims of nature. Freud believed that much of society's cultural and even economic endeavors were motivated by activities driven by the sexual and aggressive energies redirected into industrious expressions via the act of sublimation:

> The defenses . . . are ways for the psyche to protect itself from internal or external tension. The defenses avoid reality (repression), exclude reality (denial), redefine reality (rationalization), or reverse reality (reaction formations). These mechanisms place inner feelings on the outer world (projection), partition reality (isolation), cause a withdrawal from reality (regression), or redirect reality (sublimation). In every case, libidinal energy is necessary to maintain the defense, indirectly limiting the ego's flexibility and strength.
>
> (Frager & Fadiman, 2005, p. 35)

Anna Freud also developed the concept of "developmental lines." A major contribution to developmental psychology, developmental lines became a way to look at the various stages that multiple aspects of the personality tended to follow during maturation in a given environment and family structure, as well as their relationships and interdependencies with each other (Freud, 1963). For the younger Freud, the developmental lines were markers of normal, non-neurotic growth, but could also show signs of psychopathology. While develop-mental lines are interdependent and not in any practical sense separa-ble, nonetheless, observing them individually could still yield useful information about the individual child's overall developmental pro-file. One of the developmental lines that Anna Freud acknowledged was the stages of psychosexual development elucidated by her father. To this, she added the object relations line, from dependency to emotional self-reliance and adult object relationships; being fed as an infant to feeding oneself independently; excretory functions managed by caregivers to self-controlled bathroom behaviors; inability to ability to manage self-care, hygiene, and nutrition; from infantile narcissism to mature adult companionship and love relationships with others; from the exclusive identity with the body, through play with toys and hobbies, and to the adult world of work and cultural interaction; as well as physical development (which, affecting all the other lines, will impact self-image, sexuality, and confidence), sensory development, and the line for developing the psychological defense mechanisms from rudimentary through sophisticated.

The concept of developmental lines that Anna Freud pioneered was developed further by other theorists and in other models beyond the psychoanalytic (Gardner, 1983; Wilber, 1999), and we will look at concepts of development more carefully in later chapters.

Psychoanalytic Activities for Actors

So, how do we use the psychoanalytic map and psychotherapeutic tools presented above in the service of character and performance creation? The following exercises can, in general, be approached in two ways: as an individual exploration of the actor's individual psychology (self-awareness), and in service of creating a specific character or solving a particular acting problem (character awareness). Some exercises will be appropriate in one situation, while others will be totally wrong depending on the acting challenge being addressed and the psychological makeup of the actor utilizing them. You are responsible for discerning which exercises to use under your particular circumstances, and that goes for the entire contents of this book.

Much of Freud's work centered around sex, aggression, and early childhood development, particularly family relationships. So, in a general sense, when using the "Freudian lens," we will be looking at (and becoming aware of) those same dimensions in ourselves and our characters. In my opinion, a great actor will possess, first and foremost, great *self-awareness*. Self-awareness is the grounded place from where we depart on the journey of a role or characterization. Even those stars who generally appear to "play themselves" in every role they accept tend to be sensitive and in tune with their own inner terrains, and so perhaps that is the best place to start with psychology? By "setting a baseline" in our own self-understanding, we then are starting to map our own inner terrain, giving us a context or starting point from which to build characters, especially those that are different from ourselves.

As Freud's was, at heart, a developmental model, let's start by exploring Freud's psychosexual stages of development. In the following set of activities and observations, make written notes on what you find. If you prefer, you can record your journal entries on a tape recorder or digital device. These exercises can also be adapted to a classroom situation that involves groups discussion, where appropriate.

The Psychosexual Development of a Character

Start with a character you are either working on or know well. You should have already done a good deal of character history and mapping of the given circumstances to develop as detailed an understanding of the character's background as possible. Now you can walk through Freud's various stages of psychosexual development and ask yourself where the character might have had problems, or become stuck, during any of Freud's stages. Following is a brief recap of those stages and behaviors that may be related to them.

Oral Stage

Occurs during infancy when the child explores the world through the mouth and suckling. Problems or deficiencies during this stage of development can lead to an "oral fixation" later in life, the symptoms of which include issues with dependency on or aggression toward others, and problems with drinking, eating, smoking, or nail-biting, etc.

Anal Stage

The anal stage involves the period of toilet training. Problems at this stage include toilet training that is too lenient or lax, leading to an *anal-expulsive personality* in which the individual has a messy, wasteful, or destructive personality. If

the parents are too strict or begin toilet training too early, this can create an *anal-retentive
personality* in which the individual is stringent,
orderly, rigid, and obsessive, often tense or
physically grasping.

Phallic Stage

At the phallic stage, children begin to discover
the differences between males and females. This
is also the period where Freud believed that boys
begin to view their fathers as a rival for the
mother's affections, which he called the *Oedipus
complex*, a desire to sexually possess the mother
and replace the father. In girls, the roles are
reversed as a sexual desire for the father and
jealousy of the mother, which Freud called the
Electra complex. This is the period where the
conscience (superego) is developed, and problems
at this stage may result in lifelong feelings of
guilt. Freud suggested that boys who do not deal
with this conflict effectively become "mother-
fixated," while girls become "father-fixated." As
adults, these individuals may seek out romantic
partners who resemble their opposite-sex parent.

Latency Stage

During latency, the child begins to develop relationships outside of the family and direct their
energy toward external activities and social relationships. They learn how to accomplish goals
and find socially acceptable ways for gratifying
their desires by sublimating (or repressing) their
libidinal urges and directing that energy toward
things such as schoolwork or sports. Problems
at this phase might lead to difficult interpersonal relationships and a difficulty with trust
or interacting with groups and authority figures.

Genital Stage

During the genital stage, the ego and superego
have become stronger, and the individual begins to

develop strong sexual interest in the opposite (or same) sex. At this stage, the individual establishes an assortment of social relations apart from the family. For Freud, the genital stage was the last stage of development and is considered the highest level of maturity. In this stage, the individual becomes capable of the two signs of healthy adulthood, work and love. Difficulties at this stage can lead to all manner of troubles with healthy adult relationships, which can include trust issues, promiscuity, and sexual identity conflicts.

Given Freud's stage model and your contrived character history, where do you think your character might have had developmental issues or developed fixations? What are the character's relationships with their parents (alive or dead)? How would your character behave if they had an oral fixation? Or an anal-retentive personality type? How might different configurations of reactions to the various developmental stages affect your characterization? For instance, might a character with an oral fixation behave differently than the same character with more of a fixation on the anal or genital stage?

Making a decision about where along the developmental spectrum a particular character may have strong or unconscious reactions can be a very useful exercise. For instance, a character "stuck" (or with neurotic symptoms related to) the oral phase might be prone to sucking things or putting things in their mouth unconsciously, whereas a more anal character might exhibit a physical tightness or be prone to grasping props, or even repetitive, obsessive motions or actions.

Also, much of Freudian psychology centers around conscious or unconscious sexual drives and feelings. One useful application of this viewpoint is to analyze the sexual feelings, or *repressed* sexual feelings, that your character might have toward the other characters in the play, scene, or story. While this perspective may not be provided explicitly in the given circumstances of the script, it can be a very interesting lens to use in discovering one aspect of a character's drives, motivations, and internal conflicts.

A Brief Example of Freudian Text Analysis

Hamlet, Act I, Scene 2: "O, that this too, too *sullied* flesh would melt, thaw, and resolve itself into a dew. Or that the *Everlasting* had not fixed his canon 'gainst self-slaughter!" (Shakespeare & Braunmuller, 2016, emphasis added).

If we were to psychoanalyze the first two lines of Hamlet's first soliloquy (Act I), from the perspective of Freud's psychosexual developmental stages, we might note that in the first sentence, Hamlet describes his own flesh (his body) as "sullied," meaning "dirty" or "filthy." The synonyms for sullied include tainted, blemished, and contaminated (Dictionary.com, 2017), all of which could be construed as derived from anxiety surrounding Freud's anal stage. This single line also carries a desire for the self to "melt . . . and resolve" into a dew, a description very similar to what Freud believed much of religious or mystical experience consisted of. In describing the mystical reports of others:

Freud felt that these feelings . . . arose from the infant's undifferentiated view of everything as a limitless extension of the self, for whom the parental caregiver supplies whatever is necessary to fulfill the baby's needs and with whom the infant's ego merges in a feeling of narcissistic omnipotence.

(Blumenfeld, 2006, p. 59)

So, from this perspective, Hamlet is lamenting not being able to return (or regress back) to an infantile "oceanic state of bliss" before the ego had differentiated from the parent (mostly the mother figure) in the early oral phases of development.

In the second sentence, Hamlet invokes the powerful, fatherlike "Everlasting" who has fixed a canon (law) against self-slaughter (suicide). This conjures up images of a stern, even frightening (and possibly angry?) father figure who forbids a path of behavior. While these references may, at first glance, seem obscure, they make for a fine example of how the Freudian lens can be used in a line-by-line text analysis, seeking the sexual and aggressive undertones that can be either uncovered or imposed upon the language of a play. A careful reading of the text, ferreting out possible references to sex, aggression, familial relationships and overtones, can be quite fruitful in generating thoughtful and creative interpretations of a character. While it would be limiting in the extreme to *only* use this type of high-level analysis in approaching a character, particularly one as complex and nuanced as Hamlet, as *one lens* among many, the Freudian could certainly suggest interpretations that might be combined with other lenses to create a very richly textured overall performance. Many other lenses will be introduced and explored in the following chapters.

Exploring Defense Mechanisms

Revealing the nature and prevalence of psychic defense mechanisms was one of Freud's major contributions to modern Western psychology. Most people are aware, at least to some degree, of the kinds of defenses that Freud described, and the words for these defenses have passed into the common vernacular. "You're being defensive," or "That's a rationalization," or "She's projecting that feeling" are all common phrases in our everyday language. But how much do you really know about how you personally use defense mechanisms? As stated before, actors are *required* to have extraordinary self-understanding and awareness, and so knowing how your own defense mechanisms work is a prerequisite to becoming a successful performer.

A Map of Your Own Defenses

Either journal or record notes about the following introspections for later review. If any of these activities make you extremely uncomfortable or upset (beyond what you consider to be your own natural resistance), feel free to skip this exercise or the portion that seems to be causing distress. Different people have different levels of tolerance for self-reflection, so while you are encouraged to be brave in your self-explorations, you are also cautioned to respect your own limits.

Take a few moments to center yourself and turn your attention inward. Once you are fully relaxed, try to remember one of your most embarrassing or awkward moments, perhaps a time when you were caught doing something that you knew was wrong, were publicly humiliated, or were emotionally rejected by someone important to you. Try to fully recall the circumstances and emotions surrounding the event. Is this difficult for you to do? Do you find yourself resisting the memories? Can you recall if you used any defense mechanisms at the time, such as rationalization, denial, or projection? How does the memory make you feel now?

70

Now try a different memory with a different emotional quality. Ask yourself the same kinds of questions. Is it difficult to indulge the memory? If so, what kinds of internal mental defenses are you using? Can you identify any of the defense mechanisms that arose at the time? How does the memory make you feel now?

Try this exercise several times and on different days until you have notes and examples of as many of the defense mechanisms as you can identify in your own experience. Remember, these defenses include *repression* (purposefully forgetting the problem), *denial* (pretending the problem is not really a problem), *rationalization* (explaining away the problem), *reaction formation* (overreacting to a problem from the opposite direction), *projection* (blaming the problem on somebody else), *isolation* (cutting off the problem from your emotions), *regression* (responding in a childlike or immature manner to the problem), and *sublimation* (putting your energies into something else other than the problem) (Frager & Fadiman, 2005, p. 35).

Identifying Defenses in Others

Either journal or record notes about the following observations for later review.

For a week, see if you can identify defense mechanisms in other people you interact with or observe in the course of your daily life. See if you can become adept at recognizing the various defenses in others and carefully observe how others use their defenses in conversations and interactions.

Do not confront others when you recognize them using defenses, but do make careful notes on your observations. This study may well give you some ideas about how the ego defenses work under different circumstances and inform your own future character choices.

In many ways, actors are "collectors of human behavior," observing others for hints, clues, and inspirations for their own character choices. By mapping the ego defenses in yourself and others, you are building up a practical and useful "library" of unique understandings that can then be used in all sorts of creative ways in your career. Once again, more self-awareness, and an awareness of the human condition in general, is a prerequisite to becoming a successful actor.

Defense Analysis in Fictional Characters

Select a scene from one of your favorite plays or one that you are working on for class. Make notes of any of the ego defense mechanisms in your character's dialogue or scripted behavior. Would the dialogue or behavior change if the character were using different defense mechanisms? Note whether any of the other characters appear to be using defenses. Would their behavior change if they were using different defenses? Try acting out the various roles using different defense mechanisms and observe how this changes your interpretation and the interactions between all characters in the scene.

The goal is not to create a definitive way of playing the scene for performance, so much as to directly experience how a character's unconscious defense mechanisms can color how they react and behave.

In the simplest of terms, acting can be looked at as discovering and responding to the following questions, as the character: What do I want? Why do I want it? Why do I want it now? Deeply understanding and being sensitive to ego defense mechanisms, and other psychological factors we will explore in this book, can help color and add nuance to the way that you express your answers to those questions through performance.

Free Association

Freud's main technique for psychoanalysis was free association. The process is simple and can actually be adapted for individual or self-directed use. The subject of the analysis simply relaxes and begins to talk in a stream of consciousness about anything that happens to arise in their mind without any conscious direction or intentional topic. Whatever the subject says aloud is the subject matter of the free association; nothing is off limits, nothing is to be censored. By simply babbling along without a censuring of the thoughts, the subject will inevitably reveal material that has some internal significance, and even material that has been repressed in the unconscious. As the subconscious material is brought to the attention of the subject, it can be dealt with consciously, thus expanding the awareness of the subject and lessening the impact of subconscious drives and thoughts.

Do-It-Yourself Analysis

Get a digital recorder or use an audio recording app on your smartphone. Do this exercise when you are totally alone and under no pressure of being interrupted or overheard. This is a totally private exercise and requires the utmost level of honesty and self-candor.

Either lie down or relax in a comfortable chair. Take several deep breaths and close your eyes or maintain a "soft focus" where you are not looking at any particular thing, allowing the eyes to relax along with the body.

Begin to speak into the recorder and simply say whatever comes into your head. Do not censor the thoughts in any way. If at first you feel some resistance, you might acknowledge that and talk about those feelings aloud. Let your mind wander and try not to judge anything that comes out of your mouth. This may take a little practice as most of us are used to severely censoring our thoughts, and some of the content that pops out may be embarrassing or make you uncomfortable. This is OK and expected. Simply talk about those feelings and see where this leads you.

Continue talking for 15 to 30 minutes and then turn the recording device off.

Do not listen to the recording. Instead, repeat the exercise on the next day, again making a recording of between 15 and 30 minutes of your uncensored thoughts. Make a third recording on the next day, and again set the recordings aside.

On the fourth day, again in complete seclusion where you will not be interrupted or overheard, listen to the recordings and make notes in your journal. Did you notice any recurring themes? What sorts of defensive feelings did you describe? Did you say anything shocking or that you felt was "out of character" for you? Was any of the content disturbing? Did you experience any strong emotions? Did you remember anything you thought was forgotten? Did anything frighten you? Make you sad? Guilty? Was any of the content sexual? Aggressive? Related to your relationships with your father or mother? Was doing this exercise embarrassing or otherwise uncomfortable for you? If so, note why you think this was so. In relistening to the material, did any of it bring up new associations or strong emotional reactions? If so, make notes of these. Finally, write down a summary of what you think you learned or discovered about yourself during this process.

After making your notes, set them aside for a while. When you review them again with a little distance, do you have any different impressions? Does anything new come to your attention? Can you see how any of the themes or statements might relate to the psychosexual developmental phases? It can be useful to repeat this process on a monthly or quarterly basis, essentially practicing the art of uncensored free association. You will inevitably get better at the process, and the arc of personal self-discovery can be very useful to you as an actor. As I've already stated, more self-awareness is almost always a good thing.

Now that you've done a cursory analysis of yourself, try the same exercise as a character that you are very familiar with. Start by bringing that character's background and worldview to the front of your mind. It may take a bit of practice, but try as honestly as you can to free-associate *as the character*. You may find that more of your own unconscious material actually arises instead of anything that you can relate to the character, and this is OK. Simply analyze the material and make notes in your journal as before. As you get better at the process of uninhibitedly free associating, you will be able to use this as a tool for exploring some of your unconscious associations to a particular character, which may in turn spark creative choices or opportunities for unique interpretations. This kind of deep, unconscious psychological work is more about sensitizing yourself to unconscious impulses and thought processes than it is about any particular piece of content or unconscious theme.

We will now look at the theories and techniques of a number of other psychologists to see how different perspectives and practices can yield other types of results and clues about the inner worlds of the characters we build as actors.

References

Blumenfeld, R. (2006). *Tools and Techniques of Character Interpretation: A Handbook of Psychology for Actors, Writers, and Directors*. Montclair, NJ: Limelight Editions.

75

Carnicke, S. M. (2009). *Stanislavsky in Focus: An Acting Master for the Twenty-First Century* (2nd ed.). London/New York: Routledge.

Dictionary.com (2017). *Sullied*. Retrieved from www.dictionary.com/browse/sullied.

Frager, R., & Fadiman, J. (2005). *Personality and Personal Growth* (6th ed.). Upper Saddle River, NJ: Pearson Prentice Hall.

Freud, A. (1936). *Das ich und die abwehrmechanismen (The Ego and the Mechanisms of Defense)*. Wien: Internationaler Psychoanalytischer Verlag.

Freud, A. (1963). The concept of developmental lines. *The Psychoanalytic Study of the Child*, 18(1), 245–265. doi:10.1080/00797308.1963.11822930

Freud, S., & Brill, A. A. (1915). *The Interpretation of Dreams* (4th ed.). London/New York: G. Allen & Unwin/The Macmillan Company.

Frick, W. B. (1991). *Personality Theories: Journeys into Self* (2nd ed.). New York: Teachers College Press, Columbia University.

Gardner, H. (1983). *Frames of Mind: The Theory of Multiple Intelligences*. New York: Basic Books.

Hale, N. G. (1995). *The Rise and Crisis of Psychoanalysis in the United States: Freud and the Americans, 1917–1985*. New York: Oxford University Press.

Leach, P. (1997). *Your Baby & Child: From Birth to Age Five* (3rd ed.). New York: Alfred A. Knopf/ Random House.

Nagera, H. (1969). *Basic Psychoanalytic Concepts on the Libido Theory.* London: Allen & Unwin.

Pfister, J., & Schnog, N. (1997). *Inventing the Psychological: Toward a Cultural History of Emotional Life in America.* New Haven, CT: Yale University Press.

Roach, J. R. (1993). *The Player's Passion: Studies in the Science of Acting.* Ann Arbor, MI: University of Michigan Press.

Shakespeare, W., & Braunmuller, A. R. (2016). *The Tragical History of Hamlet Prince of Denmark.* New York: Penguin Books.

Wikipedia. (2017a). *Anna Freud,* September 7. Retrieved from https:// en.wikipedia.org/w/index.php?title=Anna_Freud&oldid=799377691.

Wikipedia (2017b). *Psychosexual Development,* August 14. Retrieved from https://en.wikipedia.org/w/index.php?title=Psychosexual_ development&oldid=795508651.

Wilber, K. (1999). *Integral Psychology: Transformations of Consciousness— Selected Essays.* Boston, MA: Shambhala.

76

CHAPTER 3

Carl G. Jung

Types, Archetypes, and Dreams

As described in Chapter 1, Carl G. Jung was a protégé of Freud's before their break over the nature of the libido and the unconscious (Jung, 1912; Jung & Jaffé, 1989, pp. 166–167). In his 1912 book *Wandlungen und Symbole der Libido* (*Transformations and Symbols of the Libido*), Jung described libidinal energy as a general type of psychic energy instead of a purely sexual force, as Freud had envisioned it. After its publication, the two men never spoke again.

In breaking with Freud, Jung experienced extreme professional isolation, being abandoned or criticized by almost all of his professional friends and previous supporters. The resulting emotional stress forced Jung into his own version of self-analysis that lasted for much of 16 years (Jung & Shamdasani, 2009, p. viii). During this period of self-analysis, which Jung called his "confrontation with the unconscious" and "my most difficult experiment" (Jung & Shamdasani, 2009, p. 200), he explored his own mind, both the conscious and unconscious aspects, through an exercise he eventually named "active imagination" (discussed below). The results of Jung's personal "experiment" eventually led to several of his most significant contributions to Western psychology.

One of Jung's major disagreements with Freud was over the narrow and reductionistic nature of Freud's views (Jung, 1966, pp. 27–29). Freud felt very much that people's behaviors were dictated by a mostly fixed personality that was fully formed, and unchanging, by the end of childhood. The ego was forever locked in a struggle to maintain control between the primal drives of the id and the unreasonable moral dictates of the superego, and not much could be done about it; that's just the way things are. Freud believed very little fundamental change was actually possible for the adult personality, even under the effects of psychoanalytic treatment, and that relative relief of neurotic symptoms was probably the best to be hoped for from therapy. Jung, on the other hand, believed that while psychotherapy could help people live healthier, normal lives and ameliorate neurotic symptoms, the larger point of psychological life was to integrate one's experiences with aspects of the unconscious as the person matured so as to become more whole and more "individuated" over the life span (Jung, 1966, pp. 173–174). Armed with this viewpoint on psychology, Jung came up with a very different map of the human psyche, one that included much of what Freud had discovered, and then extending it into realms far beyond mere childhood sexual frustrations and primal aggressive drives as motivators. Jung's psychology included a growth and developmental orientation that transcended Freud to include altruistic and even spiritual dimensions of personality.

Jung was a gifted writer who produced many books over his long career, some of which are quite difficult to read. Below is a very select list of Jung's contributions to psychology, many of which began with Freud's ideas and then surpassed (or directly contradicted) them. For a more complete understanding of Jung's innovative conceptions, I recommend reading Jung's original material, as cited in the references at the end of this chapter.

78

Two Realms of the Unconscious

Jung came to believe that there were two vast areas of the human unconscious, the personal and the collective. In Jung's model, the personal unconscious contains repressed material, such as painful memories, as well as unimportant or forgotten memories not retained in conscious awareness. The personal unconscious might also include aspects of the personality that had never before become conscious. So, Jung's personal unconscious looks a lot like Freud's unconscious. But then Jung added an entire other realm that included collective and "transpersonal" contents that were shared by all people, much like how we think of the instinctual drives of animals. The collective unconscious contains material that is not directly derived from an individual's personal life experience, but are universal patterns and images that have evolved over the whole of human existence. The collective realm also contains images and patterns from prehuman evolutionary development and instincts inherited from animals. These prototypical images and forms, representing the most common experiences shared by the human species, Jung called the "archetypes" (Jung, 1968, pp. 42–43).

Each archetype represents a basic psychic disposition or potential (Frick, 1991, p. 38). From the evolutionary dawn of the human race, for instance, people have shared the general experience of mother, father, birth, death, god, power, magic, the "hero" figure, the "stranger" or "outsider," and clan prejudice or ethnocentrism. These shared archetypes often will appear in people's dreams and recur in mythology from myriad civilizations across almost all periods of human history. From Jung's perspective, there are certain experiences, or at least their general forms, hardwired into the human unconscious (Jung, 1968, pp. 44–48). This concept can be very useful to the actor in that much of drama and storytelling as we know it tends to contain elements of these basic forms and potentials. Have you ever wondered why certain characters and themes so often seem to repeat themselves across different types of plays and stories? The villain, the hero, the wise sage or seer, and the self-sacrificing mother are all examples of archetypal forms.

Archetypes as such are also contentless, meaning that while they are patterns and images that tend to repeat in human experience, they are *not the experience itself.* You might say the archetypes provide the infrastructure of the personality, similar to the snowflake, where each snowflake is unique, but also every snowflake has a basic crystalline structure. And so, with humans, each person's experiences are unique. However, the general patterns into which their experiences fall are determined by the universal archetypes (Frager & Fadiman, 2005, p. 65).

A familiarity with, and general understanding of, archetypes is essential to the actor who aspires to be flexible and creative in their character interpretations. More awareness (both personal and collective) = better acting choices.

Personality Types and Functions:
The Introvert and Extrovert

Another major contribution Jung introduced to psychology were the dual concepts of *introversion* and *extroversion.* Jung believed that individuals could be characterized by one of two ways of interacting with the world around them. An introverted person tends to be more focused on internal experience, feelings, hunches, intuitions, and to generally "get their energy" from solitary activities rather than social

79

interactions. An introvert may tend to be reserved in social situations and is generally more interested in the subjective than the objective. The extrovert, on the other hand, gets their energy from interactions with others, and tends to be actively involved with people, things, and the world around them. They may be more interested in the opinions of others and "objective facts" than feelings and personal interpretations (Jung, 1971, p. 3).

While introversion and extroversion are two distinct attitudes toward the world, Jung also pointed out that neither tendency is ever wholly exclusive. There are no "pure" introverts or extroverts; everyone shares some of both qualities. A classic introvert merely *prefers* the subjective and solitary modes of engagement, but still will have the capacity to perform social tasks and interactions (unless severely impaired by emotional disorder or neurosis), and an extrovert tends to *prefer* the objective and social, but in turn will still have the capacity for some introspection and subjective judgment (again, unless severely impaired by emotional disorder or neurosis) (Jung, 1971, pp. 4–5).

In addition to the basic attitudes of introversion and extroversion, Jung identified four distinct psychological functions that represented different ways of forming judgments and making decisions, as well as ways of gathering information. Jung's functions included *thinking, feeling, sensation,* and *intuition,* and he felt that each could be experienced in either an introverted or extroverted fashion. People with a dominant thinking function tended to think in terms of objective truth and impersonal analysis, valuing consistency and abstract principles above subjective experience. Thinking types tend to be good planners and organizers, but can also be rigid and less adaptable in their thinking. In contrast, a feeling type will tend to be more interested in issues of values, such as right and wrong, or issues of justice over practicality; subjective experience will be valued more fully than facts and circumstances. For someone who is predominately a sensation type, they will tend to focus on direct and immediate experience, perception of details, and the input of the senses. Tangible experience is given priority over discussion or analysis of experience. Sensing types tend to deal with crises and emergencies well and are often considered "people of action." Intuitive types tend to see the possibilities of situations and to merge past experience, future goals, and unconscious processes so that they "add meaning" to their perceptions of the world, and because they spontaneously integrate aspects of their unconsciousness, they can seem to make leaps of understanding or comprehend things suddenly as a whole. Intuitives rely more on their imaginations than sensation types, who are more concerned with the "facts" of their experience (Frager & Fadiman, 2005, pp. 62–63).

Jung also postulated that one function would generally be more developed, conscious, and dominant in an individual, and he called this the *superior* function; as was often the case in Jung's thinking, it would be balanced in the unconscious by the opposite, least developed function, which he called the *inferior* function. By identifying various combinations of superior function and dominant attitudes, Jung developed a rather complex typology that included detailed descriptions of behaviors common to each compound type (Jung, 1971, pp. 330–407).

Jung's ideas about personality types based on the attitudes of introversion/extroversion and the functions of thinking, feeling, sensation, and intuition were taken up and extended into the form of a personality test authored by a Philadelphia housewife and mother in the mid-twentieth century. For an interesting biographical sketch of Isabel Myers, creator of the Myers–Briggs Type Indicator, you can read Annie Murphy Paul's excellent *The Cult of Personality* (2004). Myers added a fourth dimension to Jung's initial set of attitudes and functions: *judging* and *perceiving* (Paul, 2004, p. 111). Additionally, Myers specifically attempted to design her assessment instrument to evaluate healthy non-neurotics instead of patients who were in some kind of psychoanalysis or therapy. While Jung believed that psychological growth was possible throughout the life span and that his typing structure could be applied to healthy people, nonetheless he had developed his theories primarily through self-analysis and from his observations of neurotics in clinical practice. When it was first published in 1943, the Myers–Briggs Type Indicator quickly became one of the most popular personality tests in the world, and remains so today.

While the Myers–Briggs Type Indicator has come under criticism over time, as many equivalent personality tests have, nonetheless for actors looking at themselves, others they interact with, and the characters they play through a generic lens such as the Myers–Briggs types can be an extremely useful exercise. It is worth noting, however, that Jung himself offered his typing theory with the strong qualification that it was by no means intended as dogmatic or conclusive, but rather *one* way of looking at how human preferences and perceptions could be categorized (Jung, 1971, pp. 489–490). While Jung felt he had strong evidence for the existence of the psychological generalizations we have been calling types, he also knew that there was a myriad of different angles from which these patterns could be observed, and

81

therefore many typologies, even seemingly contradictory versions, were possible. Once again, from the perspective of this book, if a particular lens or model seems useful for a particular acting challenge, use it. If it seems obtuse, abstracted, or just plain wrong, ignore it and move on to another more appropriate tool. We will look at personality testing and propose some ways that it can be used as an actor's tool in the final chapter of this book.

Jung's Structure of the Psyche

Jung's model for the structure of the psyche was very different from Freud's. While Freud believed that an individual began life "*tabula rasa*" (like a blank slate) on which early childhood experience impressed the irretractable forms of personality, Jung proposed that humans were born with the forms of the psyche preplaced as the universal archetypes that we all share, and that individual experience becomes the content of both the conscious mind and the individual unconscious. Jung's model also departed from Freud's tripartite structure of id, ego, and superego. Jung theorized that the structure of the psyche was centered around a "self," which itself was an archetype that people were born with as a function of human evolution. The self-archetype represents the whole of the individual, which includes all of the conscious and unconscious contents. Jung sometimes called the self-archetype the "superordinate personality" (Jung, 1968, p. 182), which is "a psychic totality and at the same time a centre, neither of which coincides with the ego but includes it, just as a larger circle encloses a smaller one" (Jung, 1968, p. 142). The ego, which in Jung's parlance acts as an "organizing principle" for consciousness, providing a sense of consistency and direction for our lives, acts to protect that sense of psychic consistency and defend against that which is perceived as a threat, which can include contents from both the personal and collective unconscious (Frager & Fadiman, 2005, p. 67). The ego often misleads the individual in that it contains only material from the individual consciousness and tends to deny or alienate the unconscious contents that Jung believed were equally important for psychological wholeness.

Jung also separated out what the ego presents to the outside world of other people from the totality of the self and called this *the persona*. The persona is a construct we present to the world of how we would *like* to be viewed. In a way, it is the character or role we play when we relate to others. Acting itself can be conceived of as constructing a specific persona within a set of imaginary circumstances and then behaving as that persona during performance. Our persona includes our various social roles, the clothes we wear, and our personal style of expression across the multiple contexts of our life. Persona is like a mask we wear in public. In fact, the term persona is derived from a Latin term that means "mask" or "false face" (Frager & Fadiman, 2005, p. 68). In the process of social interaction, the ego begins to identify with the various faces of the persona, believing that the whole of its personality *is* the various social roles. However, in order to fully mature and reach a level of true personality integration, and by extension the potential for happiness and fulfillment, the ego must eventually release these exclusive identifications with the superficial expressions of the persona and integrate the conscious and unconscious components of self in a process Jung called "individuation" (Jung, 1968, p. 40).

Individuation then becomes the goal of successful psychological life well lived. In the process of individuation, where a mature person becomes as aware as possible of the elements of their personality, both conscious and unconscious, individual and collective, and integrates both their positive and negative aspects, the person becomes whole and fulfills their full potential as a human being. Jung believed that the purpose of psycho*analysis* (as opposed to psychotherapy, which is designed to treat illness or disorder) was to help the individual get over their own blocks to the individuation process by first helping them become aware of their own unconscious content, and then helping them to accept the innate polarities within their own personality; the aggressive versus the passive, the honest versus the deceitful, the feminine versus the masculine, etc.

The shadow was another archetype that Jung identified in the structure of personality that contains all of the material repressed by the ego from consciousness, including tendencies, desires, and memories rejected by the individual as socially unacceptable and contrary to the ideals of the persona. The shadow tends to represent the *opposite* of what we believe ourselves to be, qualities we would perceive as negative, inadequate, or undeveloped in our own personality. In other words, the shadow archetype becomes the actual shadow of the ego. In neurosis, the conscious ego rejects and denies the shadow aspect of its own personality, essentially dissociating from the perceived unsavory, yet necessary, aspects of the self-structure. Once again, for Jung, the purpose of psychoanalysis was to bring the shadow into consciousness and help the patient accept that they, as a whole human being, possess both positive and negative traits, which need to be acknowledged and integrated instead of denied and forced from consciousness. Each repressed portion of the shadow represents a part of the self, and to the extent we keep this material unconscious, we limit ourselves.

The final elements in Jung's archetypal personality structure were called the *anima* and *animus*, which represented the masculine and feminine elements of the personality. Therefore, in males, the anima represents the feminine, and in females the animus represents the masculine, both being opposite poles of a spectrum. Men who deny their feminine aspects and women who deny their masculine aspects both run the risk of being less than whole human beings (Jung, 1968, pp. 27–30). Jung's formulations around the anima and animus archetypes may well be criticized from a feminist and gender politics perspective in the postmodern view for being limited to a traditional gender roles perspective, but nonetheless, to the actor who is exploring characterization through a Jungian archetypal lens, they remain useful categorizations of common human characteristics that, like Jung himself suggested for his patients, might well be brought into consciousness and examined by the actor in the process of making character choices, regardless of the actor's orientation, identity, or expression.

Jung's model of the total personality included a "corrective function" of the unconscious, where whatever quality is developed in the consciousness (introversion/extroversion, anima/animus, etc.) will have its opposite in the unconscious. If a conscious quality becomes overdeveloped or dominant, often there will be symptoms or unconscious behaviors that emerge to oppose or correct the imbalance in the personality (Frick, 1991, p. 43). This corrective function will often lead to neurotic symptoms that can only be relieved by bringing the personality back into balance through the individuation process, and in extreme cases, where the neurosis has become chronic or debilitating, through psychotherapy.

A related concept was Jung's idea that we constantly project the contents of our unconscious, particularly those shadow qualities in ourselves that the ego might hope to deny, onto other people and our environment. Jung says, "In this way everyone creates for himself a series of more or less imaginary relationships based essentially on projection" (Jung, 1974, p. 50). He believed that most people led their entire lives blissfully unaware of this circumstance, and as long as their endless projections were "agreeable and convenient bridges to the world, they [would] alleviate life in a positive manner" (Jung, 1974, p. 51). But the neurotic, who is unable to build agreeable and convenient bridges, would ruminate and overreact to every form of imaginary slight or injustice placed upon them by the projected foe of their own inadequacies and most negative qualities seen as the characteristics of others. Only someone of extraordinary self-awareness was capable of seeing, even in part, through the projections of their own shadow elements onto others and the given circumstances of their lives. This is particularly interesting to the actor insomuch as it helps us understand that the relationships of the characters we play are also thus afflicted, and affords the actor an extra analytic tool in script analysis to think in terms of how much a character's behavior and interaction might well be a product of that character's internal unconscious shadow elements projected onto others.

Dreamwork and Active Imagination

Two of Jung's most useful tools for dealing with the unconscious are his particular style of dreamwork and the process of active imagination, both of which are of value to the actor.

Jung made several departures from Freud's view of dream interpretation. As Jung explained Freud's view, Freud tended to look at dreams in a reductionistic way, reducing all of the dream contents down to abstract versions of wish fulfillment, most often related to primal drives of sex and aggression (Jung, 1974, pp. 28–29). Freud, from Jung's point of view, was only looking at the *causal* determinants of the dream, i.e., what frustrated drive or repressed desire caused the dream to occur? Jung, on the other hand, while not denying the causal aspects of dreams, also believed that the analyst needed to look at the *purpose* of the dream in the analysand's psychic life. So, in Jungian dream analysis, we look at the exact details (manifest content) of the dream; gather amplifications and associations from the dreamer about the dream content, possibly across multiple sessions, looking particularly at the personal, cultural, and archetypal levels of the dreamer's responses; and then place the dream in the context of the dreamer's life and stage of personal development (individuation process) (Hall, 1983, p. 34). By engaging in this detailed analytic process to determine the *purpose* of the dream in the dreamer's life, Jung felt he could go far beyond Freud's more deterministic and reductionistic method of trying to interpret the symbols of the dream in terms of pregiven causal drives, needs, and wishes (Jung, 1974, pp. 31–32).

Jung also extended his ideas about the relationship between the conscious ego and the unconscious shadow into the realm of the dream, believing that the symbols in dreams came directly from the unconscious and tended to be *corrective* of the conscious contents and psychic position of the dreamer:

The unconscious is the unknown at any given moment, so it is not surprising that dreams add to the conscious psychological situation of the moment all those aspects which are essential for a totally different point of view. It is evident that this function of dreams amounts to a psychological adjustment, a compensation absolutely necessary for properly balanced action.

(Jung, 1974, p. 31)

Jung also felt that dreams could reveal important aspects or motifs from the collective unconscious. In his practice as a working psychotherapist, which lasted more than 50 years, he often noted that there were recurring motifs in his patients' dreams that had also been iterated in myriad cross-cultural examples of mythology spanning multiple millennia. In other words, many of the basic images that his patients would report in their dreams were also the images contained in classic myths from many unrelated societies down through history, leading Jung to identify them as archetypal images from the collective unconscious rather than individual contents of the personal unconscious. Once again, for the actor, this may prove an interesting lens to use in developing both a deeper self-awareness and an awareness of archetypal motifs that may recur in the dramaturgy you are asked to engage throughout your career. We will look at how this idea can be used as an analytical tool in a section below.

Overall, Jung held that dreams never expressed themselves in the logical, abstract language of waking conscious thought, "but always in the language of parable or simile" (Jung, 1974, p. 34). The job of dream analysis was to tease out the meaning or purpose of the unconscious material to the dreamer's conscious waking life, then integrate the "messages" the dream was sending to the dreamer in order to find more balance and resolve internal conflict.

Jung summarizes:

Dreams then, convey to us in figurative language—that is, in sensuous, concrete imagery—thoughts, judgements, views, directives, tendencies, which were unconscious either because of repression or through mere lack of realization. Precisely because they are contents of the unconscious, and the dream is a derivative of unconscious processes, it contains a reflection of the unconscious contents. It is not a reflection of unconscious content in general but only of certain contents, which are linked together associatively and are selected by the conscious situation of the moment. . . . If we want to interpret a dream correctly, we need a thorough knowledge of the conscious situation at the moment, that is, the material which the conscious situation has constellated in the unconscious. Without this knowledge it is impossible to interpret a dream correctly, except by a lucky fluke.

(Jung, 1974, pp. 34–35)

Luckily for the actor, the details of the "conscious situation" are available in the given circumstances of the play or script one is working on. So, this leads to an opportunity to utilize at least a portion of Jung's approach to dreamwork as a tool for the actor. For an excellent book on applying Jung's dreamwork and active imagination techniques to personal growth, see *Inner Work* (1986) by Robert Johnson.

The other approach that Jung developed for accessing the unconscious material of the psyche is called "active imagination" and is certainly one of the most potent psychological tools ever devised that is applicable to the actor's craft. Jung developed this technique during his own "confrontation with the unconscious" that began as a brutal self-analysis in the wake of his break from Freud (Jung & Chodorow, 1997, p. 21). As a result of the psychological turmoil from his split with Freud, Jung had a series of dreams and waking fantasies that much disturbed him and defied his own insight. After a period of distress, he finally decided to simply let go of his own internal resistance to these events and follow the fantasies wherever they might take him. The first thing that occurred to him was a memory from childhood when he had much enjoyed building with blocks. As strange as it seemed to him at the time, he followed his internal impulse to gather rocks along the shore of a nearby lake and began to build stone structures, like a small town, much as he had as a child. He found his own behavior, as a full-grown man playing with building blocks, to be unusual and unexplainable, but he had made a commitment to follow his impulses without judgment, and so continued the practice for some time (Jung & Chodorow, 1997, pp. 23–24).

Jung's "building game" unleashed a stream of fantasies that he began to document in notebooks, making careful notes of the fantasies themselves as well as his mental associations with the material (much like his dream analysis work with his patients). This was a powerfully emotional experience for Jung, and he felt at times that he was losing his sanity. Sometimes he would become so emotionally distraught that he would need to do yoga in order to calm his nerves enough to continue (Jung & Jaffé, 1989, p. 177):

From the beginning I had conceived my voluntary confrontation with the unconscious as a scientific experiment which I myself was conducting and in whose outcome I was vitally interested. . . . One of the greatest difficulties for me lay in dealing with my negative feelings. I was voluntarily submitting myself to emotions of which I could not really approve, and I was writing down fantasies which often struck me as nonsense, and toward which I had strong resistances. For as long as we do not understand their meaning, such fantasies are a diabolical mixture of the sublime and the ridiculous. It cost me a great deal to undergo them, but I had been challenged by fate. Only by extreme effort was I finally able to escape from the labyrinth.

(Jung & Jaffé, 1989, p. 178)

88

Jung continued this activity, consciously conjuring fantasies from his unconscious mind, documenting them, and then analyzing them for a period of 16 years. As explained in Chapter 1, much of Jung's later theoretical work and therapeutic technique arose from this work with active imagination. The most striking idea here, as it relates to the actor, is the notion that with discipline and bravery, we can confront our own unconscious and explore the images and emotions that lie beneath the surface of our conscious "ego." We will explore how we might actually go about doing that in the exercises that follow.

Analytic Psychology Activities for Actors

As in the last chapter on Freud, we will now look at some ways Jung's analytic psychology can be used as a mapping tool for your own psyche (self-exploration), as well as a set of character-building tools. Again, as with Freud, to the degree that these exercises make sense for your particular acting challenge, use them. If they seem off the mark (after taking into account your own potential resistances or defense mechanisms), then discard them for something more useful. The entire point of developing a broad psychological understanding across many different theories is to become adroit at their use in practical application. Not every tool will be appropriate or effective in every circumstance, and part of your job as either a student or professional actor is to develop an understanding of what works *for you*, and in which situations. These are not simple matters, and it will no doubt take some trial and error testing to learn what resonates for you personally. So, be patient and gentle with yourself while at the same time being brave in your self-explorations.

Archetypal Identification

Recall from above that archetypes are general patterns of common experience, much like animal instincts or collective memories, that have developed by evolution into the "hardwiring" of every human being. That being said, how do we identify (and use) these archetypal patterns? One approach is to look for the archetypal patterns that have the most impact or appeal to your own individual personality. Utilizing the journaling practice we began in Chapter 2, for instance, you can start to note what themes in movies, books, and plays affect you most strongly. The epic adventure? The tragic romance? The struggle of an individual against impossible odds? The chase and battle between good and evil? The rise to power by a queen or king? The potential list of archetypal forms is as long as the stories we tell each other in our literature and visual media. So, identify and articulate those themes that most capture your imagination, bend your heart-strings, or make you laugh heartily with understanding. Most likely, you will find that there are certain of these common, culturally shared patterns that appeal to you, and those that do not. Bringing them into consciousness is an important part of actor training.

As part of the analysis you perform in preparation for a particular role, you can look at the overall structure of the story in which your character is a part. Can you identify any archetypal themes? What *kind* of story is the author or playwright trying to tell? Additionally, can you identify any archetypal roles that the characters fulfill during the arch of the play/story? The mother? Father? Sibling? Ruler or other type of authority figure? Underling? Lover? The stranger? The destroyer? The dutiful employee? The list of possibilities for this lens are as long as the list of character types that exist in literature and stories of all ages. This is not to say that you are looking for worn stereotypes to mimic or ape during your performance, but merely that you want to identify and relate to the general patterns that may well exist there, which in turn may inform some of your specific choices as you enter the character through the actions of rehearsal and blocking. I have found, as a professional myself, it is almost always helpful to have some understanding of the overall dramaturgy I am dealing with as I begin to enter the character experientially *and* analytically.

As an additional exercise, you might try playing through a particular scene multiple times using a different archetype each time through, and see how this affects your performance. You may not keep any of these options, but this type of exercise can often suggest useful, and sometimes unexpected, choices.

The concept of archetypes can be a difficult one to fully apprehend, particularly for younger actors, and so these exercises are most likely to increase in usefulness and profundity with practice. Keep an open mind and curious imagination as you approach this work, and resist the impulse toward self-judgment or negative self-talk should it arise. A profound and embodied sense of the psychological potential of human beings is most likely a lifetime acquisition rather than a semester-long chore, so be patient with yourself and dig deeply.

Type Analysis: The Introvert/Extrovert Continuum

Placing people indiscriminately into categories or making blanket judgments about individuals has become a rightly criticized practice in our culture, particularly in the last 20 years. "Typing" or categorizing people is definitely a reductive act that minimizes individual differences and multiple perspectives. However, from the actor's point of view, having a lens that does precisely that—creates generalized categories defined by explicit features—is a very useful tool indeed. If every character was wholly unique and explicitly ignored shared cultural stereotypes, it would be very difficult to communicate stories to a mass or even regionalized audience. In fact, I would go so far as to argue that nearly all modern dramatic structures depend, to some degree, on typing, categorization, and conceptual reduction in order to communicate their stories, meanings, or messages. Even the very word character derives from "characteristic," defined as "a feature or quality belonging *typically* to a person . . . serving to identify it," which is the same order of reductionism as typing. There are post-dramatic forms that intentionally cut against rational, linear plot lines, the notion of "character" altogether, and any semblance of "psychological realism," and so perhaps those forms of dramaturgy can ignore the following investigations. On the other hand, often these nonrealistic modes of performance still present images or activities that embody or represent concepts, ideas, or human (or nonhuman) tendencies, and so still, as an orienting framework, it might be useful to understand more deeply what "the norm" is, even if only to explode the notion in some theatrical way. There are, of course, some post-dramatic presentations or theatrical events where a discussion of psychological typing will be wholly superfluous. As always, discretion is advised.

With that caveat in mind, the following exercises will explore Jung's unique contributions to psychological typology, starting with the introvert/extrovert continuum. As Jung himself was careful to point out, psychological types are indeed reductive generalizations, and no individual is purely one or the other:

There can never be a pure type in the sense that it possesses only one mechanism [introversion or extroversion] with the complete atrophy of the other. A typical attitude always means merely the relative predominance of one mechanism.

The hypothesis of introversion and extroversion allows us, first of all, to distinguish two large groups of psychological individuals. Yet this grouping is of such a superficial and general nature that it permits no more than this very general distinction. Closer investigation of the individual psychologies that fall into one group or the other will at once show great differences between individuals who nevertheless belong to the same group.

(Jung, 1971, pp. 5–6)

Starting with the very general category of introversion/extroversion, each of which is present in every personality, but with one usually dominating, we can look at ourselves, and eventually the characters we play, and then build out toward our more idiosyncratic traits and characteristics.

Test Your Type

Answer each of the following questions as either true or false based on how you *most often feel or react* to the situation described:

1. I like to be alone more than in large groups.
2. While I enjoy concerts or sporting events, I often find them draining.
3. When I study, I like it to be quiet.
4. I would rather go for a walk in nature than be in a crowded nightclub.
5. I would prefer to write an essay than give a speech.
6. I prefer class lectures to group discussions.
7. My friends consider me more shy than outgoing.
8. After a lot of activity, I recharge my batteries by spending some time alone.
9. In a classroom setting, I am more likely to wait to be called on than to raise my hand to answer a question.
10. I don't like to make decisions on impulse.
11. In a new group, I wait on the sidelines rather than introducing myself to people I don't know.
12. I prefer the company of a few close friends over being in a large crowd.
13. I prefer hearing jokes over telling them.
14. I am easily intimidated by aggressive people.
15. I can learn more studying by myself than in a group.
16. I prefer individual assignments to group projects.
17. Large parties make me nervous.
18. When making important decisions, I like to mull things over before I decide.
19. I would rather be picked than to volunteer.
20. Noisy crowds drain my energy.

Count up the number of true and false answers you made. If you had more true answers than false, you probably tend toward being more introverted than extroverted. If you had more false answers, your tendency is probably toward extroversion. A tie between the true and false responses probably means you have a relative balance of introverted and extroverted qualities; this is sometimes called an "ambivert." In any case, it is most likely that

you have a conglomeration of both qualities in
your personality. Knowing which way you *tend* to
interact with the world and others can be very
helpful information about yourself.

Now that you have some sense of your personal introverted or
extroverted tendencies, you can extend that understanding by observing and interacting with others. In your journal, make notes on your
friends' and family members' tendencies. Who do you know that is
clearly introverted or clearly extroverted? Given your own type, do you
feel more comfortable spending time with introverts or extroverts?
Does one type or the other irritate you or make you uncomfortable?
Take a week and carefully observe those around you, identifying
introverted and extroverted types and tendencies that you observe.
This careful observation work can also be extended into a classroom
or group activity where participants observe and discuss their own
proclivities and those of their classmates. Feedback from others can
often be a revealing tool for self-exploration, and the reflections of
others can often reveal previously unnoticed, or even unconscious,
aspects of our own personalities. Try some improvisations where you
play someone of the opposite type than your own. What are the physical responses in your body when you "play against" your own type?
    If you have completed the above activities, you should be starting
to become sensitized to these two different, albeit very general, types
of being in the world. So, now let's extend that understanding into
the world of character-building.
    Pick a character or scene you are working on. Is your character an
extrovert or introvert? Is the character's type different from your own?
If so, is it easy or hard for you to perform the behaviors of the other
type? This can be practiced. Try the scene playing your character as
shy and painfully introverted. Take it to the extreme and see how the
scene plays out. How does it feel in your body? Now reverse the type
and do it again, this time as a boisterous, overtly extroverted character. How were these scenes different from each other? Was one type
easier for you to play than the other?
    The more you observe and work with introversion and extrover-
sion, the more sensitive to this broad general categorization you will
become, and the more useful these understandings will be in preparing for performance. For greater detail on Jung's typological model,
see *Lectures on Jung's Typology* (Franz & Hillman, 1986).

93

Persona and Shadow

As explained above, the persona is our "public face," the version of our self we show the world, the way we would *like* to be perceived by others. The shadow, on the other hand, represents those qualities or aspects of our personality that we find unacceptable, those parts of us that we wish we didn't have, and may perhaps even deny or repress. Shadow material is often unconscious, and in many cases is projected onto others so that we see, and criticize, those qualities in the other person, while at the same time denying or remaining unaware that we may well possess the same traits our self.

Exploring the Persona

Make a list of your favorite clothes, accessories, style of makeup, hats, shoes, or anything else that you wear regularly and that you feel represents "your image" the best. Now add to that list any of your favorite sayings, oft-told jokes, modes of interacting, ways of showing off or getting attention from others, and familiar modes of interacting with others, again choosing those you feel present you in the most favorable light. Finally, write a paragraph or two describing how you think you appear to others.

Now let's take this from a slightly different perspective. Write down a more detailed description of three different masks you use in different areas of your life. Perhaps how you behave when you are at school? At work? With one group of friends or another? With groups of the opposite sex? The same sex? Are these masks different? In other words, can you identify different personas you might take on under different circumstances in your life? And going back to the earlier lists, do you wear different clothes, accessories, makeup, etc. in these different circumstances?

You have just identified some of the versions of your own persona.

Now try observing other people's personas in action. See if you can identify how people you know or have regular interactions with might behave differently under different social situations. Describe in your journal as many different personas as you can observe.

Finally, try changing your persona slightly in different situations in your life and see how it feels. You might try wearing different makeup to school one day, or wearing different clothes than you normally would. If you're usually quiet in a particular circumstance, try speaking up; or conversely, if you usually talk a lot, try being quiet and listening carefully to others for a day. Notice any feelings or reactions you may have to changing these elements of your "public self."

With these observations in hand, you can begin to build a library of different styles of persona that you can experiment with in your characterizations. For instance, how might a particular costume piece or prop affect the way a character presents themselves to others in the world of the play? Might there be a difference between how a character *thinks* she is presenting herself and how the other characters actually perceive her? A maladaptive persona, in Jung's system, might be considered a neurotic symptom and something beyond the conscious control of the character. You can look at your work with personas as a kind of "mask-work," where the mask, instead of being a physical artifact, is the social behavior and actions we take both in our lives and as our characters. A subtle understanding of the range of ways we present (or try to present) ourselves to others can be an invaluable tool in the actor's toolkit.

One of Jung's unique insights was that we tend to project onto others those qualities in ourselves we most abhor or wish to disown. In other words, we tend to project our shadow qualities out onto others rather than confront these disowned aspects in ourselves. We also tend to project our *positive qualities* that we don't think we possess onto others such as celebrities, gurus, and other hero figures. The interesting thing about this is we not only project these qualities onto others, but then we *respond* to those projections, which can lead to grand misunderstandings and strained relationships. So, now let's take that idea into our character work.

Your Character's Shadow Projections

Working with a character you are already familiar with, can you find any incidents where the character appears to be projecting traits or qualities onto (and responding to) another character?

Does your character, for instance, seem to be overreacting in some way?

Exaggerating their response to something that might otherwise be interpreted as benign?

Are there any incidents where your character seems to be sanctimonious, self-righteous, or outspokenly moral?

These could all be examples of projecting the shadow.

In some plays, the major arch of action comes down to a character being forced to confront aspects of their own personality that they originally did not believe they had. The confrontation with one's own shadow is a powerful archetype itself, and thus is a theme that regularly appears in dramatic literature.

Dreamwork

Working effectively with dreams is a skill that in most cases needs to be developed over time. Many people, when they first start off on this kind of work, have difficulty remembering what they dream. The goal with dreamwork for the actor is to gain more immediate access to our own unconscious mind and to use that material in creative and inspired ways. So, clearly, in order to do that, we must remember our dreams, and that usually takes practice. When actively pursuing dreamwork, one is often required to immediately document what they recall of a dream before going back to sleep. This activity can cost you some sleep along the way, so remember to use any of these techniques judiciously, particularly if you are in a performance cycle or other situation where your sleep will be important to your ability to accomplish your immediate goals. For more detailed instructions and exercises utilizing dreamwork and active imagination techniques, see *Inner Work* (Johnson, 1986).

The Dream Journal

Commit to keeping a dream journal for at least three months (about the length of a typical college semester).

Keep a pad of paper and a supply of pencils by your bed where you will have immediate access upon awakening. Alternatively, if you are good at typing with your thumbs, you can enter notes on a smartphone; however, smartphones emit bright light that will wake you up in the middle of the night and perhaps interrupt your sleep cycle, so consider this before you choose a medium. You can also keep your notes in an audio journal utilizing a digital recording device (which might well be an app on your smartphone).

Keep careful notes on anything you dream. Write down what you recall *immediately when you wake up*; do not wait or start your daily activities as dream memories fade rapidly. You can also draw pictures, make photo collages, write poetry or songs; any creative activity that seems appropriate for capturing the content and the sense of the dreams you have can become part of your journal. If you happen to wake in the middle of the night, particularly if a dream woke you up, make notes of your dream right then, before you fall back asleep. Do not wait for the morning as the details will almost certainly be lost.

One useful thing you can do to help you remember what you dream is to set an intention right as you go to bed every night. This means that, just before sleep, remind yourself that you are going to remember whatever you dream that night. Visualize yourself writing down your dreams in the pad you have preset by the bed. Commit to successfully capturing your dreams. Believe it or not, this is one of the most effective ways to start remembering your dreams, even if you think you never remember them.

You will quickly find that as you develop the habit of writing down whatever you remember first thing in the morning, your recollections will become increasingly more vivid and detailed. Begin by capturing any snippet or portion you can recall and then contemplate it for a moment or two. You may find that additional details arise; write these down. Include any feelings or general sensations that you recall. Note if any of the dream contents seem to be related to events in your life the day before. Also, keep track of any feelings you might have about the dream after you are awake. All of this raw material will become useful at a later part of this work.

For a while, you will simply collect data on what you can remember and what your sensory or emotional responses were while you were writing your dreams out. Most people find that as they repeat the practice of writing dreams down, they remember more and more. It can be like the doors to the unconscious mind become relaxed and don't close as tightly between sleep and waking. Often people who engage in dreamwork find that they become more intuitive and subject to creative inspiration during waking hours (all of which can be a great boon to an actor).

Once you have collected a significant number of dreams in your journal, try the following exercise.

Opening the Back Door to the Unconscious

Read through your dream journal, front to back.

Are there any themes or images that recur? Are there any particular dreams that elicit a strong emotional reaction, even when rereading them long after they happened?

You might try using Freud's free association technique from the last chapter to explore this dream material further (collecting further associations with dreams was one of the techniques Jung used with his patients).

Sit in a relaxed position, where you won't be overheard or interrupted for at least half an hour.

Read through a dream that still resonates for you and then begin to free-associate into a tape recorder or digital device any thoughts, emotions, and interpretations that come up. Try to censor none of it, but allow your mind to roam free anywhere it would like to go.

You might collect several sets of associations before going back and listening to them, so make sure you indicate which session relates to which dream.

After about a week, go back and listen to these tapes, making note of any themes, images, or emotions that strike you as significant. This exercise is not about accurate or logical analysis of the dream content. Rather, it is an exploration of the unconscious aspects of your own mind. You are now mapping areas of your own personality that you have perhaps never even been aware of before, adding more terrain and expanding the horizon of possibilities for your acting decisions.

99

If you have been working with this process for several months, as suggested at the beginning of this section, you will undoubtedly have learned some new things about yourself and your own personality. You have probably discovered a few themes that are important or significant in your life that you never suspected before. You may also have uncovered some powerful negative emotions or long-forgotten experiences that you might have preferred to leave forgotten. This is natural and very common. But as an actor, it is your job to have as much self-knowledge as possible. Self-knowledge is literally the material you work with when you act. So, look at everything you learn in this process as collecting more raw material for your work, material that will allow you to make subtle and more creative choices as your career unfolds. However, if at any point you find this work truly disturbing, feel free to discontinue it and move on to some other techniques. There are times when unconscious material can surface that is truly overwhelming or upsetting, and in these cases it is best to leave such experiences alone unless you are pursuing such work under the guidance of a trained psychotherapist or counselor.

Now that you have become familiar with this process by working with your own dreams, try creating some dreams for your character and explore them in the same ways by free-associating and looking for recurring themes and emotional connections. What if your character had significant dreams during the course of the play? How might that experience affect the character's interactions with others or their internal life?

You also might use Jung's technique of active imagination (described below) for generating a character's dream material for further analysis.

Active Imagination

Jung's active imagination exercise was based on a technique he stumbled upon during his own self-analysis. For Jung, it was a way of contacting the unconscious more directly than through dream images. You might think of the technique itself as a type of self-hypnotism or deep meditation where the barriers to unconscious contents are intentionally lowered and the person is essentially "inviting" the unconscious to come forward or "befriending" their unconscious. Both of these metaphors fail in some way to capture the actual experience of activating one's own imagination in this way, as engaging this exercise is experiential and *not conceptual*. The value of working with active imagination, for the actor, is that it provides access to a wider range of self-knowledge and opens up a plethora of possible creative choices in the acting process that would be unlikely to arise from a conscious-only effort. Getting to know or "befriending" your own unconscious in this way will expand your own personality and has the potential to open up creative reserves you may well never have known that you had.

So, how does one "activate" their imagination? Jung was often vague on the specifics of his process, generally preferring to apply it directly to his patients as a tool of analysis. However, he did occasionally explain the method in writing:

This process [of active imagination] can, as I have said, take place spontaneously or be artificially induced. In the later case you choose a dream, or some other fantasy-image, and concentrate on it by simply catching hold of it and looking at it. You can also use a bad mood as a starting point, and then try to find out what sort of fantasy-image it will produce, or what image expresses this mood. You then fix this image in the mind by concentrating your attention. [This is where previous practice at meditation techniques would be helpful.] Usually it will alter, as the mere fact of contemplating it animates it. The alterations must be carefully noted down all the time, for they reflect the psychic processes in the unconscious background, which appear in the form of images consisting of conscious memory material. In this way conscious and unconscious are united, just as a waterfall connects above and below. A chain of fantasy ideas develops and gradually takes on a dramatic character: the passive process becomes an action. At first it consists of projected figures, and these images are observed like scenes in a theatre. In other words, you dream with open eyes. . . . It is very important to fix this whole procedure in writing at the time of its occurrence, for you then have ocular evidence that will effectively counteract the ever-ready tendency of self-deception. A running commentary is absolutely necessary in dealing with the shadow, because otherwise its actuality cannot be fixed.

(Jung, 1977, paragraph 706)

Using these basic instructions as a guide, try the following exercise. As with the free association exercise in the previous chapter, do this exercise when you are totally alone and under no pressure of being interrupted or overheard. This is a totally private exercise and requires the utmost level of honesty and self-candor. You can use a digital recorder or an audio recording app on your smartphone to document the session, or you can make written notes as you go along, whichever is most productive for you.

Active Imagining

Either lie down or relax in a comfortable chair. Take several deep breaths and close your eyes or maintain a "soft focus" where you are not looking at any particular thing and allowing the eyes to relax along with the body. If you meditate, you might try clearing your mind by focusing on the breath for a few moments.

At some point, images will start to appear in your mind. You can "seed" this activity by intentionally bringing a recent dream or vivid fantasy to mind and holding it there. Try to keep whatever subject you are starting with firmly in your mind's eye. Shortly, as Jung suggests, your mind will begin to wander and the images you have been concentrating on will change and morph; stay with this process and make careful notes about what comes up (this note-taking will help you continue to concentrate on the images as they arise and help you from becoming distracted from the exercise). Try not to censor anything. Remember, you are allowing the unconscious contents of your own mind to surface into consciousness, so don't resist the process. This will very likely require some practice, so you should plan to repeat this exercise over several sessions.

As new images arise, you may find the urge to censor or ignore certain images becoming very strong. This usually indicates your own defense mechanisms activating. Try to follow whatever comes up, even if it is uncomfortable or just seems "stupid." Much unconscious content will not follow the rules of logic.

Continue to make notes or recordings until the session is over.

How did that go? Was any of the imagery exciting? Frightening? Embarrassing? Did any strong emotions come up in response to your imaginings? If so, make notes of these.

As with the dreamwork, after you have collected material from several sessions, go back over your notes in detail and document your emotional response to what you have written. Does this review bring up any additional emotions or images that seem significant? If so, write them down.

The point of the exercises is more about exposing the contents of your unconscious mind than to understand or analyze them in a logical sequence. So, keep an open mind and be brave in the face of your own impulses to censor or deny what is coming up. However, I will reiterate my caution from the dreamwork exercise here. If at any point you find this work truly disturbing, feel free to discontinue it and move on to other techniques. There are times when unconscious material can surface that is truly overwhelming or upsetting, and in these cases it is best to leave such experiences alone, unless you are pursuing the work under the guidance of a trained psychotherapist or counselor.

One variation on the above active imagination exercise is to utilize the same open state of awareness as cultivated while "simply imagining whatever comes up," and instead create a dialogue between yourself and a character you are working on. For this variation, relax and prepare yourself in the same way as before, only now speaking out loud to your character, asking them questions, and starting a legitimate conversation. Then switch roles, becoming the character, and responding to whatever questions you have just been asked. In this way, you can use active imagination to "play both parts" of the conversation. It is important to let the conversation emerge as spontaneously as possible, avoiding censoring or preplanned dialogue, and instead just seeing where your unconscious takes both of you, the character and the actor.

The other interesting advantage of Jung's active imagination is, once mastered as an exercise, it can be used as a waking substitute for dreaming as a portal to the unconscious. This allows the actor to utilize the process as a tool not only for self-understanding, but for working with characters. It is much easier, for instance, to create a series of dreams "as a character" by using active imagination than it is to actually "seed" your own dreaming process to investigate the dream material of a character's psyche. So, consider using active imagination to collect and explore your characters' dreamworlds. At first, you are likely to experience significant internal resistance to this process. But with practice, the defenses tend to soften, and you may be surprised at what you find your own imagination is capable of.

In traditional modern actor training pedagogy, an actor's overall instrument is considered to be composed of body, voice, and imagination (Bartow, 2006, pp. xxvi–xxvii; Hodge, 2010, p. 81; Zazzali, 2016, p. 44). The above exercises represent a potentially very powerful way of *directly training* the imaginative component of that triadic model by, at least partially, opening the conscious imagination to the realm of the unconscious.

References

Bartow, A. (2006). *Training of the American Actor*. New York: Theatre Communications Group.

Frager, R., & Fadiman, J. (2005). *Personality and Personal Growth* (6th ed.). Upper Saddle River, NJ: Pearson Prentice Hall.

Franz, M.-L. V., & Hillman, J. (1986). *Lectures on Jung's Typology*. Dallas, TX: Spring Publications.

Frick, W. B. (1991). *Personality Theories: Journeys into Self* (2nd ed.). New York: Teachers College Press, Columbia University.

Hall, J. A. (1983). *Jungian Dream Interpretation: A Handbook of Theory and Practice*. Toronto: Inner City Books.

Hodge, A. (2010). *Actor Training* (2nd ed.). London/New York: Routledge.

Johnson, R. A. (1986). *Inner Work: Using Dreams and Active Imagination for Personal Growth*. San Francisco, CA: Harper & Row.

Jung, C. G. (1912). *Wandlungen und Symbole der Libido: Beiträge zur Entwicklungsgeschichte des Denkens*. Leipzig: F. Deuticke.

Jung, C. G. (1966). *Two Essays on Analytical Psychology* (Vol. 7). Princeton, NJ: Princeton University Press.

Jung, C. G. (1968). *The Archetypes and the Collective Unconscious* (Vol. 9). Princeton, NJ: Princeton University Press.

Jung, C. G. (1971). *Psychological Types* (Vol. 6). Princeton, NJ: Princeton University Press.

Jung, C. G. (1974). *Dreams*. Princeton, NJ: Princeton University Press.

Jung, C. G. (1977). *Mysterium Coniunctionis: An Inquiry into the Separation and Synthesis of Psychic Opposites in Alchemy* (2nd ed.). Princeton, NJ: Princeton University Press.

Jung, C. G., & Chodorow, J. (1997). *Jung on Active Imagination*. Princeton, NJ: Princeton University Press.

Jung, C. G., & Jaffé, A. (1989). *Memories, Dreams, Reflections* (rev. ed.). New York: Vintage Books.

Jung, C. G., & Shamdasani, S. (2009). *The Red Book: Liber Novus*. New York: W.W. Norton & Co.

Paul, A. M. (2004). *The Cult of Personality: How Personality Tests Are Leading Us to Miseducate Our Children, Mismanage Our Companies, and Misunderstand Ourselves*. New York: Free Press.

Zazzali, P. (2016). *Acting in the Academy: The History of Professional Actor Training in US Higher Education*. London/New York: Routledge.

CHAPTER 4

Alfred Adler

Inferiority and the Individual

Alfred Adler (1870–1937) was another early associate of Freud's who eventually broke away to pursue his own vision of the human psyche (Adler, 1956). Although they had never met, Freud invited Adler to join an elite group of physicians and psychiatrists (later known as the Vienna Psychoanalytic Society) in 1902 after Adler had publicly defended Freud's recently published *The Interpretation of Dreams* (Freud & Brill, 1913; first published in 1900) from attacks in a local newspaper. While Adler attended this group for more than eight years, and was its president in 1910, he was never personally close to Freud, and left the group in 1911, in protest, with nine other members, and would shortly form his own organization, the Association for Individual Psychology, under which title he would continue to formulate and disseminate his own ideas (Bottome, 1957). While it is oft-misstated that Adler was a student or pupil of Freud's in the beginning, this is not true, and was an idea that Adler himself vehemently denied for the rest of his life (Hoffman, 1988, p. 105).

Adler's individual psychology was based on a much different set of views than Freud's darkly sexual and deterministic vision. Adler felt that childhood sexuality, while certainly important, took a backseat to the individual's drives for power and superiority, as well as the relationship of the individual to society (Adler, 1924). Individual psychology was the first version of an "ego psychology." Adler's focus on conscious, rational processes, outward behavior, goal-seeking, and values separates his work from "depth psychology," which is much more interested with the dynamics of the unconscious mind and its causal relationship to neuroticism. Adler's individual psychology was to have a major impact on family therapy, child guidance, education,

105

and psychotherapy (Frick, 1991, p. 21). His theories have become so absorbed into the fabric of twentieth-century psychology as a field, and our shared cultural language, that often Adler has been forgotten as the source of those influences. Adler made a serious impact on the psychology of his day and was a noted influence on many other famous psychologists who followed, including Carl Rogers, Rollo May, and Abraham Maslow (Ansbacher, 1990; Hoffman, 1988, p. 102). However, after his death in 1937, his influence and notoriety began to wane, and it was not until near the end of the twentieth century that Adler's ideas and reputation began a resurgence of popularity.

Following are some of the main concepts that Adler contributed to psychology.

Will to Power

Borrowing Friedrich Nietzsche's term "will to power" (Nietzsche & Lessing J. Rosenwald Collection, Library of Congress, 1908; first published in 1883), Adler made the *striving for superiority* the central theme of his psychology (Adler, 1958). According to Adler, young children feel a strong sense of inadequacy, weakness, and frustration when surrounded by adults with their relative control over bodily functions and the environment. From the child's perspective, power is the first "good thing" and weakness the first "bad thing" that they confront in their psychological life. The child's struggle to attain power and autonomy is their earliest compensation for this feeling of inferiority. Adler felt this will to power was much more central to human motivation and development than prepubescent sexual conflict (à la Freud), and this fundamental difference was at the heart of his break with psychoanalysis. To conceptualize this concept, he coined the term "inferiority complex," which has since found its way deeply into the popular vernacular (Frager & Fadiman, 2005, pp. 95–96). He also developed the notion of "compensation" for feelings of inferiority, which he felt drove much of human striving and accomplishment, something that Freud might well have reduced to the sublimation of inappropriate unconscious sexual desires. Moderate feelings of inferiority Adler considered normal, and in adults might well lead to admirable accomplishments when tempered with appropriate social concern (the genuine caring about others). But strong feelings of inferiority were the drivers of neurosis and could easily lead to maladaptation and unhealthy self-centeredness.

In the inherent striving for power, individuals could either show a healthy bent toward accomplishment and a striving for self-perfection (a foundational notion of Abraham Maslow's theory of self-actualization, discussed later), or a much less healthy desire to dominate others or impose control over them. Both of these adaptions can have very useful implications in character-building in certain contexts. We will explore the application of these various lenses later in the chapter.

In Adler's writing, he often used the term "aggression" to describe an individual's attempts to achieve power; however, his use of the word was more in the spirit of initiative to overcome obstacles than as a form of outright hostility. Later in his life, as his theory evolved, he began to look at the will to power and aggression used in its pursuit more as part of a general motivation toward superiority and perfection (Adler, 1970). Adler came to believe that all healthy individuals are motivated to strive toward perfecting their potentials and continuous self-improvement. For Adler, the overriding goal of superiority had its roots in Darwin's evolutionary theory, which proposed a continuous and implicit effort to adapt to the environment or face extinction (Frager & Fadiman, 2005, p. 96).

Life Goals and Lifestyle

Another area of Adlerian thought that has found its way so deeply into our shared cultural milieu as to be taken for granted is life goals and lifestyle. Individual psychology holds that people develop specific, overriding life goals that become the focus of their internal striving and external achievements. These life goals are influenced by personal experiences, values, attitudes, and personality traits, and are not necessarily consciously held, but can very well influence our decisions and behaviors as unconscious frameworks and drivers (Adler, 1927). Life goals in general tend to be unrealistic, but can become neurotically overinflated if the person suffers from too great an inferiority complex. One of Adler's favorite questions to ask his patients was, "What would you do if you had not got in this trouble?" Inevitably, the patients' answers would reveal what their symptoms were helping them to avoid in their life (Frager & Fadiman, 2005, p. 97).

Adler, following the philosophy of Hans Vaihinger, who proposed the concept of *social fictions* as critical determinants of human behavior, also brought the idea into psychology, where he postulated that our life goals are inherently *fictional*. What he meant by this was that people, confronted with the facts and experiences of life, tend to create systems for organizing and relating to those experiences (which may or may not be based on an accurate interpretation of reality or their personal circumstances). Then they assume that these self-created fictional beliefs are *the unalterable truth* about the world that they confront. These self-fictions can have a powerful influence on lifestyle, fundamentally orienting one toward suspicion and aggression or compassion and trust. In the end, these fictional beliefs become some of the strongest influencers on our behavioral orientation toward the world. According to both Adler and Vaihinger, who had influenced him, people are more affected by their *expectations*, formed based on their own social fictions, than they are on their actual experiences. This position poses some interesting questions for character-building. For instance, how much of a character's behavior is governed by what they *expect* to get under the circumstances of the drama, as opposed to what actually *happens* to them during the action of the story? Depending on a character's deepest orientations toward the world (suspicious, optimistic, alienated, etc.), their responses within any particular scene could be quite different.

In many ways, Adler's concept of the life goal is similar to Stanislavsky's "super objective" (Stanislavsky, 1989, pp. 293–295; text reset 2003) except in the context of a person's life instead of a character's given circumstances in a particular play or script. A person's life goal becomes their hidden motivation, a way of defending against current feelings of inferiority by providing a bridge from the unsatisfying "now" to the bright, powerful, and fulfilling "future." In the neurotic, fantasies of great personal superiority and scenarios of inflated self-esteem receive more attention than more grounded goals involving real achievement, leading to self-defeating behaviors and alienation from others. It is almost always an interesting exercise to envision a character's overriding life goal and then play it out in both healthy and neurotic expressions through the lines of the scene.

Lifestyle, for Adler, was the unique way in which an individual chose to pursue their life goal. It is an integrated and repetitive pattern of adapting to and interacting with a person's life in general, a type of orienting framework that drives action and desire, the answer to the question "What do you *really* want?"

Early Childhood Recollections and the Birth Order Affect on Development

Adler believed that one of the most important keys to understanding someone's personality was their earliest recollections. He felt that one's earliest recollections and memories, far from being random occurrences, were telling reflections that express and reinforce the most important aspects of the current personality and lifestyle. Oftentimes these memories might not reflect accurate recollections of linear events, so much as important indicators of one's life goals, feelings of inferiority/superiority, philosophy of life, and anxieties. It is your consistent *current* lifestyle that informs what your earliest recollections will be and how you interpret and express them. Having his patients ponder and reveal their earliest childhood memories was an important technique that Adler used in therapy to unearth hidden goals and motivations.

Another highly useful perspective Adler introduced through his individual psychology was the notion of birth order and its affect on psychological development. From a postmodern perspective, Adler's birth order analysis was based exclusively on the nuclear family model, which has declined significantly in Western culture since Adler made his formulations. In 2006–2010, the probability of a first marriage lasting at least 10 years was 68% for women and 70% for men. Looking at 20 years, the probability that the first marriages of women and men would survive was 52% for women and 56% for men in 2006–2010. Based on a study released in 2012, these levels were virtually identical to estimates based on vital statistics from the early 1970s (Copen, Daniels, Vespa, & Mosher, 2012). Obviously, there are far more incidents of nontraditional nuclear family relationships than in Adler's time, and these various combinations and adaptations can be taken into account by a creative actor attempting to formulate a family order schema as part of the character development process. However, here I will present the four types of familial relationships Adler used in his original speculations.

According to Adler, the order of birth (within a traditional nuclear family structure) was an important factor in childhood development, and thus on the ways that adults interpret and interact with the world. Depending on the birth order, the psychological environment, even for children growing up in the same household with the same parents, can be significantly different. These different kinds of family constellations can lead to very different coping and goal-seeking strategies, as well as overall lifestyle.

The firstborn, or *oldest child*, must eventually face a "dethronement" crisis when a new sibling arrives in the family. This would also be the case whether the family was divorced or single-parent. With the arrival of the new brother or sister, the oldest child will most likely feel displaced, their power and control (over who gets attention, for instance) lessened or demeaned. As a result of this power crisis, oldest children may later in life enjoy demonstrations of authority, tend toward conservativism, and exaggerate the importance of rules or laws. Adler noted that an older child was more likely to act out or become a "problem" child than children born farther down the family hierarchy (Frick, 1991, p. 27). If the family structure is stable and the oldest child feels loved and prepared for the arrival of the sibling, the more negative potential aspects of dethronement may be mitigated. As with most of Adler's other theories, the relative sense of security or inferiority is the deciding factor between neurotic or healthy responses in the personality.

The *second child* position comes with a different set of challenges and developmental hurdles. The second child must share the family's attention from the very beginning of life. One of the primary motivations in a second child's development is to first catch up and eventually surpass the older sibling. The second child can often behave as if they were in a race or competition with the older sibling, and thereby set their goals unrealistically high as a result. Adler's generalization for the second-born child was that often the second-born was more talented and successful than the oldest child in a family.

The *youngest child* has the advantage of the example of their older siblings, and, much like the second child, tends to be highly motivated to exceed the accomplishments of the older siblings. Adler noted that the ultimate success of a youngest child over the older siblings was a common theme in many myths and fairy tales from across cultures (what Jung would identify as an archetype). However, because of an overexaggerated desire to excel, the youngest child runs the risk of never fully developing a central ambition or life goal, dissipating their energies in later life across too many aspirations and interests. The youngest child, according to Adler, also tends to be pampered, which he considered a detriment to holistic development, and as a result might fail to develop a solid sense of independence, leading to feelings of inferiority later in life.

By contrast, an *only child*, having no siblings with whom to interact, may tend to focus all of their feelings on the mother and father. According to Adler, only children are often pampered, again an impediment to proper development, and may become timid and non-adventurous as a result of an overprotective home environment, leading once again to feelings of inferiority. In Adler's judgment, only children tended to be spoilt and ran a risk of becoming neurotically self-centered and attention-craving as adults.

While family structures may have changed significantly over the last 100 years, the affects of family dynamics on early childhood development have not. So, Adler's lens of birth order dynamics still makes an intriguing perspective to bring to character analysis and development. Does your character show qualities of an "oldest child"? Second or "middle child"? How about "youngest child" or "only child"? This type of birth order analysis can be particularly useful in looking at realistic characters whose family relationships are part of the dramatic structure of the play.

Social Context and Cooperation

For Adler, the human being was a *social being* and could not be understood outside of that context. A healthy person is someone who takes a *social interest* in others and the community in which they live, while a neurotic is self-centered and driven by a desire to dominate others out of a need to ameliorate deep-seated feelings of inferiority. This social interest, sometimes translated as "community feelings," is a critical sense of connection with the human community, an interest in the interests of others (Frager & Fadiman, 2005, p. 100). Without this community feeling, the individual is doomed to feeling isolated, alone, and alienated from others, and will generally perceive the world as a hostile and dangerous place.

Adler's idea about social interest and community feelings grew out of an evolutionary perspective where cooperation with the community in food-gathering, hunting, and defense against predators was the most effective adaptation to the environment and a necessity for the survival of the species. Therefore, cooperation, from Adler's perspective, was a biological necessity. Only by cooperating with the community and becoming a productive member of society can an individual hope to conquer their own feelings of inferiority, or their actual biological inferiority in relationship to the environment. A lack of cooperation will ultimately result in feelings of inadequacy and failure, which are at the heart of all neurotic and maladaptive lifestyles.

Adler's basic emphasis on cooperation and "fitting in" with society may seem somewhat at odds with the idea of individualism and the "outsider" orientation to which many actors aspire, and on some levels it is. However, once again, as an interesting lens through which to view the world of a character, and that character's relationships and orientations within the world of the story, this perspective can be very enlightening, and remains a good tool for assessing a particular character's sense of self.

Individual Psychology Activities for Actors

Adler introduced a number of concepts to Western psychology that were predicated on a view of humans as *socially embedded* rather than reducible to the components of their psyches. In other words, Adler felt that you could not evaluate (or help) people outside of their social context, a very different view from either Freud or Jung, who both were more interested in the affects of the unconscious mind on conscious life. In the following exercise, you will be asked to answer a number of questions about your feelings and behavior that touch on many of Adler's most salient perspectives. By answering these questions honestly, you will develop an "Adlerian portrait" of your personality that can act as a starting point for exploring yourself, your attitudes related to the world in which you live, and the characters you wish to create within the social constructs provided by the given circumstances of the play/script/story.

The Adler Inventory

Below are a number of statements followed by related questions. Read the statement, and then answer the questions as fully and honestly as you can. You may want to write your answers in your private journal for later review.

1. All behavior occurs within a social context; therefore, people cannot be studied or understood outside of their social context. Cooperation and community feeling is a biological/evolutionary necessity, not a contrived social construct. It is important for the individual to develop a feeling of being an integral part of a larger social whole.

   Questions: What are the most important ways you fit in with your current social environment? Where are you most useful/helpful to others? In what social contexts are you most comfortable?

   List the social groups to which you belong. How would you be different without them? How would you be different in other social groups? What are the social groups to which you wished you belonged?

In what areas of your life are you an "outsider"? Where do you not fit in, and are you comfortable or uncomfortable in that role? In what social contexts do you wish you fit in better?

2. A person's psychological whole is more important than the individual components of consciousness. All aspects of the personality are subordinate to the person's overriding life goal and lifestyle. The central motivation for the individual is to strive for perfection or superiority, which is another evolutionary quality of natural human growth.

   Questions: In what areas of your life are you actively striving for perfection? What do you desire the most to improve about yourself? What are your weakest areas of self-development?

   Articulate, as best you can, your single most important life goal. What are some of your lifestyle choices that are helping you reach toward it? What behaviors hold you back from that goal?

3. Behavior is based on how we *perceive* reality, not necessarily reality itself. Our life goals are often fictional constructs based on an ideal we have invented from the perceptions, emotions, and circumstances of early childhood.

   Questions: In what ways are your most important life goals unrealistic or overly idealistic? Can you remember when your life goal first developed or became conscious, or the circumstances that most led you to strive toward your life goal in general? If your childhood had been different, how might your current life goal be different?

You can repeat this inventory for a character you are developing to create a baseline assessment of the character's social engagement and awareness.

Earliest Recollections Exercise

Write down your earliest recollections. Take some time to contemplate this carefully and recall as many details as possible. Try to describe both the circumstances and your feelings at the time, as best as you can recall. Keep in mind you are writing down *specific memories* (i.e., on my first day of school, a group of other kids made fun of my clothes, which made me cry in the hallway and feel embarrassed), rather than general reports (i.e., I remember we always drove to my aunt's house for Thanksgiving dinner).

Read over your entries and try the following suggestions:

If your memories seem inconsistent, or even contradictory, look for recurring patterns or unifying themes. Make notes.

Trivial events may actually be more meaningful than spectacular ones. Try to identify which memories hold the greatest emotional charge or affect your outlook today. Make notes.

In your recollections, does the world seem safe and comfortable? Or is your environment hostile and threatening? Are your memories mostly warm and pleasing, or are they of accidents, punishments, and confrontations that make your world in these reflections seem dangerous or unfriendly? Make notes.

Were any of your memories about the birth of a sibling? If so, were there any feelings of competition or jealousy that you recall (dethronement issues)? Make notes.

In your recollections, are you usually alone, or in a group with family members or friends? Are you cooperative or competitive? Feeling secure or insecure? Make notes.

In your recollections, are you an active participant or passive observer? Make notes.

Is one of your recollections about the first day of school or first time at any social institution? If so, is this a pleasant or unpleasant memory? Does it reflect how you feel today about entering a new social situation? Make notes.

If you were able to complete this exercise in some detail, you now should have some interesting self-knowledge about your own sense of security (or insecurity) and orientation toward the world. This is all very useful material for contrasting with the lives of the characters you play. You can start, for example, by asking yourself: How is my character's orientation to the outside world similar or different from my own? How relatively secure or insecure do they feel?

Adler tended to be forward-focused instead of looking at the past as a source of motivation. He felt that people's hopes for the future had a greater impact on their current behavior than where they had already been in life. He was always trying to understand what people's dreams for the future were, and to help them have a better self-understanding and style of life that was more likely to help them achieve those goals rather than hinder their journey.

115

Life Goals and Your Daily Activities

In your journal, write down a list of what you currently think of as your most important life goals. Do not be overly concerned if they seem generic, abstract, or trivial; just write what comes into your mind without judgment. You may want to consider different aspects of your life, such as the personal, family, career or school, social, community, and spiritual.

On a new page, write a brief essay about how you would like to spend the next five years of your life. Cover things you would like to accomplish, adventures you would like to have, and how you would generally hope to actualize the life goals you have already explored.

Now imagine that you just found out you have three months to live. Write another brief essay about how you would spend the rest of your time. Who would you visit? Would you deliver any overdue apologies or make amends to those you had harmed? What experiences would you seek out in the short time you had left? Are any of your choices different than in the essay about the next five years? Did you learn anything about what you feel is *most* important to you?

Finally, consider all of the goals you have explored in the previous pages and write down the three you consider the *most important* to you. Are there any common themes among these goals? Are they socially oriented or personally focused? Are these goals also on your first list? Are these goals different in some way from the goals in your essays, and if so, how?

116

After completing this exercise, you should have a clearer view of your personal goals and how they relate to your daily life. You may find that your daily behaviors align with and support what you feel to be most important. Or you may find a dissonance between what you commonly do and "what you really want." This is all important self-information for an actor to have. As with most of the other exercises in this book, you can repeat the process from the fictional perspective of a character you are investigating to give you a fresh perspective on what that character might want and feel.

The Wishing Exercise

Pretend you have been given three wishes. They are granted by magic, and you can have anything your heart desires, except that the wishes should be in the realm of human attainability. In other words, while they may be fantastic leaps in imagination from your current position, they should still remain possible in the realistic world; *someone* could believably attain what you ask for.

Now write down your three wishes.

Starting with the first one, write this single wish out in detail, with the benefits, consequences, and implications if this wish were your most important life goal. What would you do to attain this goal? How would it affect your current relationships? What kind of changes, if any, would you make if this were your central life goal?

Repeat this for each wish on your list.

After you are through, go back and read what you have written. Does any one of these now seem more appealing than the others? Is any one of them more achievable than the others?

Make note of any feelings you might have had while doing this exercise. Did the detailed exploration of your wishes (life goals) bring up any surprising emotions? Were you inspired? Disturbed? Investigate your feelings and write down what you find.

The three wishes exercise is another perspective on exploring your personal life goals and becoming sensitized to the power of the concept of a life goal in general.

Dominance/Power Relationships (an Improvisation Exercise)

Work with a scene partner or imagine the other characters' responses. Work with a scene you are already familiar with. Perform the scene (or run an improv with conflicting objectives for each player) with one character feeling in control or powerful, and the other feeling insecure or inferior. After you complete the scene, run it again, only this time switch who feels the power and who is insecure.

Notice any difference in the relationships between the characters? Usually, this is a very useful exercise in exploring both the dynamics of an unbalanced power relationship as well as the internal feelings related to dominance and inferiority.

You can try this exercise another time, only in this version have the players play against their primary feeling of either power or insecurity by hiding it (compensating) from the other character during the course of the scene. Does that change the emotional tone or choices of actions in the scene?

Birth Order and Cooperation Improv

After discussing Adler's model of birth order dynamics, experiment with improv to discover how these play out in an imaginary life situation. Assign a group of actors a scene that involves solving a conflict or accomplishing an important task. Each player is assigned a birth order, first child, middle child, youngest child, or only child. Play the scene or improv out under these circumstances. Now have the players switch birth order roles and do the scene again.

For discussion, explore how each player felt enacting the scene from each perspective. Did one role provoke feelings of aggression or dominance more than another? Was there one role that was more comfortable or familiar than another? If so, was that role correlated with the actor's actual birth order or not?

118

Adler's individual psychology provides us with a useful and very different set of perspectives from the other theorists we have explored so far. This material, as with the rest, can best be used in the dual purpose of providing self-realization and understanding, as well as an exploratory method of building a character.

References

Adler, A. (1924). *The Practice and Theory of Individual Psychology*. London/New York: K. Paul, Trench, Trubner & Co/Harcourt, Brace & Company.

Adler, A. (1927). *Understanding Human Nature*. New York: Greenberg.

Adler, A. (1956). *The Individual Psychology of Alfred Adler: A Systematic Presentation in Selections from His Writings*. New York: Basic Books.

Adler, A. (1958). *What Life Should Mean to You*. New York: Capricorn Books.

Adler, A. (1970). *Superiority and Social Interest: A Collection of Later Writings* (2nd ed.). Evanston, IL: Northwestern University Press.

Ansbacher, H. L. (1990). Alfred Adler's influence on the three leading cofounders of humanistic psychology. *Journal of Humanistic Psychology*, 30(4), 45–53. doi:10.1177/002216789003000404

Bottome, P. (1957). *Alfred Adler: A Portrait from Life*. New York: Vanguard.

Copen, C. E., Daniels, K., Vespa, J., & Mosher, W. D. (2012). *First Marriages in the United States: Data from the 2006–2010 National Survey of Family Growth*. Retrieved from www.cdc.gov/nchs/govdelivery.htm.

Frager, R., & Fadiman, J. (2005). *Personality and Personal Growth* (6th ed.). Upper Saddle River, NJ: Pearson Prentice Hall.

Freud, S., & Brill, A. A. (1913). *The Interpretation of Dreams*. London: G. Allen & Company.

Frick, W. B. (1991). *Personality Theories: Journeys into Self* (2nd ed.). New York: Teachers College Press, Columbia University.

Hoffman, E. (1988). *The Right to Be Human: A Biography of Abraham Maslow*. Los Angeles, CA/New York: J.P. Tarcher/St. Martin's Press.

Nietzsche, F. W., & Lessing J. Rosenwald Collection, Library of Congress (1908). *Also sprach Zarathustra: ein Buch für Alle und Keinen*. Leipzig: Insel-Verlag.

Stanislavsky, K. (1989). *An Actor Prepares*. New York: Routledge.

119

CHAPTER 5

Karen Horney

Psychoanalytic Social Theory

Karen Horney (1885–1952), pronounced /ˈhɔːrnaɪ/, was another psychoanalyst who eventually broke with Freud and created her own set of depth psychology theories. She is often categorized as a "neo-Freudian," a term used to describe a group of mid-twentieth-century American theorists who attempted to extend Freud's psychoanalytic concepts into the realm of the social and cultural while downplaying his original emphasis on biological determinism (Rycroft, 1995, p. 60). Horney is also credited by many as the first psychoanalytically oriented feminist. In her early work, while acknowledging Freud's contributions, she severely criticized Freud's formulations as patriarchal, particularly his notion of penis envy, and wrote extensively during the 1920s correcting and adapting Freud's theories. Much of this early work on a female-centric view of traditional psychoanalysis was forgotten until her papers were republished in *Feminine Psychology* (1967), which garnered her much posthumous praise for being a visionary leader of the feminist movement and ahead of her time (Chodorow, 1989, pp. 2–3; Paris, 1994).

For the purposes of applying Horney's theories as acting tools, we will focus on her two later phases, what we will call Horney's new paradigm and her mature theory (Frager & Fadiman, 2005, p. 120). For more on her feminist phase, see both *Karen Horney: A Psychoanalyst's Search for Self-Understanding* (Paris, 1994) and *Feminism and Psychoanalytic Theory* (Chodorow, 1989).

In revisioning psychoanalysis to consider social and cultural impacts on psychic development, rather than Freud's overriding view that personality was fixed in the first few years of life, well before social influences fully come to bear, Horney constructed a much different map of the human mind. She also moved the focus of her therapeutic techniques, which influenced many who followed, from the person's historical past to the present life circumstances and structure of the personality. This was a significant break with traditional psychoanalysis, with its nearly exclusive focus on uncovering past, mostly static, events. Much of contemporary psychotherapy today follows Horney's example of present-focused investigation of the dynamic personality. Below, we will introduce some of Horney's most salient contributions.

Basic Anxiety and a Developmental Schema

While Horney did not deny the importance of early childhood development, she shifted her focus from prepubescent sexual frustration to family conflicts that made the young child feel insecure, unsafe, or unloved. Horney felt that it was these conditions that eventually led to what she termed "basic anxiety," the feeling of helplessness in a hostile world, which later on, as adults, people try to reduce by using the pursuit of love, power, or detachment as a type of generalized defense strategy (Horney, 1937):

121

[Basic anxiety develops when] the environment is dreaded as a whole because it is felt to be unreliable, mendacious, unappreciative, unfair, unjust, begrudging, and merciless. . . . The child . . . feels the environment as a menace to his entire development and to his most legitimate wishes and strivings. He feels in danger of his individuality being obliterated, his freedom taken away, his happiness prevented. In contrast to his fear of castration [Freud] this fear is not fantasy, but is well-founded on reality.

(Horney, 1939, p. 75)

To some degree, everyone suffers from basic anxiety; it is a natural response to the world in general, and to some extent everyone adopts the pursuit of love, power, or detachment as coping mechanisms, also a natural adaption. However, when these defensive solutions (discussed below) become overly compelling or obsessive, they create "vicious circles" that only serve to create more anxiety and maladaptation to the reality presented by life (Horney, 1937, p. 114). So, for Horney, neurotic problems stem from basic anxiety, which spawns maladaptive patterns of behavior, which in turn heightens the level of basic anxiety, all of which are influenced along the way by ongoing experience, eventually constellating into adult defensive strategies (the pursuit of love, power, or detachment) and neurotic character structures. It is these neurotic character structures that cause people suffering and alienation from the world, and the point of therapy is to help people relinquish their defenses—which keep them from identifying their authentic likes, dislikes, hopes, fears, and desires of the heart—so that they can get in touch with and befriend their "real self" (Horney, 1939, p. 11).

In contrast to Freud, with his fixed-traits-from-childhood model, Horney's focus on the dynamic interaction between an individual's basic patterns and the impact of the culture around them was a truly developmental model of the psyche where the present structure of personality was based on the sum total of all life experience to date, and not merely a mechanistic response generated by deterministic forces; people can and do *change* over the course of their lifetimes.

Neurosis, in Horney's view, was the alienation from the *real self* by the unconscious use of defense mechanisms and coping strategies (see below) for avoiding basic anxiety. The real self is not a static entity or consciousness, but a set of intrinsic potentials, including temperament, basic talents and proclivities, capacities, and biologically determined predispositions, that need favorable environmental circumstances in order to fully develop and become actualized within the mature personality.

Toward, Against, and Away from Others

Horney, as a psychoanalyst, was mostly concerned with neurotic character structures and personality traits that caused people problems in coping with life. As actors, this is a major area of interest to us as well, given the dramatic and comedic possibilities of neurotic behavior and motivation so often found in dramatic literature and theatrical expression of all kinds. Certainly, not all characters are neurotic in their constitution, but a solid understanding of how people cope with the world in both adaptive and maladaptive ways is a significant advantage to the actor who must be a student of *all* human nature. Such an understanding will widen and deepen the number of choices you have available in creating and enacting character decisions.

In Horney's paradigm, there are three fundamental solutions that people adopt to deal with their basic anxiety. While healthy people can adopt some form of all three solutions depending on what feels appropriate to the situation, neurotics tend to fixate or overly depend on one particular strategy, which ultimately becomes a maladaptive defense and creates additional anxiety as it alienates the neurotic from others and the person's *real self*. Each solution involves a general group of behaviors and personality traits, a particular view of what "justice" is, and a set of beliefs about human nature and human values, as well as a "deal" or "bargain" with fate wherein the person follows a course of action in the world believing that compliance with the terms of the bargain, by way of their chosen solution, will be rewarded and their actions justified "in the end."

The compliant solution, or *moving toward* other people, is the attempt to gain affection or approval from others or to control others by imposing dependency upon them. The neurotic version of moving toward people involves a strong need to be wanted, desired, protected, loved, attached, and cared for by others. They may adopt subservient roles and be overtly self-effacing and self-depreciating. The compliant person feels weak and helpless in the world and moves toward those who can provide the protection against a hostile environment they feel they cannot conjure on their own. Their bargain with fate is that if they are good, meek, and non-aggressive with others, and shun pride and glory of their own, then they will be well treated by the world and other people. These people may be compulsively religious as part of their emotional defense mechanisms, viewing the world as displaying a providential order where virtue and self-sacrifice are rewarded, and perhaps believing that there is a higher or transcendent justice that goes beyond human understanding and their current life circumstances.

The expansive solution, or *moving against* people, is essentially the opposite of the compliant solution. The neurotic version of moving against people involves a craving for power, an assumption that others are generally hostile, and a drive to outsmart or exploit others before one is exploited themselves; there is an aggressive drive to succeed and achieve status and prestige. In her 1950 book *Neurosis and Human Growth*, Horney identified three distinct sub-solutions or styles of moving against people: narcissistic, perfectionistic, and arrogant-vindictive.

The *narcissistic solution* involves an air of self-aggrandizement and charm as a tool for manipulating others. They often have great confidence in their own abilities and talents and feel there is no game or challenge they can't win. They may speak incessantly about their own accomplishments and demand admiration and constant reassurance of their value from those around them. While seemingly arrogant and boastful, much of the narcissist's bluster is really a defense against insecurity and hidden feelings of inadequacy.

People who adopt the *perfectionistic solution* tend to have extremely high moral and intellectual standards by which they judge and look down upon others. They take great pride in their excellence and own superior drive and rank others as more or less inferior in comparison to their own deeds and moral standing. Judgmental and uncompromising by nature, the perfectionist may well hold others to impossibly high standards and despise them when they fail to live up to their unrealistic expectations, which is another way of externalizing or projecting their own insecurities onto others. Their bargain with fate tends to be legalistic and rigid, where they feel that if they are fair, just, and apply "the rules" evenly to everyone, they in turn will be treated fairly by other people and life in general. "This conviction of an infallible justice operating in life gives [them] a feeling of mastery" (Horney, 1950, p. 197).

The *arrogant-vindictive solution* is most commonly adopted by people who feel a strong need to "be right" and to have vindictive triumphs over others. Arrogant-vindictive personalities tend to have grown up under harsh circumstances and feel the need to punish others for wounds and injuries they have suffered in the past. As Horney put it, the world of the arrogant-vindictive person "is an arena where, in the Darwinian sense, only the fittest survive and the strong annihilate the weak" (Horney, 1945, p. 64). They often subscribe to the principle that "might makes right," and they tend to be competitive, ruthless, and cynical in their relationships with others. They are emotionally tough and hard on the outside, and look at the expression of emotion or feeling as a sign of weakness. Their bargain with fate is essentially with themselves; they don't count on anyone or anything to get them what they want except their own wits, guile, and muscle (Frager & Fadiman, 2005, p. 128). Other people are almost always a disappointment, and so they rely on their own inner vision and judgment, ignoring traditional morality and their own softer feelings as they "do battle" with the world to achieve their self-directed goals.

The detachment solution, or *moving away* from people, is a highly individualistic approach to life where the person values freedom and self-sufficiency above everything else. Detached people tend to have a general estrangement from others and crave emotional distance. They prove themselves by not needing help, emotional or otherwise, from others. They tend to avoid effort and worldly achievement, and get much of their validation through their own imagination and internal ruminations rather than through acknowledgment of others. They are

124

often "loners" and keep others at a safe distance from their true feelings and emotions. Their bargain with fate seems to be that if they expect little or nothing from the world, they will be asked for little or nothing in return, therefore being left to their own devices without bother or interference; if they don't try, they can't fail.

The Idealized Image and the Tyranny of the Shoulds

Horney believed that we construct an *idealized image* of ourselves that we endow with "unlimited powers and exalted faculties" (Horney, 1950, p. 22). The idealized self is constructed in the imagination using the lens of the primary defensive posture (compliant, expansive, detached) as its model. Therefore, an idealized self based on the compliant solution might consist of qualities such as unselfishness, generosity, saintliness, nobility, sacrifice, etc., and glorify helplessness and martyrdom, whereas an idealized self based on the expansive solution might aggrandize qualities such as invincibility, superior intelligence, and a tough, realistic exterior immune to fear and softer emotions, better equipped to deal with life's challenges than others. The detached idealized self "is a composite of self-sufficiency, independence, self-contained serenity, freedom from desires and passions" (Horney, 1950, p. 277). In many cases, the idealized self, regardless of which solution informs it, may be based, in whole or in part, on an historical, religious, or culturally important figure who embodies the ideal principles of the image the person has created in their imagination. Unfortunately, even though the qualities of the idealized self may seem admirable, the construct is actually an impossibly perfect ideal, which, when we don't fully live up to it, makes us feel worse and even develop self-hate.

125

Once the idealized self-image is formed, usually in childhood, the person sets out on a quest or *search for glory*, attempting to actualize or bring into reality the perfect version of the idealized self, a quest that, of course, is doomed to fail. The idealized self despises the real self for its (natural) faults and inability to attain perfection, and this leads to what Horney called the *tyranny of the shoulds*. A person, based on their primary defensive posture, has created an idealized self that "should" be lived up to. However, in addition to being an impossibly high ideal, the idealized self also includes aspects of the other defensive orientations, leading to internal conflicts and inconsistencies that make how a person ideally "should" behave/act/think an impossible set of contradictions as well. For Horney, this suggested the notion of an inescapable tyranny that creates vicious circles of anxiety for the neurotic or, at a minimum, must be rectified and accepted if a healthy person ever hopes to be happy and satisfied with life.

Horney went further, as a social critic, and pointed out that the dominant American culture (of the 1930s and 1940s) was often a major contributor to the development of neurotic character structures. She identified three major trends that she felt were major contributors to neurosis in American culture.

1. The irrational pursuit of material possessions and monetary gain (beyond sustenance), that were falsely associated with satisfying our basic needs for security, power, and self-esteem.
2. An exaggerated competitiveness with others, built into the fabric of capitalistic society, that permeates all of our relationships and impairs our basic abilities to love, share, learn, and play.
3. An insatiable need for love and external validation, combined with an unrealistic expectation that acquiring such love will resolve all of our conflicts and feelings of deficiency we experience as a result of living in our society.

(Frick, 1991, p. 57)

From our own postmodern vantage point, we can observe that these embedded cultural characteristics have only accelerated and intensified over the last three-quarters of a century since Horney's time, and the alienation and false striving that they produce, has only grown with the addition of other techno-socio factors such as social media networks, cable television, and the 24-hour news cycle, the near dissolution of the nuclear family model, globalization, identity politics, and the ethics of late capitalism in general. Even though the interactions between the self and society were complex and substantial during Horney's lifetime, it could be argued that that complexity, and subsequent impact on personal development, has grown significantly. It is left to the individual actor to add whatever contemporary social influences they might identify to Horney's basic models.

Psychoanalytic Social Theory Activities for Actors

Karen Horney's work forces us into the present moment and makes us confront the external, social forces that affect our current personality structure and the way we tend to interact with the world. Instead of exclusively looking into the unconscious for influences from childhood development (Freud) or archetypal images (Jung), Horney invites us to examine our current-state posture toward the world around us and our relationships with others in that context. For the actor, this provides yet another lens for viewing our personal psychological makeup, as well as multiple potential perspectives on our characters' inner lives.

Directions of Movement

In your journal, write down examples from your own past of the three directions of movement, *toward*, *against*, and *away* from other people. Pick situations that are strong in your memory and have a powerful emotional charge, if you can. This is a private entry, so try to be as honest and brave in your self-reflections as you can. You might look at major events in your life, such as the breakup of a relationship, a change in school or job, a conflict where you felt humiliated or wronged, or a time where you realized that you were in the wrong. Seek out circumstances where your behavior best illustrates Horney's three solutions or strategies, compliancy/dependency, aggression/dominance, withdrawal/isolation/resignation, and write down each in detail.

Now ask yourself what your generally *preferred strategy* is for dealing with the world, and write down your answer, along with several examples that illustrate this trend for you.

How is behaving in this way an asset for you? In what ways is it a successful strategy? Try to find several examples where using this solution was the very best choice for dealing with a life situation.

Now look at how your preferred strategy is a negative for you. Try to remember times where you took this approach and it held you back or affected your relationships in ways that were not positive.

Finally, using the situations you have recalled above, spend some time imagining how these situations might have been different using the other solutions or strategies.

The point of the above exercise is to bring into awareness how you use these solutions in your own life, when they are a successful coping mechanism, and when they might be unconscious defenses. In better understanding these basic strategies for interacting with others, we can then apply them to the dramatic circumstances of the characters we play.

Once you have completed this exercise for yourself, you can go through it again for a character you are familiar with or are currently working on. How do these solutions affect the way a character interacts with others in the world of the play or movie? Is one strategy more appropriate for this particular character than the others? Does your character adopt multiple strategies throughout the events in the drama depending on the given circumstances? Or does the character unconsciously and maladaptively stick with one solution, even though it causes damage and conflict, as with a neurotic personality?

The Real Self Exercise #1

Find a quiet, comfortable space where you can be alone. You can record your thoughts on paper or into a digital recording device for later playback. Relax and concentrate on your breath for a few minutes, allowing your mind to clear and settle.

Look for the most basic goals/things that are fundamentally important to you. Investigate areas such as family, relationships, long-term career, housing and income, religious or spiritual beliefs, political ideals, feelings about children and marriage/life partnerships, race and gender issues, social status and identity affiliations, etc.

Make a detailed list of those goals and ideals that are most important to you and that you feel will endure over time; in other words, the values you hold as most fundamental.

Review your list and see if you can identify any groupings or general themes that run through the list.

Now make a similar list of those things and qualities that you think are the most abhorrent, disgusting, or unjust in the world and other people. What are the opposite of your goals and values?

Compare your two lists. How would you state in a few sentences what you think is most important and what you think most needs to change or be eliminated in the world? How can you achieve your own most important goals and develop those qualities in yourself, and what can you do to help with the problems and injustices you have identified?

Finally, look at your list of goals and values, and see if some are wholly unrealistic or even grandiose. Are there others that are more realistic or attainable than others? If you can make clear distinctions between the two categories, you may well be looking at descriptions of both your idealized self and your real self.

129

If you have done a careful and honest job of looking at those things you most value and most wish to see changed or eliminated from society, you should have a very useful map of your own internal value structures and some insight into what both your real and ideal self-image looks like. In life, this type of self-understanding can be useful in guiding you to make healthy and self-actualizing choices and decisions. As an actor, it provides you with an excellent basic map to compare your individuality with the characters you will play, and understand the similarities and differences between the two.

The Real Self Exercise #2

As in the last exercise, find a quiet, comfortable space where you can be alone. You can record your thoughts on paper or into a digital recording device for later playback. Relax and concentrate on your breath for a few minutes, allowing your mind to clear and settle.

Try to remember yourself as a teenager, age 13 or 14. Pick a particular day during that time and go through as many details of that day as you can remember. See if you can recall your friends, what you did at school and for fun. What sort of music did you like? What did you talk about? What were your secrets? Who did you have a crush on? How did you get along with the members of your family? Were you part of team sports, clubs, or other groups? What was important to you at that time in your life?

Once you have captured as many details as possible about your inner and external life at that time, turn your memory back even further. See if you can recall yourself at 5 or 6 years old. If not 5 or 6, then the youngest you can remember, and go through the same exercise again, recalling details about your friends and family relationships, your likes and dislikes, and the ways in which you recall seeing the world.

Now that you have two clear pictures of yourself at earlier stages in your life, compare the two and note the differences between your childhood and adolescent selves. How had you changed over time? What social forces or significant events do you feel most influenced the changes that you found between childhood and adolescence? Note particularly how your relationships with both friends and authority figures, such as your parents or teachers, might have changed over time.

Finally, compare these two images of yourself with who you are today. Are there any differences? Do you feel more or less authentic as a human being? Is it easier or harder for you to express your ideas or feelings honestly with others? Note any significant changes between your younger selves and your sense of self today.

In this exercise, you have been trying to bring into consciousness different versions of your self-image at different developmental stages during your life. You have also been looking, in detail, at the way that self-image might have changed due to the influences of the external and social world around you. You may also have discovered some insights into the way your internal self-image has evolved over time and how perspectives (on the self and the world) tend to change over time and at different life stages. Once again, this heightened self-perspective can be very useful information for the actor who would bring subtlety and nuance to their character work. As with most of our other exercises, this can be repeated using the imaginary circumstances of a character's younger life, either provided by the writer in the text or imagined by the actor in pre-performative research.

Examining Neurotic Claims and Patterns

Think about a time when you wanted something very badly that you either could not have or it would have otherwise, from a rational perspective, been impossible for you to attain. How did you behave when it became clear that you would not get what you wanted? Did you become angry? Resentful? Did you plot some form of revenge? How did you respond when your pride or feelings were wounded? Were you reasonable or unrealistic? Did you express yourself outwardly or keep your feelings to yourself? Try to remember how your body felt during the moment of greatest disappointment. Did you experience guilt or shame over your behavior? Make notes for yourself about this experience.

Now try to remember a time when you were asked to do something for someone else that you really didn't want to do. Did you do what you were asked, or did you get out of it somehow? Try to recall your thoughts and feelings about the person who asked you to do the task. Once again, were you angry, resentful, or vengeful? Did your own actions in the situation cause you shame or pride?

Try to recall a time when someone disappointed you greatly or failed to live up to your standards of behavior. Pick a situation that had a high emotional charge for you, something that really made you indignant and judgmental. Try to recall your feelings and thoughts when you discovered the

131

disappointing behavior. What did you say or do to express your feelings?

Finally, pick an instance where you knew you were in the wrong or had somehow significantly violated your own moral code, a situation such as lying, cheating, or stealing. Did you get caught? How did you feel about what you had done? Did you act to cover up your guilt? What was your specific behavior and thoughts? Were you self-condemning or did you try to shunt the blame onto others? Really try to investigate your true feelings around the event.

Now that you have run through this experience using yourself as a basis, you might try applying this style of analysis to a character you are working on or one with which you are already deeply familiar. Run through the question list from this exercise again and see if you can answer them for the character. This will probably involve creating some rather detailed character biography; however, when properly done, these biographical imaginings can lead to very playable moments in the context of the script. Like with most of the exercises in this book, you become familiar with the perspectives or emotions that arise through the exercises utilizing your own individual history first, and then practice applying these exercises to fictional circumstances. With repetition, this type of work becomes a natural and reflexive part of your preparation for a role.

Horney believed that by studying your own reactions and feelings under stress and in situations of high emotional charge, we could learn about our own neurotic tendencies and patterns. Certainly, it is important for an actor to understand a wide range of potential reactions to stress and emotional pressure as the vast majority of drama and comedy, at least in the Western world, surrounds extraordinary or extreme circumstances and how characters respond to them in the world of the story. A careful study of neurotic or maladaptive behaviors can provide a very useful set of character tools for the astute actor.

References

Chodorow, N. (1989). *Feminism and Psychoanalytic Theory*. New Haven, CT: Yale University Press.

Frager, R., & Fadiman, J. (2005). *Personality and Personal Growth* (6th ed.). Upper Saddle River, NJ: Pearson Prentice Hall.

132

Frick, W. B. (1991). *Personality Theories: Journeys into Self* (2nd ed.). New York: Teachers College Press, Columbia University.

Horney, K. (1937). *The Neurotic Personality of Our Time.* New York: W. W. Norton & Company.

Horney, K. (1939). *New Ways in Psychoanalysis.* New York: W. W. Norton.

Horney, K. (1945). *Our Inner Conflicts: A Constructive Theory of Neurosis.* New York: W.W. Norton & Company.

Horney, K. (1950). *Neurosis and Human Growth: The Struggle Toward Self-Realization.* New York: Norton.

Horney, K., Kelman, H., & Association for the Advancement of Psychoanalysis (1967). *Feminine Psychology.* London: Routledge & Kegan Paul.

Paris, B. J. (1994). *Karen Horney: A Psychoanalyst's Search for Self-Understanding.* New Haven, CT: Yale University Press.

Rycroft, C. (1995). *A Critical Dictionary of Psychoanalysis* (2nd ed.). London/ New York: Penguin Books.

Erik Erikson

Life Span Development

Erik Erikson (1902–1994) was born in Germany to a Danish mother and German father. He was raised in the Jewish faith, a fact that later forced his emigration from Europe to the United States during the rise of Hitler, and converted to Christianity after his marriage. His formal education ended at 18 and for a time he studied and taught art. In a twist of fate, he was invited to teach art and other subjects to children at a new school formed in Vienna, Austria, for families who had come there for psychoanalysis. Through this affiliation, he met Anna Freud and other prominent members of the psychoanalytic community, and eventually entered psychoanalysis himself with Anna Freud in the house she shared with her father, Sigmund Freud (Frager & Fadiman, 2005, pp. 173–174).

Erikson's most important contribution to Western psychology was his introduction of the life span developmental model, where he adapted traditional psychoanalytic theory to extend across the entire life span from childhood through old age. While many have grouped him with the *neo-Freudians*, Erikson himself preferred the more neutral title of *post-Freudian* (Frager & Fadiman, 2005, p. 175). As with many of the early psychoanalysts who followed Freud, Erikson both accepted and criticized Freud's theories, and ultimately expanded them into areas far beyond Freud's original limited vision. Erikson's three major innovations to Freud's theories included the idea that along with stages of psychosexual development, individuals also go through simultaneous psychosocial and ego-development stages; personality development continues throughout a person's life span, and is not wholly fixed after early childhood; and that each stage of development can have either a positive (healthy) or negative (neurotic) outcome that affects all following stages.

In Erikson's model, each stage of development culminates in a crisis between two potential extremes that must be successfully solved in order to move on to the next stage. In solving this developmental crisis, the individual gains a particular competence or virtue that is useful (in its healthy versions) during all later stages of growth.

In addition to his life span developmental model, Erikson introduced the notions of *identity* and *identity crisis* into psychology and other social sciences. Identity, for Erikson, was a broad and inclusive term that included the ego as a central agency or organizing principle for the personality, the sense of individuality and continuity of experience, as well as the process of identifying and internalizing the rules and ideals of social groups with which the individual might be affiliated. An identity crisis is a mental state where the individual, even if only on a temporary basis, has lost or is in between a solid sense of identity and appropriate social affiliation. Erikson first identified these concepts when working with World War II veterans in a rehabilitation clinic in San Francisco. His patients were easily upset and unbalanced by external stimuli. They were often quickly startled and exhibited bodily symptoms such as hot flashes, heart palpitations, and intense headaches, symptoms today we would associate with post-traumatic stress disorder (PTSD). "There was a distinct loss of ego identity. The sameness and continuity and the belief in one's social role were gone" (Erikson, 1968, p. 67). Interestingly, Erikson looked at the identity crisis, which can emerge repeatedly at different times in life, as an opportunity for the individual to make adjustments, either positive or negative, to their sense of identity as they adapt throughout their lives to changing circumstances and the various developmental stages (Feist & Feist, 2006, p. 248).

135

The development of a solid sense of identity is a process that takes place over several of the developmental stages (described below) and has both psychological and social dimensions. An individual's development of their sense of "sameness" and continuity of experience is based, in part, on a belief in the sameness and continuity of a worldview that is shared by their significant others and that part of society they identify with the most. In the search for this consistent sense of personal identity, both conscious and unconscious factors come into play. A stable sense of identity can only develop if certain environmental support factors, including physical, mental, and social preconditions, are available. Also, the development of a sense of identity cannot be delayed as the future stages of healthy development depend on the sense of identity in order to succeed. In other words, external factors such as war, serious family disruption, or trauma can derail or delay the development process. Additionally, identity development relies on the past, present, and future hopes and the actual life situation of the individual. First, a person must acquire a clear sense of identification in childhood. Second, the choice of vocation or career identification in adulthood must be reasonably aligned with actual opportunities available within the environment. Finally, the adult must feel some sense of assurance that their chosen role will remain viable in the future, both as an individual function but also in the broader world of their society (Erikson, 1980, pp. 120–130).

One other major multidisciplinary contribution Erik Erikson made was the popularization of *psychohistory*. Psychohistory is the study of:

psychological motivations of historical persons and events. It attempts to combine the insights of psychoanalysis with the research methodology of the social sciences to understand the emotional origin of the social and political behavior of groups and nations, past and present.

(Wikipedia, 2018)

Psychohistory remains a controversial activity, and there are no departments dedicated to psychohistory in any major institution of higher learning, even though some history departments have run courses in it. It is sometimes criticized as a pseudoscience; however, it is most interesting to actors for its practices of forensic analysis of historical (and therefore potentially fictional) events and individual motivations, much like classic character analysis is performed on the imaginary circumstances of a play. Erikson wrote, or delivered as lectures, several classic psycho-biographical studies, also called verbal portraits (Capps, 2014), that included detailed psychoanalytical analysis of important historical figures, including Martin Luther (Erikson, 1958), Maxim Gorky (Erikson, 1993, pp. 359–402), Adolf Hitler (Erikson, 1993, pp. 326–358), George Bernard Shaw (Erikson, 1968, pp. 142–155), Sigmund Freud (Erikson, 1968, pp. 196–208), and Mahatma Gandhi (Erikson, 1969), which won him the Pulitzer Prize and the National Book Award.

Developmental Stages, Polarities, and Virtues

As stated above, Erikson's model extended psychoanalytic theory across the entire life span and beyond mere psychosexual development. Whereas Freud had mostly identified psychological stages with physical body parts (the mouth, penis, and anus, for instance), Erikson looked at stage growth as both physically embodied and environmentally/socially influenced. For Erikson, each stage of a person's development is progressive, depending on the completion of the stage before it as its basis. Unsuccessful completion of development at one stage will influence and inhibit growth at all later stages. Erikson also held that healthy development required adequate circumstances in the environment to support growth, including family structure, economic and cultural opportunity, and lack of trauma or serious disease.

Each of Erikson's stages are characterized by a conflict between two polarities or extremes that ultimately becomes a crisis that must be resolved in order to develop a virtue, strength, or competency at that stage, and thus move on. For instance, Erikson called the first stage of development *basic trust versus basic mistrust* (the polarities), where the ability to trust others and one's environment (the competency) is contrasted with an inability to do so. So, in this first stage, during infancy, the child's main developmental task, or crisis to be resolved between the polarities, is to develop trust and a sense of security; a failure to succeed at this task will result in an inability to trust that will affect the individual for the rest of their life.

Erikson felt that development followed an epigenetic scheme, meaning that the developmental cycle followed a predetermined sequence that unfolded in a naturally progressive order, much like an embryo grows into a fetus and a fetus into a baby; each stage built upon the last. Erikson's developmental schema was based on two primary assumptions:

(1) That human personality in principle develops according to steps predetermined in the growing person's readiness to be driven forward, to be aware of, and to interact with a widening social radius; and (2) that society, in principle, tends to be so constituted as to meet and invite the succession of potentialities for interaction and attempts to safeguard and to encourage the proper rate and the proper sequence of their unfolding.

(Erikson, 1964, p. 270)

While the polarities described in the names of each of Erikson's stages appear to be wholly positive or negative in nature, Erikson was careful to warn that this is not necessarily so. He explained that the extremes of either pole are actually unhealthy and maladaptive, and that the goal of personality development is to find a balance or appropriate ratio between the two extremes (Frager & Fadiman, 2005, p. 191). For instance, looking at the qualities of basic trust and basic mistrust, even though "trust" may seem a wholly desirable trait, someone who is too trusting may be gullible and just as out of touch with reality as someone who is neurotically mistrustful. A healthy person is able to discriminate between situations where trust in another has been earned and another situation in which they may be taken advantage of. It is the balance between relative trust and relative suspicion that helps a person successfully navigate their way through life's interactions with others. In all of the following stages, successful development is in finding the *balance* between the poles that yields the virtue or competency needed to navigate life and move on to the next stage; too much of one extreme or the other can be equally unhealthy.

The first three of Erikson's stages are in basic agreement with Freud's first three stages, although they extend beyond the body part identity into the social sphere and characterize development in more universal human themes.

Stage 1: Basic Trust vs. Basic Mistrust

In the first stage of life, an infant is totally helpless and dependent on others for its care and survival. During this stage, the first "other" an infant is likely to encounter is the mother or a motherlike care provider. Through the mother's care and nourishment, both physical and emotional, the baby learns a basic sense of trust or mistrust for the world. As with Freud, Erikson acknowledged that much of an infant's interactions and explorations at this stage are through the mouth. Development of basic trust "implies not only that one has learned to rely on the sameness and continuity of the outer providers, but also that one may trust oneself and the capacities of one's own organs to cope with urges [such as hunger]" (Erikson, 1964, p. 248). At this stage, an infant's feelings of relative security and insecurity will be highly influenced by the interactions with and quality of care received from the primary care provider.

The virtue or competency that is developed through the infant's struggle with the dichotomy of trust and mistrust is *hope*. In Erikson's view, hope becomes the lifelong belief that fervent wishes are attainable despite life's difficulties, challenges, and the dark urges of primal drives. Hope becomes a basic strength that is relatively independent of specific goals, desires, and wishes. As the child matures to further stages of development, this virtue is verified and reinforced in different ways; positive experiences inspire new hope, etc. At the same time, a healthy balance between the two poles that created hope will imbue the individual with the capacity to endure the inevitable disappointments that life brings, ultimately helping the child develop realistic dreams and expectations for life. Later in

138

life, hope is cultivated by social institutions such as religion, inspirational figures and literature, or spiritual communities. The mature version of hope in the grown adult is *faith*, which is often reinforced by religious rituals and practices designed to support, deepen, and restore a sense of faith, often in the face of catastrophe or loss.

Stage 2: Autonomy vs. Shame and Doubt

Erikson's second stage parallels Freud's "anal" period and occurs generally in the second and third years of life. The polarities that the child must confront at this stage are *autonomy* vs. *shame or self-doubt*. Much of this development is based on the child learning to grasp and let go of things. This includes the physical grasping and releasing of objects in its environment with the hands, as well as the process of toilet-training, controlling and releasing the bowels. It is a time of maturing muscular control, learning new skills such as walking, climbing, and holding on to objects, and communicating more effectively through language. The child gains more control over its environment and begins to be able to make choices, such as what toy to pick up or throw away, which begins to build a sense of autonomy. At this stage, most children discover, and often cherish, the use of the word "no."   139

Successfully achieving a sense of autonomy and self-control yields the virtue of *will*, the power to control one's drives and use judgment and discrimination in interacting with the environment. Failure to successfully develop the strength of will leads to a sense of shame and doubt, the other extreme of this stage's polarity. Shame is the sense of self-exposure and a feeling that one's deficiencies are apparent to everyone. Shame, at this stage, can also be associated with the child's attempts to stand, wherein they feel unstable, small, and powerless compared to the adults around them. Doubt emerges from the fact that the child has a physical "front side" that it can see and conceptualize, but also possesses a hidden and unseeable "back side," which is an unknown territory and yet comes to the fore, and often dominates the parent/child relationship during the toilet-training period, which must be mastered in order to successfully become more autonomous. Repeated failures at toilet-training tend to breed various levels of shame and doubt, and the process must be successfully mastered in order to develop the strength of will discussed above. Will, then, becomes the ground for self-restraint, regardless of the unavoidable experiences of shame and doubt that life inevitably deals.

The important strength of will is what allows us later in life to accept, with a semblance of dignity, the rule of law, and to join with society in following rules presupposed to be based on justice without collapsing our sense of self and our individuality in the process. Ultimately, social institutions, such as the rule of law, give concrete form to our ego's control of our drives, for without such individual and institutional restraints there would be mayhem and chaos instead of a "social order."

A personal sense of autonomy and the ego-strength to confront both shame and doubt head-on, through the exercise of will, are critically important qualities for an actor who is often, in the course of their work, called upon to enter uncertain circumstances and reveal potentially uncomfortable aspects of themselves (through their characters) that may take them far from their personal comfort zones. Actors are often asked to take emotional "risks" in performance, and a strong sense of autonomy and the power of will are essential prerequisites for doing so with dramatic abandon.

Stage 3: Initiative vs. Guilt

In this stage, which is equivalent to Freud's phallic, and generally unfolds between 4 and 6 years of age, the two dominant polarities that must be negotiated are *initiative* and *guilt*, and the virtue/strength developed by successfully mastering the stage-specific crisis is *purpose*.

At this stage, the child's primary activities are *play* and *fantasy*. The favorite word often shifts from "no" to "why." The child makes tremendous leaps in terms of language, imagination, and mastery over environment, learning to plan for the future. This new power inevitably comes with feelings of guilt as the child develops a conscience and the capacity for self-observation, self-guidance, and self-punishment. In order to successfully overcome the crisis of this stage, the child needs to learn to set limits, which produces the strength/virtue of a sense of purpose. The act of play provides a model for the child to practice planning and directed effort toward a longer-term goal, what will become the "work ethic" in later years. Purpose, then, for Erikson, is the courage to pursue goals even in the face of possible defeat, guilt, and the fear of punishment.

Stage 4: Industry vs. Inferiority

In Erikson's fourth life stage, ages 6 through 11, the polarities are *industry* and *inferiority*. This stage is roughly equivalent to Freud's latency stage and is typically when the child's main school years begin. Developmentally, the child moves beyond the family relationships that have been the primary focus up until now and enters the larger social system outside of the home. At this point, the child's main activities shift from play and fantasy to organized instruction and the modeling of what, in adult life, will become the workplace or career. In recent decades, the beginning of school activity has begun earlier with widely available pre-K programs (at least for the middle class), and so our contemporary society may be moving this stage up from what was typical when Erikson formulated his ideas.

At earlier stages, the child could play at activities with little concern for the outcome or results of the effort, but as the socialization process begins in earnest, this shifts to a sense of satisfaction and accomplishment for a job well done. The child is expected to master various tasks and skills and may well be graded or evaluated for their efforts. The opinions of others take on more importance. Children who don't succeed or fail to demonstrate the same level of mastery as their peers may develop feelings of inferiority or inadequacy, setting the groundwork for the major crisis or developmental challenge of this stage.

The virtue or strength developed by successfully mastering this stage is the feeling of *competence*, which is based on pride in workmanship, acquisition of practical life skills, and general capacities, many of which are culturally defined by the educational institutions provided by the society.

141

Stage 5: Identity vs. Identity Confusion

As the child becomes an adolescent, Erikson's model of development begins to exceed Freud's and enter areas that the later had either ignored or not explored. Adolescence, which in Erikson's model extends into the early twenties, is a time of great confusion and experimentation. This is the period when a stable ego structure finally emerges from all of the experiences and crises of the earlier stages. The polarity at this important stage is between *identity* and *identity confusion*. The sense of identity includes the integration of past identifications with present impulses, aptitudes, skills, and the opportunities that the social milieu provides. This is often a time of experimentation with various roles, and the adolescent may enter a type of psychological "moratorium" while shifting between or sampling various possibilities (Frager & Fadiman, 2005, p. 182). According to Erikson:

The sense of ego identity . . . is the accrued confidence that the inner sameness and continuity prepared in the past are matched by the sameness and continuity of one's meaning for others, as evidenced in the tangible promise of a "career."

(Erikson, 1964, pp. 261–262)

Social limitations and pressures can have a strong impact on the adolescent at this point. They may have difficulty imagining a suitable career or appropriate role for themselves in society. Doubts about sexual attractiveness and sexual identity are common. There may also be an "overidentification" with youth culture or popular media figures to the point where the individual seems lost or without a solid identity of their own.

The strength that finally emerges from this crisis of identity is that of fidelity or continuity, the ability to sustain loyalty in spite of the inevitable contradictions between value systems. The process of resolving this conflict and coming to a firm sense of "who I am" allows the individual to incorporate the culture's ethical values and belief systems into their own unique viewpoint that feels as if it has fidelity and substance over time. After this adolescent stage, the person may well have other episodes of identity crisis as they navigate the challenges of other stages and enrich and expand their sense of self to meet the varying needs of other stages, but adolescence is usually the first major struggle of this type in the life cycle. The idea that the sense of identity can change and even grow throughout the life cycle was one of the major enhancements Erikson appended to Freud.

142

Stage 6: Intimacy vs. Isolation

In Erikson's sixth stage of development, *intimacy* versus *isolation*, the young adult develops a growing independence from parents and schools, builds adult friendships and intimate relationships, and develops an adult sense of responsibility based on a relatively stable ego identity acquired in the last stage. It is this ego identity that gives the adult the confidence to commit to more mature, ongoing relationships, partnerships, and intimacy with other people. This is often the first stage where a truly intimate love relationship begins that is significantly different from earlier sexual and self-identity explorations. However, without the ability to commit to an intimate and mutually revealing relationship, the young adult may fall prey to isolation from others and a perpetual superficiality that prevents the individual from feeling a strong connection to and meaning from their relationships with others. If the individual's sense of identity is weak or feels threatened by intimacy, they may turn away from or even become hostile toward those who would love them.

The strength/virtue of the sixth stage is love, and Erikson argued that it was the greatest of the virtues cultivated during the life span. Love takes many different forms during the life cycle. Early in life, the infant loves the mother as caregiver; later, love expands to the parents and family; in adolescence, it becomes infatuation. When real intimacy develops between adults, love includes a shared identity and a validation of each partner in the other (Frager & Fadiman, 2005, p. 183).

Stage 7: Generativity vs. Stagnation

The stage of *generativity* vs. *stagnation* spans most of the period of adult life, and involves widening the circle of care to extend beyond individual and private concerns to include the broader society and future generations. It is the period of the adult work life, of families, childrearing, and saving for retirement. This stage is characterized by creativity, both in the personal and professional domains, and a care and concern for those things we create and the younger generations who follow. If the sphere of care and productivity does not widen, the individual risks suffering boredom, lack of direction, and a general stagnation in life. The consequences of stagnation can lead to depression and self-loathing.

The virtue of this stage is *care*, the core of which is generally focused on children, and later grandchildren. Care, at this stage, includes not only the direct offspring, but also ideals, ideas, and creations. As adults, humans "need to be needed," otherwise, they tend to become narcissistic and self-absorbed, which can lead to deep loneliness and alienation. Erikson believed that as a psychosocial species, we need to teach others in order to feel fulfilled in our own identity, particularly during this seventh stage of life.

143

Stage 8: Integrity vs. Despair

The final stage in Erikson's model looks at old age and is characterized by the polarity between *integrity* and a sense of *despair* or loss. For Erikson, ego integrity in old age included the acceptance of the individual's unique life cycle and history of defeats and victories, and a growing sense of order and meaning in life and the world that we inhabit. Old age is a time for confronting ultimate concerns and perceiving a unity across the entire life experience. It is also a time, when successfully met with grace and appropriate humility, for accepting others and lifestyles that may be widely different from our own. The other extreme, which must be transcended and cannot be avoided in this stage, is despair and a catastrophic loss of meaning. When people fall prey to despair, they may develop a strong fear of death and a feeling that it is too late to start over, or develop contempt and a ridged disgust for other value systems, institutions, and lifestyles. Finding a balance between the acceptance of integrity and the existential horror of despair during the declining years becomes the crisis that must be solved in Erikson's eighth and final stage of life.

If the aging adult is successful in solving the crisis of this stage, they develop the virtue/strength of *wisdom*. Wisdom helps maintain the sense of value the individual feels in their accumulated knowledge and experience. Someone who has developed wisdom may tend to be held up as a model of wholeness and completeness, an inspirational example for younger generations to aspire toward. The sense of wholeness that comes with wisdom may also ameliorate some of the inevitable feelings of helplessness and dependence that generally mark old age and the process of death (Frager & Fadiman, 2005, p. 184).

Life Span Development Activities for Actors

Erikson approached psychology and his theories of life span development more like an artist, which he was in his youth, than a data-driven scientist. Thus, his theory is elegant and uses imagery that evokes an emotional tone or a subjective sense of recognition rather than research studies and laboratory results to justify its perspectives (Feist & Feist, 2006, p. 267). From a postmodern perspective, Erikson's formulations do little to take into account feminist, gender, power, class, and inclusion concerns that we might see as central today. While Erikson, during his time, actually did explore multiple cultures in the process of formulating his ideas, he can nonetheless be criticized as limited in the scope of his vision. One could say that his model of "ideal" development was more an attempt to describe functional fit within the middle and upper middle classes of Western (U.S. and European) culture in the middle of the twentieth century than a wide-ranging, multiculturally consistent set of universal stages. One of his main limitations was his dedication to the model of psychoanalysis. While his brilliant reformulations of Freud, to take into account social and developmental factors that Freud himself either denied or ignored, helped expand the usefulness and functionality of psychoanalytic theory, it nonetheless remains bound by those theories' limitations (Frager & Fadiman, 2005, pp. 194–195). As stated previously, all of the theorists detailed in this book are, to varying degrees, products of their own times and embedded in cultures that have been radically modified by, or simply no longer exist in, the postmodern era. Therefore, some adaption or "bracketing" may be necessary to make theories such as Erikson's fully useful today. With that in mind, let us now investigate Erikson's map of developmental stages with respect to our own unique experiences and apply it to the task of exploring character.

144

A Chart of Individual Development

Review Erikson's eight stages of development and identify the stage you currently think you are at.

In your journal, write a few paragraphs about your relationship to each stage that you have already completed up until now. You may not be able to recall specifics from your earliest developmental stages (or perhaps you can?), but explore your own *current* feelings toward trust/mistrust (do you have hope?), autonomy/shame or doubt (what is your strength of will?), initiative/guilt (describe your sense of purpose in life), industry/inferiority (do you feel competent or insecure in your own abilities?), identity/identity confusion (do you have a strong sense of "who you are" or are you still struggling to answer that question?), intimacy/isolation (have you developed a central love relationship or are you lonely and isolated?), etc.

Once you have noted your current feelings about each of your own stages of development so far, go back and see if you can identify how you solved each stage's crisis and identify where you think your balance is between the two polar extremes of each stage. For instance, do you consider yourself more of a trusting person, accepting others at "face value"? Or are you more suspicious of other people's motivations until they have "proven themselves" over time? Make notes on each stage and then make a list that you feel best describes your personal, unique orientation based on Erikson's descriptors. ("I am basically trusting of others; however, I often doubt my own abilities to succeed without help; I have a strong sense of purpose and clear goals of what I want to accomplish in life; and I am working hard to hone my talents so that I can become the best actor I can possibly be; however, I am still looking for an intimate relationship that I can share with another.")

145

As with many of the other exercises in this book, once you have completed this exercise based on your own experiences and feelings, you can repeat it for a character you are working with, using the given circumstances of the script (or ones you derive for yourself from the facts presented in the story). What sorts of developmental challenges has your character had to deal with? How might they behave if they had particular difficulty solving one of Erikson's crises? Might the character's circumstances growing up have inhibited or interrupted "normal" development? Is your character more trusting or suspicious? Confident or insecure? Purposeful or aimless? Do they have a strong sense of self, or are they struggling with their own identity? Are they loved or lonely? The more you work with these polarities and strengths/virtues, the more obvious and apparent they will become as ways to categorize and understand various types of behavior and possible underlying motivations.

Observing Others' Development

146

For the next week, observe those around you carefully. Make notes in your written or audio journal to document what you find. Using Erikson's basic model of development, try to identify where people in your life and environment seem to be in terms of their life stage. Look for particular examples of people who are either at, or perhaps show problems resulting from difficulty completing, the various stages such as trust/mistrust, autonomy/shame, identity/ identity confusion, intimacy/isolation, etc.

How does someone with basic trust issues behave? Is their basic mistrustful attitude adaptive (they are savvy and not easily taken advantage of) or maladaptive (they reject others out of hand and quickly engage in conflict or blame)? What about someone with either a strong sense of identity or a person who seems confused about "who they are"? Do they behave with confidence and self-direction? Or are they shy, erratic, or unpredictable?

Also, observe people who are much younger than you, such as children, and people who are older and clearly at later stages in the life cycle, perhaps your grandparents or an aging mentor, and see if you can identify their goals and concerns based on their life stage. How are their interests, things they care about, and things they talk about in conversation different from yours? Can you either remember yourself at that previous stage or imagine yourself at the later stages? How does it feel when you interact with people at totally different developmental stages than your own?

This type of analysis may be a bit general, but it will definitely tune your eye toward recognizing the differences in people's behaviors and give you a new way of understanding what challenges (and opportunities) might have influenced them along their path in life. To make the exercise more specific, you might choose to look at the members of your immediate and extended family and see if you can identify some of the different stages and conflicts. The advantage of using family members and people you have known all your life is that you tend to know their personal histories in more detail and may have observed them over many different progressive stages, which gives you a richer portrait of the developmental journey.

Exploring Trust and Autonomy

A classic exercise, often used in acting schools, is the "trust walk" (Boal, 1992).

Basic instructions: With a partner, decide who will be the "blind" participant and who will be "sighted." The participants will exchange roles in the second half of the exercise. The blind participant, or "follower," is blindfolded and is instructed to keep their eyes closed beneath the blindfold for the duration of the exercise. The sighted participant, or "leader," slowly spins the follower in circles several times so that the follower does not know in which direction the walk will begin.

The leader, through a series of verbal and nonverbal directions and cues, leads the follower on a walk through the environment, carefully protecting them from any harm or danger, while simultaneously providing the follower with a rich, varied, sensual experience. The exercise can take place inside, outside, or a combination of both, but the area of the exercise should be clearly defined in advance so that the blind follower is never exposed to any physical dangers (such as busy streets, sharp objects, or sudden drop-offs, etc.).

The leader talks or guides by physical touch, such as hands on shoulders, the follower through the environment, introducing them to various objects and obstacles that they must together navigate or experience. Activities can include touching unknown objects, exploring them through the sense of touch, tasting or smelling (nontoxic) items of food, etc., and unusual sound environments. The emphasis should be on a sense of adventure and exploration; however, the primary purpose of the exercise is to allow and encourage the follower to place complete trust (and responsibility) on the leader during the experience.

The walk experience can last anywhere between 15 and 30 minutes. Once complete, the participants change roles, and the follower now becomes the leader and the leader dons the blindfold.

Once both participants have completed the walk experience, they can debrief each other or make detailed notes about their internal reactions to the exercise.

For the follower: Was it easy or difficult to relinquish control to the leader? Were there moments when it was difficult to follow the instructions? Did any emotions surface during the exercise? Was the experience of trusting someone with your physical safety comfortable or perhaps frightening? Which role did you feel more comfortable in, leader or follower?

For the leader: How did the responsibility for the other person's safety feel? Was that level of control over another frightening, or did it give you a sense of power? Did any emotions arise for you during the exercise? Did you have any thoughts of misusing your power or intentionally misleading your charge? Are you normally a person who likes to be in control or do you prefer to "be taken care of"?

Another variation on the trust walk is the "parent–child exercise."

Basic instructions: With a partner, decide who will be the parent and who will be the child.

In this exercise, the roles *will not* be reversed. After the completion of one cycle of the exercise, partners should be switched with someone else to play the opposite role. This eliminates any concern for bias or retribution between the team members and more fairly should allow for a genuine participation in each role.

For a period of time (half a day would be optimal if practical, but a one-hour session will suffice), the parent will instruct the child in what to do in every activity. (Basic limits on what kinds of demands the parent can make should be established at the outset, such as no participant should be forced to harm themselves or others, they should not be asked to perform acts that would embarrass them personally or otherwise compromise their dignity, etc.) The idea is to proceed through typical life tasks and situations, except that the "child" wholly submits to the will and command of the "parent." The child is not allowed to refuse or to suggest activities or actions and, within the proscribed limitations previously set forth, must comply with every direction or order given by the parent.

As in the trust walk, the activities engaged should be varied and wholly at the discretion of the parent participant. Potential activities might include eating a meal, taking a walk, engaging in some kind of game or play task, creative activity such as dancing, singing, or drawing, climbing a tree, rolling on the ground, etc. The parent participant should be creative in designing activities for the child participant.

After the session ends, a similar journaling or debriefing among the participants takes place, where each carefully observes their own responses to the roles they have just played.

For the child: What was it like to have all your actions and choices dictated by someone else's whim? Did any memories from childhood surface? Were they pleasant or unpleasant memories? Did you find it easy to relinquish your will to

149

another? Or did you find yourself resisting? Did this exercise bring up any emotions?

For the parent: What is the experience of having complete control over another like? Was the feeling of dominance pleasant or unpleasant? Did the exercise bring up any emotions? Did you ever have the impulse to misuse your power? Are you normally a person who likes to be in control or do you prefer to be told what to do?

Hopefully, Erikson's developmental viewpoint will give you yet another perspective to add to your kit of lenses for observing human behavior. We will also see a developmental structure used by our next theorist, Abraham Maslow, who was influenced by Erikson, as well as Adler and Horney, among others, in building his own model of human motivation and psychological functioning.

References

Boal, A. (1992). *Games for Actors and Non-Actors*. London/New York: Routledge.

Capps, D. (2014). *Erik Erikson's Verbal Portraits: Luther, Gandhi, Einstein, Jesus*. Lanham, MD: Rowman & Littlefield.

Erikson, E. H. (1958). *Young Man Luther: A Study in Psychoanalysis and History*. New York: Norton.

Erikson, E. H. (1964). *Childhood and Society* (2nd ed.). New York: Norton.

Erikson, E. H. (1968). *Identity, Youth, and Crisis*. New York: W. W. Norton.

Erikson, E. H. (1969). *Gandhi's Truth: On the Origins of Militant Nonviolence*. New York: Norton.

Erikson, E. H. (1980). *Identity and the Life Cycle*. New York: Norton.

Erikson, E. H. (1993). *Childhood and Society*. New York: Norton.

Feist, J., & Feist, G. J. (2006). *Theories of Personality* (6th ed.). Boston, MA: McGraw-Hill.

Frager, R., & Fadiman, J. (2005). *Personality and Personal Growth* (6th ed.). Upper Saddle River, NJ: Pearson Prentice Hall.

Wikipedia (2018). *Psychohistory*, February 7. Retrieved from https://en.wikipedia.org/w/index.php?title=Psychohistory&oldid=803639929.

CHAPTER 7

Abraham Maslow

Motivation and Humanistic Psychology

As discussed in the first chapter of this book, Abraham Maslow (1908–1970) was a seminal figure in twentieth-century psychology whose work marked the turning point from reductionistic and highly academic forms of psychology, primarily focused on pathology and mental disease, to a much broader view of the human experience and the more positive potentials of human development. Maslow began his career as a staunch behaviorist, studying dogs and later chimpanzees, before coming under the influence of both Freud and Adler. In developing his own theories, Maslow would synthesize the work of many of his intellectual antecedents, in addition to Freud and Adler, including Max Wertheimer and Kurt Koffka (Gestalt psychology); Kurt Goldstein (who first coined the term "self-actualization"); social anthropologists Margaret Mead, Ruth Benedict, and Ralph Linton; social psychologists and psychoanalysts Karen Horney and Erich Fromm; and others, many of whom he came to know personally in roiling intellectual circles of New York City in the late 1930s (Hoffman, 1988, pp. 87–110).

151

Maslow came to believe in a radical type of holism, in direct contradiction to both behaviorism and psychoanalysis, that focused on the discrete elements of psychological functioning often to the exclusion of much human experience, where the person was looked at as a whole, integrated system—each part fully interrelated to and interdependent on the other parts of the whole. For Maslow, one could not separate out external behavior from internalized values and subjective experience; they were all simply different, and inseparable, dimensions of the same event in reality: the psychological life of a human being.

Maslow's primary concerns became understanding and conceptualizing a psychology that covered the full range of human experience, especially the most mature and healthy of the population. Instead of concentrating on the mentally ill, as most psychologists previous to him had done, Maslow became interested in studying the psychological traits of the most highly developed and mentally healthy people he could find. This led him to develop a theory of human motivation that extended from feelings of deprivation and struggle with basic needs, such as food and shelter, through the entire spectrum of human endeavor to include those rare individuals who might change whole societies by their actions, such as great historical leaders or sainted religious figures. Effectively, his theory of motivation integrated the findings of behaviorism and Freudian psychoanalysis (and its extensions), along with the holism of Gestalt psychology and the functionalism of William James and John Dewey, to create a model that Maslow considered both holistic and dynamic (Maslow & Frager, 1987, p. 15).

Following are some of the contributions Maslow made to Western psychology, many of which became foundational to the humanistic psychology movement, and later the transpersonal psychology movement, described in Chapter 1.

Maslow's Hierarchy of Needs

Maslow postulated that human motivation is a multi-tiered affair, where one level of need must be satisfactorily fulfilled in order for the next higher level to emerge, creating a hierarchy, or predictable order of emergence, that is developmentally driven across the life span (Maslow, 1943a, 1943b). At the bottom of this hierarchy are what Maslow termed "physiological needs," such as food, water, and oxygen, followed by sleep and the need for sex. Explained in the simplest of terms, if a person is starving or dying of thirst, it is unlikely that they will pay much attention to their needs for good company or conversation and position in the community until they have solved the problem of hunger or thirst.

The other higher levels of psychological needs that emerge after the physiological needs are met include (in this order): safety, security, and stability needs (such as shelter and a stable, predictable social system); love and a sense of belongingness (this includes family and intimate relationships); self-respect and esteem (a standing in a community of peers or "a place in society"); and growth needs where the individual develops and makes use of their inherent potentials and talents (this process Maslow called "self-actualization").

Maslow believed that the more basic needs, such as the physiological and security needs, must be fulfilled before the less critical but psychologically important needs could emerge.

Maslow often portrayed his hierarchy as a pyramid where the more basic physiological needs made up the larger base, and the higher levels stacked on top in ever-smaller layers until the pyramid's apex was topped by the self-actualization needs at the pointed pinnacle, visually demonstrating the idea of tiered emergence:

It is only in the healthiest, most mature, most evolved individuals that higher values are chosen and preferred consistently more often . . . [M]an's higher nature rests upon man's lower nature, needing it as a foundation and collapsing without this foundation. That is, for the mass of mankind, man's higher nature is inconceivable without a satisfied lower nature as a base. The best way to develop this higher nature is to fulfill and gratify the lower nature first. Furthermore, man's higher nature rests also on the existence of a good or fairly good environment, present and previous.

153

(Maslow, 1968, p. 173)

In further exploring the "higher" and "lower" needs of humans, Maslow developed the terms "deficiency needs" (referring to the lower, more fundamental needs of his hierarchy) and "growth needs" (referring to the higher, more psychologically based needs) (Maslow, 1968, p. 27). Deficiency needs, also sometimes called "instictoid" or basic needs, share a series of qualities, including: (1) if the fulfillment of the need is missing (such as food or shelter), it tends to lead to disease, illness, or death; (2) if the need is fulfilled, it tends to prevent illness or restore health; (3) the need's fulfillment tends to be preferred by the deprived person over other potential satisfactions; and (4) the need tends to already be fulfilled, or mostly fulfilled, in the healthy person (Maslow, 1968, p. 22). In other words, deficiency needs are most recognizable by the fact that when fulfillment is lacking, there is a strong desire or yearning, and the need causes the organism distress accompanied by an immediate drive to fulfill the need or perish. Maslow also considered neurosis, in its many forms, to be a disorder caused by deficiency of certain basic needs, which then would include the needs for safety, security, stability, love, a sense of belongingness, self-respect, and self-esteem in the category of basic or deficiency needs (the lack of which can cause illness and psychological distress, as described above) (Maslow, 1971, pp. 382–390).

Growth needs, on the other hand, are constitutionally different from deficiency needs. Growth needs tend to emerge when the deficiency needs are relatively well fulfilled, and the person is basically healthy as a result. One of Maslow's main points is that *humans are never really fully or permanently satisfied*, without needs and motivations of any kind, and that once a more basic need is met, a higher-order need will inevitably emerge. His hierarchy was essentially an attempt to predict what needs would emerge, and in what order, as the human being evolved throughout the life cycle. Growth needs, then, are the needs for self-actualization and the fulfillment of higher potentials. Growth needs are less basic than the deficiency needs, because one will not die from lack of wisdom or a charitable heart, but one most certainly will die from a lack of food, water, or air. Nonetheless, once the basic needs have been satisfied and the growth needs have emerged, their fulfillment becomes just as motivating and important for happiness and psychological health as the physiological needs are to the health of the organism (Maslow, 1968, pp. 24–27).

154

Maslow's model is one of the first *metamodels* to be proposed in Western psychology, integrating the basic ideas of depth psychology (Freud, Jung, Horney, etc.), behaviorism (which he did not reject so much as criticize for its extreme limitations), Gestalt psychology (which was holistic at its core), and social and personality theory. Each of these previous "maps" of the human psyche are included in some way in Maslow's formulations, and then expanded or amended by becoming part of the broader whole. For instance, Maslow includes Freud's concerns about sexual development at the physiological needs stage of his hierarchy. For Maslow, many of Freud's ideas still operate as originally proposed, or amended by the neo-Freudians, but are included, side by side, with the other models that address other areas or perspectives that fall into Maslow's broad general categories. The social and family concerns of Karen Horney and Alfred Adler can be located in Maslow's safety and belongingness and love categories. Jung's individuation process fits nicely at Maslow's self-actualization level, etc. The actor can now use this map, which essentially includes most of the other maps we've already looked at, as a way to analyze character motivation from a much broader perspective than generally suggested by the highly constrained models that underlie Stanislavsky's work and the Freudian-influenced American Method purveyors that followed him.

Self-Actualization

Early in his career, Maslow became intrigued with two of his favorite mentors, Ruth Benedict and Max Wertheimer. For Maslow, these were two extraordinarily mature, self-possessed, and self-satisfied human beings, and he admired them both personally. He began making notes on them as a way of trying to understand their unique personalities, for which his studies in traditional psychology offered little or no explanation. Eventually, this personal project yielded a thought experiment that would become one of his most important explorations in psychology (Maslow & Frager, 1987, pp. 125–128). As early as 1940, while contributing to a book on abnormal psychology, Maslow began to explore the notion of the personality of the "normal," well-adjusted, and highly functioning human being (a subject few had even considered in psychology at that point). He wrote an entire chapter on the normal personality, outlining desirable qualities such as adequate self-esteem, reasonable self-knowledge, the ability to receive and express love, and the capacity to question the rules of the governing society. In his chapter, he even included a brief section on "The Ideal Personality and Goals" (Maslow, Mittelmann, & Murphy, 1941). Maslow felt that the ideal personality would be somehow defined by positive values and heightened levels of personal development, another subject rarely studied by the psychology of that day. However, he was unable to find much research to support his position and had to summarize his point with a vague call for science to someday take up such a study (Hoffman, 1988, pp. 152–153). This story marks the beginning of Maslow's lifelong quest to understand healthy as well as extraordinary psychological functioning and to create a comprehensive meta-map of human motivation.

155

In his seminal 1954 book *Motivation and Personality*, Maslow wrote a rough definition of the concept of self-actualization. He described a self-actualizing person as someone who was using their talents and individual capacities to their fullest. Such a person would be doing the very best they were capable of in meeting life's challenges and their own personal goals, being all they could be in their unique life situation.

With this description, Maslow was trying to describe the very pinnacle of his hierarchy of development, those individuals whose basic physiological and psychological (deficiency) needs had been met by both a successful developmental path and an accommodating environment. At first, Maslow believed that self-actualization was a very rare human accomplishment, and his initial investigations were around trying to identify the unique characteristics of individuals who were capable of attaining such a rarified state. But, eventually, he adjusted his thinking. He realized there was no real reason that self-actualization should be all that rare. Instead, he became convinced that almost everyone was capable of self-actualization, as long as their life circumstances were properly supportive and they had adequately met their basic deficiency needs. In other words, the self-actualizing person was not someone who was special or particularly gifted, but rather was a normal person whose environment and circumstances had not interfered with the process of development by depriving them of their basic needs.

This new viewpoint was one of the keys that unlocked his hierarchy of needs and helped include the other schools of psychology that had come before into his metamodel of motivation. From this perspective, then, everyone has the potential to mature to the point of self-actualizing their unique potentials, but quite often that process is blocked or stunted by unfavorable life conditions (as noted by Adler and Horney) or developmental obstacles or neurotic pathologies (à la Freud and the psychoanalysis schools). Maslow also suspected that the process of self-actualization might require a maturity that is often only gained by those who have lived a full life up through middle age and beyond, and might be an inaccessible developmental stage for the young and immature. In his initial formal attempts to study self-actualized individuals, Maslow screened over 3,000 college-aged students and found only one wholly acceptable candidate and less than two dozen other possible future subjects that he characterized as "growing well" (Maslow, 1970, p. 150).

Maslow's view of self-actualization was a very positive one compared to many of the psychologists that had come before him who had concentrated on, or at least developed their data from, populations of the neurotic or mentally ill. Maslow wanted to look at the human being as innately growth-oriented. To him, humans had an intrinsic need/motivation to utilize and excel at what they were *capable* of doing, to use their capacities and talents to the fullest extent possible, and like many other psychologists he believed that the basis of psychological processes were driven in part by evolutionary forces first described by Darwin; self-actualization, then, is ultimately an evolutionary drive shared by the whole human species.

Over time, Maslow's studies of self-actualized, or self-actualizing, individuals came to include approximately 18 mature and exceptional people, some of whom were personal friends, as well as several historical figures, including Abraham Lincoln, Thomas

Jefferson, Albert Einstein, Eleanor Roosevelt, Jane Addams, William James, Albert Schweitzer, Aldus Huxley, and Baruch Spinoza (Frager & Fadiman, 2005, p. 349). In studying these people, Maslow found that, just because they fit the criteria of mature, self-developed, and self-actualizing that he had set up, these individuals were not necessarily "perfect" in their behavior or even free of major personality flaws. They tended to have strong commitments to a career or cause outside of themselves and an individualized set of self-affirmed values, but at times they could pursue their goals relentlessly, even ruthlessly. Their work could take precedence over other concerns, such as family commitments or the feelings of others. They sometimes took their sense of independence to the extreme and were, on the whole, subject to many of the same problems that "average" people were, such as guilt, anxiety, sadness, conflict, etc. However, Maslow's self-actualizers also exhibited many unique and rare qualities, which included:

1. More efficient perceptions of, and relations to, reality.
2. A general acceptance of self, others, and nature.
3. Heightened spontaneity, simplicity, and naturalness.
4. Problem-centered approach as opposed to ego-centered approach to life situations.
5. A quality of detachment and the need for privacy.
6. Autonomy expressed as an independence from culture and environment.
7. Freshness of appreciation of the basic good in life.
8. A tendency toward mystical and peak experiences.
9. A deep feeling of identification, sympathy, and affection for the human species.
10. Deeper and more profound interpersonal relationships.
11. A "democratic" character structure or acceptance of differences.
12. Healthy discrimination between ethical issues such as good and evil.
13. A philosophical, unhostile sense of humor.
14. Creativeness, originality, or inventiveness.
15. A transcendency (or even resistance) of any particular culture.

157

(Maslow & Frager, 1987, pp. 128–145)

Maslow went even further in his final book, published posthumously in 1971, *The Farther Reaches of Human Nature*, to describe eight ways people tend to self-actualize or behaviors that lead toward self-actualization.

Concentration or Absorption

By this, Maslow meant to become fully and selflessly engaged with any activity, without the limiting concerns of ego-awareness or self-consciousness. This concept is particularly salient for the actor, who, in the course of successful performance, must become completely absorbed in the actions of the role, forgetting the "self" and any feelings of embarrassment for a while, and concentrating only on the life and objectives of the character while the cameras roll or the audience sits in the theater.

Making Growth Choices

Maslow described life as a process of choices, some of which could be defensive, toward safety, toward fear, etc. The other alternative to a fear choice could be considered a "growth choice," a choice to take some risk, a choice to take an unknown path, a choice to discover something new in the course of life. This idea is quite obviously in line with traditional actor training, "putting oneself out there," and even implies that acting itself might be considered a type of self-actualizing behavior.

158

Self-Awareness

Maslow suggested that most people respond to their environment and the events of their lives often by listening to the voices of their mother, father, or the authority of society and tradition, instead of the more authentic voice of their true self, the "impulse voices" that allow the self to spontaneously emerge. He would sometimes suggest to his students, as a way of making this point, that the next time someone offered them a glass of wine and asked how they liked it, instead of looking at the bottle's label for a clue, they should shut their eyes and "make a hush," so that they could look within themselves and shut out the noise of the world as they savored the taste of the wine on their tongue and made their own decisions about whether they liked it or not.

Honesty

As Maslow put it, "when in doubt, be honest" (Maslow, 1971, p. 46). He felt that honestly looking inside the self, instead of automatically relying on external influences such as cultural norms and expectations, was a way of taking personal responsibility and a path toward self-actualization.

Using Judgment

Maslow felt like the previous four self-actualizing behaviors added up to, with use over time, an improving judgment or discernment in making life choices. He believed that listening to the self in matters of taste and preference required some bravery and a daring to be perceived as different, unpopular, or nonconformist. Such confidence and willingness to act with integrity upon issues requiring personal judgment, Maslow felt, was a self-actualizing behavior and a step toward ever-growing maturity.

Self-Development

Self-actualization is not a static goal or end state, but an ongoing, evolving process of actualizing (using to their fullest) unique potentials at any time and in any amount. Self-development often requires effort sustained over time, such as in improving intelligence by arduous study, or mastering similar challenges. So, part of Maslow's perspective on self-development related to the amount and quality of effort being applied in the service of improvement and growth.

Peak Experiences

Maslow became interested in a general type of human experience often called "mystical" and what he termed "peak" experiences, which tend to be transient moments of powerful feelings of wholeness, absorption, or deep (even spiritual) engagement with the events of life. Maslow felt that these seminal moments of experience could be explicitly self-actualizing, especially when properly supported by the individual's environment. He also thought that people who were centered at the self-actualizing level of his hierarchical model tended to have peak experiences, or at least become aware of their occurrence, more often than people who were struggling to deal with the fulfillment of lower-order needs. We will explore Maslow's work on peak experiences in the next section.

Identifying and Reducing Ego Defenses

The final item on Maslow's list of self-actualizing behaviors involved getting to know the self on yet a deeper level by identifying and essentially relinquishing ego defenses, so that the individual can see the "actual self" more clearly and with less delusion.

One other aspect of self-actualization that interested Maslow was what he came to call the *Jonah complex* (Maslow, 1971, pp. 35–40).

The Jonah complex, named after the biblical character who tried to avoid the responsibilities imposed on him by god and was eventually swallowed by a whale, is the "fear of one's own greatness" or "the running away from one's own best talents" (Maslow, 1971, p. 35); in other words, the fear of success or self-actualization. Maslow would demonstrate this tendency to his students by asking which of them were planning to write a great novel, become a senator, or even President. Inevitably, the members of the class would giggle uncomfortably, blush, and otherwise avoid answering the question seriously. Then Maslow would ask, "If not you, then who else?" In the same vein, he would challenge his graduate students in psychology as to which of them were secretly planning to write an important book on psychology. And, as with the others, his graduate students would become uncomfortable and in one way or another put off answering the question. To which Maslow would then point out that they were indeed being trained as psychologists, and so therefore why the reticence to commit? To this confrontation, the graduate students would generally respond with stunned silence. Finally, he would offer a prophecy that if they intentionally planned to become less than they were capable of by evading or minimizing their own true potentials, they would probably find misery and disappointment in the rest of their lives.

160

Self-actualizing as a process and self-actualizing behaviors, as just described above, can make for a fascinating lens through which to approach characterization of certain roles. In much drama, as well as psychology, we tend to look at the dysfunctional or aberrant more often than the extremely healthy, high-performing, or transcendent aspects of experience or personality. What, for instance, might motivate a Gandhi, an Einstein, or a Jesus? Perhaps Maslow's descriptions of self-actualization can give us some clues or lead us to think in detail about what motivates and drives characters into realms that may well be beyond the normal, extraordinary, or even spiritual in nature.

Peak Experiences

As briefly described above, Maslow explored a group of experiences that could be qualified as mystical, transcendent, or in other ways extraordinary moments in a human life when the experiencer felt most alive, most whole, connected to all existence, or most fully absorbed in some activity or event. In Eastern spiritual traditions, these moments of extreme clarity and perception are often characterized as episodes of "enlightenment."

Peak experiences can be very intense and transformative, as implied above, or more mundane and common in nature, but with the common thread of being some of the best and most complete moments in life; temporary snapshots of life at its most full and complete.

Maslow made a study of such experiences and became convinced that almost all people had them, in varying degrees of regularity and intensity, but some people were more inclined to ignore or deny them for various psychological reasons. He even speculated that the world's great religious traditions had been founded upon descriptions of the peak experiences of a small number of sensitive and lonely sages and saints (people such as Moses, Jesus, and Muhammad), who were then recorded in the supernatural and ethnocentric terms of their day in texts that were then misinterpreted in dogmatic and legalistic ways that degraded the full significance of the original experience into meaningless rites and rituals (Maslow, 1964).

For Maslow, peak experiences could be transformative and evolutionary moments in a person's life when new potentials for growth could be opened instantaneously and the individual could leap ahead in terms of actualizing their unique potentials. His interest in spiritual, mystic, and peak experiences, and their potential to help self-actualize the individual, eventually became a major interest for him, leading to the founding of yet another school of psychology, transpersonal psychology, which was the first Western school of psychology to take seriously these types of experiences and study their psychological effects in detail.

Humanistic Psychology Exercises for the Actor

Maslow described human motivation with a metamodel of hierarchical needs, the lower of which were more fundamental to physical survival and the higher were more important to psychological happiness and fulfillment once the lower needs were adequately met. As actors, we might look at the motivations of our characters as driven, at different times and under different given circumstances, by these varying types/levels of need. For instance, how might a character act or interact differently if they were extremely hungry as opposed to extremely lonely, or under the stress of being hated by their family members as opposed to accomplishing something of great value or importance to society? Maslow's model of needs and hierarchical needs fulfillment can add much depth to the way we answer questions of motivation for our characters by making those answers more specific than general.

The Different Feelings of Need

Maslow listed what he considered the needs of every human being in an order (hierarchy) from most fundamental/basic (for physical survival) through most important to advanced development and happiness/contentment with life. These basic categories include (in this order):

1. Physiological needs (food, water, air, sleep, etc.).
2. Safety, shelter, security, and predictability of environment.
3. Belongingness and love (family, romantic, and friendship relationships).
4. Esteem and position in society (having a job/career, a sense of purpose, a "place in the world").
5. Self-actualization (being the best you can be, fully developing talents and abilities, a purpose beyond self).

In your journal, list for yourself the ways in which you are *currently* either fulfilling or not fulfilling each category of needs.

Next, write down the feelings you have when each of these needs is not being met (i.e., what it feels like to be hungry, in physical danger, in a fight with a loved one, losing a job or being kicked out of a social group, not doing your best or procrastinating on something important to you, etc.).

Now observe others who you feel are operating at each level of the hierarchy, and describe their behavior. (Examples might include someone who is starving for lack of food, someone who is homeless, someone who is divorced or otherwise estranged from their family, someone who has lost their job or otherwise experienced a loss

162

in status, or someone who is afraid of their own
potential or success.) How does each person behave
or interact with others? How do they go about trying to fulfill their most current pressing need?
Does their current situation cause them to act in
extreme or socially unacceptable ways? How might
you react if you were in a similar situation?

In a different entry, write a description of
where you most often locate yourself on Maslow's
hierarchy today. What needs are regularly fulfilled for you (do you usually have enough food
and sleep?) and what do you spend most of your
time pursuing (romantic relationships, moving up
in job or career, self-improvement, etc.)?

After this exercise, you should have a more specific idea of how
each of Maslow's levels of need affect individual behavior and motivation. For instance, how might a character react differently in a
scene if they were extremely dejected or humiliated? Secure or insecure about where they were going to sleep that night? Or, how about
extremely fulfilled and self-satisfied? Successful and hopeful for the
future? Understanding the diversity of what can, and does, motivate
people can be a very useful map in charting the arc of a character
through a particular set of given circumstances.

Exploring Self-Actualization

Make a list of your greatest talents and potentials.

If you were wildly successful in your life and
career, how might you use those talents? Imagine
yourself 20 years in the future, doing exactly
what you've always dreamed of doing. Are you a
star of stage and screen? Do you have a family?
How are you able to help others with your success?

Create the brightest picture of yourself that
you can imagine and write it down in detail.

Now select the person that you know or are
very familiar with who best represents someone that is self-actualized or in the process of
self-actualizing. (You can refer to the list of

15 qualities that Maslow associated with self-actualizing people in the previous section to give you ideas of what to look for and examine.) This might be a mentor, teacher, or an older adult you admire very much. How do they interact with others? What qualities do they exhibit that inspire you or that you want to imitate? How do they set an example for others? List the specific examples that you feel represent the best or most mature aspects of this person's personality.

Now compare the two descriptions. How is the idealized image of yourself as self-actualized different from the example of the person you view as already self-actualized or self-actualizing? How are they the same? Do you share the same talents, or are your talents different? How might the example of a self-actualized person help you actualize your own talents or abilities?

164

Owning Your Jonah Complex

Using the list of your best qualities and talents you made at the beginning of the previous exercise, explore the ways you avoid or prevent yourself from actualizing those talents and potentials. What talents or positive qualities do you deny in yourself or won't admit to having? What sorts of things do you self-deprecate yourself to others about? Do you have any hidden talents that you've never revealed to others? Make a written list of these talents and any behaviors you use to hide or avoid using them.

Maslow envisioned self-actualization as a never-ending, ongoing process of self-development throughout the life cycle. How might a character be affected at different stages of that process? One lens to use might be to ascertain just how self-actualized a character might be during the time frame of the play or drama. Do they become more self-actualized as a result of the events in the script? Or are they resisting their own growth and their "better selves" as in a Jonah complex? What happens to a character who begins on a relatively positive growth path but is suddenly thrown into a state of desperate need from a lower, more fundamental level such as hunger or a threat to security or family? Maslow's hierarchy and self-actualization can both serve as dynamic lenses with which to analyze and build a character.

The Experience of a Peak

Find a private place where you can relax and won't be interrupted for at least half an hour. Let your body relax and your mind turn inward; just breathe for a few minutes. Once you are centered and present in the moment, try to recall one of the best moments of your life, a time where you felt most alive, engaged, and whole. It may have been an experience that involved a "flow state," such as during an athletic competition or other kind of high performance. It may have been an emotional high or moment of spiritual feeling. Whatever the experience is, concentrate on it and try to bring as many details to mind as you can. Remember the physical sensations, any emotions or heightened feelings, sudden realizations of mental understandings that became clear in that moment. Really try to recapture as much of the experience as memory will allow.

165

Write down notes about the experience.

Now consider how having that experience has changed your life and/or the way you see the world. What has remained transformed for you? What do you understand more clearly about yourself, and perhaps others, since you had this experience? Have you ever had this experience, or something like it, again? Have you ever shared this experience with someone else? And if so, how did you feel when you told them the story?

As with many of the other maps and lenses we have explored in this book, working with the ideas, examples, and feelings that come up during the exercises will make them more familiar to you in an experiential sense, and make these ways of working more available to you in preparing a character or the act of performance.

References

Frager, R., & Fadiman, J. (2005). *Personality and Personal Growth* (6th ed.). Upper Saddle River, NJ: Pearson Prentice Hall.

Hoffman, E. (1988). *The Right to Be Human: A Biography of Abraham Maslow.* Los Angeles, CA/New York: J.P. Tarcher/St. Martin's Press.

Maslow, A. (1943a). A preface to motivation theory. *Psychosomatic Medicine,* 5, 85–92.

Maslow, A. (1943b). A theory of human motivation. *Psychological Review,* 50, 370–396.

Maslow, A. H. (1964). *Religions, Values, and Peak-Experiences.* Columbus, OH: Ohio State University Press.

Maslow, A. H. (1968). *Toward a Psychology of Being* (2nd ed.). Princeton, NJ: Van Nostrand.

Maslow, A. H. (1970). *Motivation and Personality* (2nd ed.). New York: Harper & Row.

Maslow, A. H. (1971). *The Farther Reaches of Human Nature.* New York: Viking Press.

Maslow, A. H., & Frager, R. (1987). *Motivation and Personality* (3rd ed.). New York: Harper & Row.

Maslow, A. H., Mittelmann, B., & Murphy, G. (1941). *Principles of Abnormal Psychology: The Dynamics of Psychic Illness.* New York/London: Harper & Brothers.

CHAPTER 8

Ken Wilber
Integral Psychology

Ken Wilber (1949–) is an American philosopher and writer who has produced over 20 books that have been translated into dozens of languages. He began his publishing career as a transpersonal psychologist (a field described in Chapter 1) by proposing a "spectrum of consciousness" model that attempted to integrate the modern understandings of developmental psychology with the philosophies of Eastern and Western spiritual traditions (Wilber, 1977). Wilber, in other words, attempted to marry scientific reason and spiritual experience in a description of reality that took into account both seemingly contradictory positions and, at the same time, treat both positions seriously, a feat that many have tried yet most have failed to accomplish.

167

Wilber himself apparently has an exceptionally high IQ (as did Abraham Maslow before him) and is a voracious researcher who, after having dropped out of medical school around the age of 23, began a detailed literature review of such diverse fields as psychology, Western and Eastern philosophy, anthropology, biochemistry, the history of science, religious history, cultural studies and postmodernism, and art and literary criticism. In addition to his studies, Wilber is a serious meditator, and studied with a number of renowned meditation teachers concurrent with the development of his theories (Wilber, 1999c, p. x).

Quadrants, Levels, Lines, States, and Types

Wilber has gone through several stages in his work, evolving what eventually became known as *integral theory*, a worldview that seeks to account for all of the fundamental dimensions of reality, internal/external, individual/collective, in a comprehensive holistic synthesis or meta-theory, similar to what Maslow attempted for psychology, but with much broader implications. According to Wilber, any map or model that attempts to integrate all the fields of human endeavor into a cohesive understanding that honors and includes the greatest number of perspectives must, at a minimum, take into account:

Quadrants. The subjective (or interior perspective), the objective (or exterior perspective), and an individual and collective perspective (from both an interior and exterior viewpoint), which can be represented by a grid with four *quadrants*. Each quadrant of this grid represents an irreducible, fundamental aspect of reality at any given moment in time.

Levels represent the various progressive *stages of development* that living beings (particularly humans) evolve through, from pre-personal to personal to transpersonal. Various descriptions of levels or stages of psychological development, for instance, have already been described by many of the theorists we have covered in this book, including Erikson and Maslow. Levels, or stages, is essentially the idea that development of almost anything progresses through a series of patterns, generally from less complex to more complex, while including but exceeding each previous level in the progression; another term for this might be "growth hierarchy."

Lines are the discrete domains or characteristic qualities of individuals (such as intelligence, emotional, interpersonal, moral, spiritual, physical, etc.) that can develop through their own levels or stages generally independent of the other lines. (As you will recall, Anna Freud introduced the idea of developmental lines into psychology.) So, for instance, you could have a person who is highly developed intellectually but with very low interpersonal skills. Another example might be a highly skilled athlete whose body has been developed to a very high degree but who might have very low moral development or little emotional control. Lines typically develop through an identifiable sequence of levels or stages.

States refers to "states of consciousness." There are many different states of consciousness that people are capable of experiencing. For instance, when you wake up in the morning and go about your business, you are in what is considered a "normal" waking state of consciousness. But at night, when you go to sleep, that waking state transforms into something completely different.

168

A third state of consciousness, radically different from those first two, is the dream state. Consciousness can also be altered from the "normal" waking state by various external forces or environmental elements. For instance, sleep deprivation, starvation, concussion, or brain damage can all have an altering effect on consciousness. Think about spinning in circles until you become dizzy as an intentional way of altering consciousness. Another example of an altered state of consciousness would be the influence of intoxicating drugs or alcohol, which can significantly change the normal waking state, altering perceptions and thought processes. Also, a set of *discrete states of consciousness can be generated* by activities such as extended meditation and deep yogic practices that disclose very different types of perceptions and cognitions from normal waking consciousness. Such states can include "enlightenment" or "spiritual" experiences, which historically have been described as changing the personalities of their experiencers in fundamental and potentially long-lasting ways.

Types is a kind of catch-all category for things such as male/female, introvert/extrovert, and other types of distinctions of difference and phenomena that don't fit in the other four concepts.

So, by including all of these basic dimensions or perspectives, what Wilber calls an AQAL (pronounced "aw-qwal") approach—which is shorthand for "all quadrants, all levels, all lines, all states, and all types"—one can create a radically holistic representation of reality that seems to be able to explain, and integrate, almost every human discourse or philosophy, belief system or spiritual tradition, academic field or worldview, as well as physical reality from the Big Bang to modern human history, as a single grand set of true-but-partial perspectives on a completely cohesive and harmonious universe. In other words, to the degree that you subscribe to Wilber's comprehensive view, the argument between Plato and Aristotle, religion and science, and a lot of other folks has finally been resolved.

The AQAL Approach and Integral Psychology

The above may seem like an awful lot to bite off and chew in a book about psychology directed at actors, so let us focus on one explicit application of Wilber's integral theory. In 1999, Wilber published *Integral Psychology*, which utilized his integral theory (AQAL approach) as a lens for integrating over 100 schools of psychology and spiritual traditions (often considered Eastern psychology) into a single overview of the human experience. It was a massive endeavor, and brought to fruition Abraham Maslow's dream of a meta-theory of psychology that would honor, and make sense of, all of the previous schools of psychology, from Freud to Adler, to Horney to Erikson and beyond, while including the farther reaches of humankind (spiritual and religious, what Maslow called "peak experiences") that were only being discovered and investigated for the first time, in the West, in Maslow's day.

The AQAL approach begins with the premise that no human being is capable of generating 100% error. Therefore, there is *something* true about every idea, vision, or perspective. Wilber uses his metamodel as a type of infrastructure to "bolt on" other people's theories and ideas, and get the varying truths to align and agree with each other. That doesn't mean that there are not contradictions among various viewpoints (religion versus science, for instance), but viewed from a high enough level, and utilizing the various fundamental perspectives that Wilber has identified as organizing generalities, most systems of thought can actually be brought into some level of agreement.

170

Starting with his first approach, the *spectrum of consciousness* view, Wilber theorizes that consciousness evolves or develops (across all its potential lines) from preconscious to conscious to superconscious (what in Eastern philosophy has traditionally been called "enlightenment" or unity consciousness). In other words, consciousness tends to "unfold" or evolve through a series of stages that are progressive, and the earlier of those stages have been studied by Western psychology (Freud's model of the unconscious, Erikson's model of development, etc.), whereas the later stages of consciousness development have mostly been the subject of Eastern religious and spiritual philosophies. However, all of these stages are part of a unified developmental whole.

Western psychology has tended to ignore or deny the spiritual realms of human existence (and development), while Eastern views of human experience, such as Buddhism and Hinduism, have tended to only focus on the latter, more advanced stages of spiritual development and ignore aspects of the ego, the unconscious, and sociocultural developmental factors that Western psychology has tended to explore. For Wilber, both views are essentially correct; they are just looking at *different stages or levels of development across different lines* and not getting the whole picture. Another way to view this is that Western psychology, for the most part, has looked at development in lines such as psychosexual (Freud), psychosocial (Horney and others), and individual or ego (Jung, Anna Freud, etc.), while Eastern philosophy's domains of concern have primarily been the spiritual line or consciousness itself, all of which are legitimate (and mostly independent) lines of development in human beings. Wilber's stroke of genius here is in demonstrating, through a detailed review of the research, that *all of these perspectives*, Eastern and Western, are pointing at the same grand unfolding of consciousness, only usually from limited viewpoints that only account for one or two of these developmental lines at a time, while trying to ignore or deny the others. When all of the possible lines are taken into account (Wilber has identified over 20), and their general features or stages of development are mapped, suddenly the myriad forms of Western psychology (several of which we have already reviewed in this volume), and many of the spiritual systems from the great religious traditions of the world, seem to fit together in a larger puzzle that describes human experience and growth as a unified whole, from body to mind to spirit (Wilber, 2000a, 2000b, 2000c). This is the power and elegance of Wilber's integral (AQAL) model.

171

Taking all of this into account, then, Wilber built a series of charts that correlated nearly 100 systems, both Eastern and Western, with each other across a number of dimensions suggested by the AQAL approach (Wilber, 1999b, pp. 197–217). He also noted that as people grow through their own developmental stages, they can have problems or deficiencies that cause pathology. In fact, Wilber proposed that many of the mental diseases that Western psychologists have identified are actually associated with different stages or levels of development, and that individuals, depending on their stage of development, might be subject to different types of mental pathology. In other words, things can go wrong in an individual's life at any stage of development and, depending on the stage, cause different forms of mental sickness. For instance, a person who was severely abused as a young child may never develop a fully stable ego structure and be subject to a borderline personality disorder for life. But another person who had a relatively stable and secure childhood, and has had the opportunity to develop through several life stages into an otherwise "healthy" adult, might suffer the loss of a job or a painful divorce that challenges their feelings of stability and self-worth (Maslow's belongingness and esteem needs; Erikson's generativity vs. stagnation) and fall into major depression, a different type of mental pathology.

For the actor, Wilber's integral theory is a very rich stew indeed, offering numerous perspectives on characterization rarely found in any version of contemporary acting theory. As a part of this book, I will barely be able to scratch the surface of these subject matters, and so recommend a full reading of Wilber's work to any serious actor who wants to expand their own worldview and capacities to understand the human experience. Several of Wilber's books can be found in the references section that follows this chapter.

Integral Psychology Exercises for Actors

Perhaps Wilber's most important contribution is his quadratic model of reality and consciousness. The quadrants, as stated above, represent four fundamental perspectives that cannot be reduced, or ignored, in any full accounting of existence-in-time. Fundamentally, Wilber's quadrants are the internal and external views of the individual and collective aspects of reality. These four views can be expressed by a grid divided into four parts (quadrants), labeled starting in the upper left-hand corner (and proceeding clockwise): individual (internal), individual (external), societal or systems (external), and communal or cultural (internal). Below is a representation of Wilber's quadrants applied to the actor (upper-left quadrant) within a theatrical context.

The quadrant model (or lens) provides a very powerful way of analyzing and understanding or interpreting the theatrical event. By taking into account each of these irreducible perspectives in approaching a play, film shoot, or other type of theatrical expression, we can get a much more comprehensive view of "what is going on in the moment" than merely the actor's individual perspective (which is wholly included in the upper left-hand quadrant view), the director's objective perspective (which is wholly included in the right-hand side of the model), or the audience's subjective perspective (which is wholly included in the lower left-hand quadrant view). Therefore, Wilber's quadratic model becomes a way of capturing all of the fundamental elements (or perspectives) of a production, making it a very powerful tool that includes, among several other items, all of the psychological theories we've investigated to this point.

Upper-left quadrant—"I" space	Upper-right quadrant—"it" space
The actor	The actor's technique
Individual experience	Movement
The monologue	External behavior
Emotions and feelings	Vocal control and expression
The motivations of character	Dance, combat, other forms of physical control and dexterity
Character's worldview	
Lower-left quadrant—"we" space	Lower-right quadrant—"its" space
The scene	The theater, sound stage, or location
The cast	
Dialogue	Cameras, lighting, special effects
The stage/camera crew	Physical forms of distribution and promotion (movie theater, TV, Broadway, Internet, etc.)
The audience	
The given circumstances shared by all characters	

(Left-hand quadrants—internal) (Right-hand quadrants—external)

Lower quadrants—collective

173

Figure 8.1 The theatrical event expressed in Wilber's quadrants

Source: © Kevin Page

Experiencing Wilber's Quadrants

The "I" Perspective

Working alone, perform a monologue that you already know well. What is your internal experience of performing that speech? What are your emotions? What images run through your head as you say the prescribed words? How does your body feel? What is the sensation of movement? How about your voice? What does it feel like when the speech speeds up or slows down? When the inflection rises or falls? Bring yourself as fully as you can into the present moment while performing this monologue, and whatever sensory or mental impressions you have of your personal experience (which includes the inner monologue of the character) is the "feeling" of the *upper left-hand quadrant*, the sensation of the purely subjective, the experience *of* the experience.

The "We" Perspective

Now think of how it feels to be a part of a large crowd or the audience at a concert, the cheering, the shouting, the spontaneous applause; the feeling of being drawn together with a group to act as one is the feeling of the "we." This is the internal experience of the intersubjective dimension or the collective "we" perspective.

The "we" perspective is entering into the collaborative process of a production, the working with a scene partner, the director, and the rest of the cast and crew to "get the scene right."

Perform a scene with a scene partner (or multiple scene partners). What is the interaction like between the various players on the stage? What is the feeling of nailing your blocking, of getting the timing just right, of affecting and being affected by the other players as you move through the actions and the moments of the scene together? Does it feel like a dance? Or like playing in a band? You can perceive the sensation of the "we space" when you enter a conversation and discuss a just completed scene in terms of "How good were *we*?" "How can *we* make the scene better?" "Were *we* funny or just boring?" "I think *we* should pick up the pace here." So, the perspective represented by the lower left-hand quadrant is the internal experience of the intersubjective or communal during performance (or rehearsal).

The "It" Perspective

Now consider all of the props you dealt with in the course of the scene you just completed. Perhaps run through the scene again, this time focusing on the physical actions that constitute the forms and rhythms of the scene. What is the timing of that upstage-left cross? How do you physically handle that teacup you drink from? How do you sit in that chair? What are the technical elements of the stage fight near the end? Focus on the physical, repeatable behaviors and technical requirements of performing this scene on this stage or in front of these cameras. How closely do you hit your mark? What is your distance from the camera lens for your close-up? How many times must you repeat these exact actions before the director calls cut and you "have it in the can"? These are all examples of the upper right-hand quadrant, the "it" dimension of reality (or in this case, performance). Understanding and mastering the technical elements of any performance is another indispensable element of being a good actor. Notice that all of the internal, emotional, and interpersonal activities of the scene (the left-hand side of the model) are all still taking place simultaneously, but technical (external) execution is also an integral part of successfully completing the scene as an actor and as part of a cast or ensemble.

The "Its" Perspective

Along with your specific physical interactions with the set, props, and other actors during a performance, you are also performing in a certain space and under certain conditions. These conditions are informed by the infrastructure or context for the overall production and the production's delivery into the public sphere. In other words, your individual performance may be a part of a movie, TV show, stage play, or Internet video. Whatever the case, your performance happens under certain circumstances, and each of those sets of circumstances has different sets of requirements that an actor must understand and be able to execute in order to successfully complete their job on a set or during a live performance. These circumstances, and commensurate requirements for success, are what are "contained" in the lower right-hand quadrant of Wilber's model.

For most roles, an actor must audition. Understanding what that protocol is under various conditions is very important. An audition for a role in a movie that takes place in a professional casting studio in front of a casting director and a video camera is very different than singing 16 bars from a Broadway show tune on a stage in a spotlight when auditioning for a musical. The same can be said for the general rules of a film set or a 500-seat theater; they are very different sets of rules, dealing with wholly different infrastructures and environments, and a successful actor needs to fully understand which circumstances she is in (and what processes and behaviors are expected of her) if she wants to successfully win and execute an acting job. These concerns and protocols represent the "its" or "systems" dimension of the acting process, and it is fundamentally different from the other three dimensions we have already investigated.

To experience this directly, compare two acting experiences you have had, one on a stage with a live audience, and the other on a film or TV set where you have performed a scene multiple times in front of a camera or cameras. How are the circumstances and expectations different? How do you have to adjust your performance to meet the different requirements? Make a list of these differences in protocol and performance venues for later reference. If you have not yet had experience in these various domains, it is highly recommended that you do, so that you will understand the professional, external behaviors that will be required from you during your career.

Using Wilber's quadrant system as a way of understanding and analyzing the requirements of a particular acting challenge is

176

perhaps one of the most potent tools ever developed that can be applied to the actor's craft, simply because it requires you to investigate and deal with all of the important aspects of performance and does not allow you to ignore or remain ignorant of any of them. I have known many very good actors who were deeply personal in their emotional, mental preparations and performances, but lacked the practical, common knowledge of auditioning or film set protocols, so that they simply were not hired for certain jobs (and therefore never gained that experience). Using Wilber's quadrants forces the actor to be prepared for the work at hand, both technically as well as psychologically.

Your Character's Lines of Development

One of the major components of Wilber's AQAL model is the perspective of development across multiple, mostly independent, lines that represent qualities or aspects of the human personality and consciousness. The idea is that these relatively discrete lines, most of which have been identified and studied by various researchers in Western psychology, develop through a set of relatively fixed stages that unfold in a predictable sequence that generally subsumes earlier stages within the later and more mature stages. In this sequence of development, one stage proceeds from the previous, and no stage can be skipped or bypassed. So, for instance, a child's cognitive development, as described by Jean Piaget (Piaget, 1977, 1978; Piaget, Elkind, & Flavell, 1969), proceeds through four distinct stages: the sensorimotor, preoperational, concrete operational, and formal operational. In the *sensorimotor* stage, infants gain knowledge of the world from the physical actions they perform within it (movement, touch, sucking, etc.). In the next stage to emerge, *preoperational*, the child acquires language and develops the capacity for symbolic thought, although still retains the knowledge and learning that occurred in the previous stage. In this stage of cognitive development, the child learns "object permanence," or the fact that things continue to exist even when they are not physically present and in view. At this stage, even though the child has greatly evolved since birth, they still cannot understand concrete logic and cannot mentally manipulate information, which is the next major growth stage. In the *concrete operational* stage, beginning around age 7, the child begins to develop logical thinking abilities, something that was not possible in the early stages, and therefore is an emergent of this more hierarchically advanced stage. In other words, in order to develop logic, one must first have the structure of language, and in order to develop language one must first have some control of their sensual impressions of the world around them; this is what is meant by "one stage proceeds from the previous and no stage can be skipped or bypassed." At the concrete operational stage, the child becomes able to incorporate inductive reasoning, which involves drawing inferences from observations in order to make generalizations. However, at this stage, they still struggle with deductive reasoning, which uses a generalized principle in order to predict the outcome of an event; this ability to "abstract" does not emerge until the next stage. *Formal operational* thinking involves the logical use of symbols related to abstract concepts. This form of thinking includes "assumptions that have no necessary relation to reality" (Piaget, 1950). At this stage of cognitive development, the now adolescent is capable of hypothetical and deductive reasoning. In other words, they develop the ability to think *about* thinking and abstract thought.

Piaget's model of cognitive development, even with certain flaws that have been pointed out by later researchers (Callaghan, 2005; Lourenço & Machado, 1996), remains a good example of a line of development that unfolds fairly independently (although it may to some extent be a prerequisite for some other lines). For instance, cognitive development will generally progress in the stages just described, regardless of development in other lines such as kinesthetic (athletic), musical, emotional, moral, spiritual, etc.

As mentioned above, Wilber, building on the work of other theorists, including Piaget, Kohlberg, Kurt Fischer, Abraham Maslow, Carol Gilligan, Howard Gardner, etc. (Wilber, 1999b, p. 29), identified more than 20 developmental lines that he felt were significant in terms of understanding individual psychological growth (the upper left-hand quadrant in his quadratic model). Some of these mostly independent lines include: morals, affects, self-identity, psychosexual development, cognitions, ideas of good/evil, role-taking, socio-emotional capacity, creativity, altruism, spiritual development, joy, needs (à la Maslow), logico-mathematical competence, kinesthetic skills, empathy for others, etc. The interesting thing about Wilber's (and other developmentalists') theories about lines of development is in the aforementioned "independent" quality, meaning that if each line can develop relatively independently from the others, then overall development ends up being a completely unique and individual affair, with each person highly developed in some areas, modestly developed in others, and perhaps deficient or severely underdeveloped in yet other capacities or qualities. One hypothetical example of this kind of "uneven" development might be the successful politician who has developed strong communications and interpersonal skills (enough to get elected to high public office), and yet has very poor moral development or even pathologies in psychosexual development. Such a person might wield great power and command much respect from peers and constituents, yet become embroiled in a sex scandal where they abused their position of power to inappropriately solicit a sexual relationship. Another hypothetical case might be the world-class athlete who has developed their kinesthetic senses, reflexes, musculature, hand–eye coordination, etc., but has spent very little time and effort on other forms of education and cognitive training, so that their reading and reading comprehension is very low.

179

Building a Developmental Lines Profile

Start by taking a careful look at yourself. Assess the areas or skill sets that you feel represent your strongest or most developed qualities. (You might start by looking over the list of developmental lines that Wilber has identified above, but feel free to list your own as well.) Make notes in your written or audio journal. Now add to that list the areas or skill sets where you feel you are only "average" or could definitely use some improvement or growth. Finally, list the areas where you are the weakest, have deficiencies, or aspects of yourself that actually cause you problems. We will call this your developmental lines profile (DLP).

Now look at your DLP and ask yourself which of these lines you could improve with some form of effort. If you are out of shape, for instance, you

could always add exercise into your daily routine.
If you feel you are a little low on empathy, perhaps you could dedicate some time to charitable
works or helping others. The point of this exercise is to identify your own unique DLP and to use
it to find ways to improve or balance out your
talents and gifts.

Once you have some familiarity with your own
developmental lines and DLP, try building a DLP
for a character that you are working on or that you
already know well. Use the given circumstances of
the script or the content of the dialogue to suggest those developmental lines where the character
may be overdeveloped or underdeveloped. Perhaps
there are some areas where the character may be so
underdeveloped that they exhibit pathology (such
as in the hypothetical politician above).

How do various character DLPs inform or change
the ways you might play a particular scene? What
if your character was very smart or educated? Or
not very smart at all? Would this change anything
in your performance? What if your character were
excessively moral and honest by nature? Or, conversely, what if they were a moral despot with a
sociopathic disregard for other people's feelings? Experiment with different combinations of
developmental lines and see what they bring up in
terms of creative possibilities.

As mentioned above, Wilber has written dozens of books and
has been very prolific in applying his integral theory to multiple
disciplines and areas of criticism. As such, I have only been able
to touch on a minor fraction of what Wilber has taught that might
have significant value to the actor. I would go as far as to say that
a full application of Wilber's theories to the actor's craft might well
represent the first theory since Stanislavsky's to be comprehensive
enough to capture the full subtlety and range of the serious actor's
art. However, it would take an entire book (and perhaps a series of
books) to explicate the possibilities. Until then, I highly recommend
reading Wilber's original works in other areas such as psychology
(Wilber, 1999b), consciousness studies (Wilber, 1999c; Wilber,

Engler, & Brown, 1986), postmodernism and philosophy (Wilber, 2000b), anthropology and cultural studies (Wilber, 1999a), and meditation practice (Wilber, 2016). One word of warning on reading Wilber; some of his works are *very academic* and can be challenging, if not flat-out difficult, to read. He has, however, also written books to introduce his theories that are intended for a more general audience (Wilber, 2000a, 2007). These titles may be a better place to start with Wilber, and then explore his more challenging work once the basic concepts are clear to you.

References

Callaghan, T. C. (2005). Cognitive development beyond infancy. In B. Hopkins (Ed.), *The Cambridge Encyclopedia of Child Development* (pp. 204–209). Cambridge: Cambridge University Press.

Lourenço, O., & Machado, A. (1996). In defense of Piaget's theory: a reply to 10 common criticisms. *Psychological Review*, 103(1), 143–164. doi:10.1037/0033-295X.103.1.143

Piaget, J. (1950). *The Psychology of Intelligence*. London: Routledge & Kegan Paul.

Piaget, J. (1977). *The Development of Thought: Equilibration of Cognitive Structures*. New York: Viking Press.

Piaget, J. (1978). *Behavior and Evolution*. New York: Pantheon Books.

Piaget, J., Elkind, D., & Flavell, J. H. (1969). *Studies in Cognitive Development: Essays in Honor of Jean Piaget*. New York: Oxford University Press.

Wilber, K. (1977). *The Spectrum of Consciousness*. Wheaton, IL: Theosophical Publishing House.

Wilber, K. (1999a). *The Atman Project: Up from Eden*. Boston, MA: Shambhala.

Wilber, K. (1999b). *Integral Psychology: Transformations of Consciousness—Selected Essays*. Boston, MA: Shambhala.

Wilber, K. (1999c). *The Spectrum of Consciousness: No Boundary—Selected Essays*. Boston, MA: Shambhala.

Wilber, K. (2000a). *A Brief History of Everything: The Eye of Spirit*. Boston, MA: Shambhala.

Wilber, K. (2000b). *Sex, Ecology, Spirituality: The Spirit of Evolution* (2nd rev. ed.). Boston, MA: Shambhala.

Wilber, K. (2000c). *A Theory of Everything: An Integral Vision for Business, Politics, Science, and Spirituality*. Boston, MA: Shambhala.

Wilber, K. (2007). *The Integral Vision: A Very Short Introduction to the Revolutionary Integral Approach to Life, God, the Universe, and Everything.* Boston, MA: Shambhala.

Wilber, K. (2016). *Integral Meditation: Mindfulness as a Way to Grow Up, Wake Up, and Show Up in Your Life.* Boulder, MA: Shambhala.

Wilber, K., Engler, J., & Brown, D. P. (1986). *Transformations of Consciousness: Conventional and Contemplative Perspectives on Development.* Boston, MA/New York: New Science Library/Random House.

182

CHAPTER 9

Personality Testing and Pathology

In this chapter, we will look at the broad general area of psychological testing, and specifically at the subset of testing tools called personality inventories. Psychological testing has been an important, and often controversial, aspect of Western psychology since nearly its beginnings. The history of endeavors to understand, categorize, explain, and predict human behavior, as well as justify giving advice, goes back as far as the practice of astrology. In the fifth century BC, Greek philosopher Hippocrates of Kos developed a system for understanding human nature based on a series of internal "humors" or bodily fluids, the balance of which it was thought would determine mood and disposition (discussed in Chapter 1). In the nineteenth century, phrenology became wildly popular. Phrenology was purported to be able to characterize and predict behavior by analyzing the bumps on a person's skull. In each age, it seems, there has been some attempt to categorize people, to allow prediction, to enable swift judgments about others, to justify social structures, and to answer the question of why people are as they are.

With the coming of the twentieth century, and the "age of science," the next iteration of human analysis turned to quantification by psychologists, often driven or informed by theories, such as Freud's psychoanalysis, or research, but sometimes driven purely by the creativity and imaginations of the test developers who conjured up "tests" that merely seemed plausible to their contemporary audiences (much as humors and phrenology had seemed plausible in their own times). Contemporary psychological and personality testing remains controversial for a number of reasons, not the least of which are that such instruments are often used by courts and employers to decide a person's fate or future. For an excellent discussion on the history and criticism of psychological testing, see *The Cult of Personality* (Paul, 2004).

For the actor, certain personality tests can prove interesting explorations and provide alternative ways of looking at our own consciousness, similar to those experiential exercises we have already tried in previous chapters. In other words, to the degree that they are accurate (one of the qualities of such tests that is often questioned), the results can help an actor "set a baseline" for later comparison against the characters they play. For instance, if you have reasonably reliable data that suggest your own tendency toward being introverted and shy, it will be highly useful to understand this tendency (and work against it) when asked to play a bombastic extrovert. However, as with all theories and approaches to psychology we have explored thus far, the caveat remains to use only those approaches that seem most relevant to you and support the acting problem you are actually confronted with. If the results of a particular personality test seem to be useless or irrelevant to you, they probably are, and should be discarded in favor of one of the other approaches that seems to fit your situation better.

184

Psychological Tests vs. Personality Inventories

There are several types of psychological test. The first category is a clinical diagnostic instrument used only by licensed professionals as "a systematic procedure for obtaining samples of behavior, relevant to cognitive, affective, or interpersonal functioning, and for scoring and evaluating those samples according to standards" (Urbina, 2014, pp. 1–2). These types of test usually force the respondent to make yes-or-no statements and the results are evaluated against normative scales based on statistical analysis of large groups of people who have taken the test previously. This is the definition of a traditional "psychological test." In contrast, instruments that do not force a right/wrong or pass/fail response in sampling behavior, but instead rely on some form of self-evaluation or multiple-choice answer scheme, are considered inventories, questionnaires, surveys, etc. (Urbina, 2014, p. 3). For our purposes, those that deal with evaluating personality traits will be called personality inventories or personality tests and will be our main concern as it relates to the actor. Usually, a psychological test is focused on diagnosing mental disorders or disease, whereas a personality test is interested in assessing various characteristics or tendencies of the individual's personality, and therefore is more useful in the process of character-building. We will look at the subject of mental disease in a later section.

The Myers–Briggs Type Indicator

As noted in Chapter 3, the Myers–Briggs Type Indicator (MBTI) is a test developed by Isabel Briggs Myers and her mother, Katharine Briggs, that attempts to apply, in practical terms, Jung's theories regarding personality type to nonclinical, non-neurotic populations. The MBTI assesses Jung's original introversion/extroversion attitude dichotomy, along with the polarized sets of functions, thinking/feeling and sensation/intuition, then adds a final dichotomy, judging/perceiving. When the test is scored, it yields one of 16 *personality types* that are identified by a set of four letters representing the dominant features from each dichotomy (polarity). For instance, an INTJ-type (standing for [I]ntroverted-[N]Intuitive-[T]hinking-[J]udging) would have an original mind and great drive to understand ideas that they were interested in. They would quickly see patterns and develop long-range explanatory perspectives. INJTs tend to be skeptical and independent and hold themselves (and others) to high standards of competence and performance. In contrast, an ESTP-type ([E]xtroverted-[S]ensing-[T]hinking-[P]erceiving) learns best through doing and action. They tend to be flexible and tolerant and take a pragmatic approach that is focused on immediate results. Theories and conceptual explanations bore an ESTP-type. They want to act energetically to solve problems and focus on the here and now. They tend toward spontaneity and seem to enjoy each moment that they are active with others. ESTPs may enjoy material comforts and exhibit a strong sense of personal style.

Each MBTI participant receives a customized assessment report that details the results of the test across a number of dimensions. MBTI assessment reports usually include a description of each polarity and which pole from each pair the participant seems to favor, introversion/extroversion (the way you direct and recharge your energy), sensing/intuition (the way you take in information), thinking/feeling (the way you make decisions and come to conclusions), and judging/perceiving (the way you approach the outside world); the individual's four-letter code and a brief description of likely qualities; a chart that depicts how relatively strong or weak the identification with each category is (one might be "strongly extroverted" but only "moderately intuitive," etc.); and then a more detailed type description section that articulates the individual's type characteristics, and how that type tends to behave and interact with others.

According to the Myers–Briggs Foundation, the publisher of the MBTI test, type theory indicates that different people will exhibit different preferences (which can be assessed), which naturally will lead to different interests, views, orientations, behaviors, and motivations. According to the MyersBriggs.org website, people can use their understanding of their own type to help them appreciate their differences with others and influence the ways they interact with different types of people. To the degree that this is true, it would certainly make type theory a useful tool for actors to investigate their own personalities and the alterations that might be required for a particular character.

The MBTI test sorts for preferences along only four polarities, and does not attempt to assess mental illness or dysfunction; it also does not purport to measure traits, abilities, or overall character. The MBTI test is available to the public online (for a fee: www.mbtionline.com), and includes the detailed, personalized test assessment report (MBTI Online, 2017). As a professional actor myself, I have often found it useful to understand the Myers–Briggs types in general, and my own typology in particular.

The "Big Five" Personality Factors

Another more recent approach to assessing personality characteristics through standardized testing instruments is called the *Big Five* personality factors. The Big Five model, instead of relying on clinical observations and research as most of the personality theorists we have looked at so far have done, was based on a statistical analysis of dictionary words that researchers felt described human personality.

A British professor of psychology, Raymond B. Cattell, emigrated to the United States in 1937 as a research assistant at Columbia University, later moving on to a series of positions at other prestigious institutions such as Clark University, Harvard, and finally the University of Illinois. Cattell was an empirically minded psychological researcher with a notoriously rigorous work ethic (Paul, 2004, pp. 172–173). He became enamored with an idea called the *lexical hypothesis*, which was first put into action by the American psychologists Gordon Allport and H. S. Odbert as an experiment in defining the human personality. Around 1936, Allport and Odbert set out on an ambitious project to filter through *Webster's New International*

186

Dictionary, unabridged, and look for words that describe differences between people's personalities. They suggested that the individual differences that are most important in people's private and social lives will eventually become encoded in language; the more important such a difference, the more likely it is to become expressed as a single word. This idea, which became known as the lexical hypothesis, led them to attempt to derive a comprehensive taxonomy of human personality traits by filtering down and extracting approximately 4,500 adjectives from their dictionary search, which described nonphysical differences that could be considered observable and relatively permanent traits.

Cattell, working a decade later, began with Allport and Odbert's list, and applied several techniques, including factor analysis, a statistical method for quantifying and identifying groups of related items using mathematical operations, as a way of reducing the unwieldy number of adjectives down to just 16. Eventually, Cattell created a test he believed could reliably measure his "universal index of natural elements" of personality, and titled it the *Sixteen Personality Factor Questionnaire*, or 16PF (Paul, 2004, p. 178). Now in its fifth edition, the 16PF is a 185-question test aimed at discerning healthy personality traits, problem-solving abilities, and preferred work activities in otherwise healthy, non-pathological test populations.

The 16PF became a hugely popular, and commercially successful, test that proliferated far beyond the psychologist or counselor's office to include industry and the employer's market. Large corporations began to regularly use the 16PF, and other similar instruments, to make hiring and promotion decisions, and an entire new industry, organizational psychological test publishing, was born. There are naturally powerful criticisms on both sides of the validity and ethical issues that such endeavors raise. For actors, once again, these types of tests represent yet another set of maps and models (different perspectives) that can perhaps be used to look at self and character from different angles.

Over the years, many other researchers used factor analysis and other statistical means to continue to investigate human personality traits through standardized testing (as opposed to direct interview and clinical interactions) as a way to empirically categorize human nature. Many of these researchers began to reduce the number of fundamental personality characteristics from 16 down to five or less factors that they acknowledged as the *most* fundamental.

In 1978, psychologists Paul Costa Jr. and Robert McCrae introduced a testing instrument that they claimed fixed the universal core

187

of human personality at just three factors, *neuroticism, extroversion,* and *openness* (to experience), taking the first letter of each factor, NEO, as the acronym for their test. Later, however, they added back two additional factors that they felt had been incorrectly excluded from their first iteration, *agreeableness* and *conscientiousness,* and republished their test, which included all of what are now called "the Big Five factors," under the title *NEO Personality Inventory—Revised,* or NEO PI-R. The NEO PI-R is a 240-question self-assessment survey that is very similar in structure to its predecessor, the 16PF, or even the *Minnesota Multiphasic Personality Inventory* (MMPI-2), which is a 567-item test designed to evaluate and categorize mental patients with serious psychiatric disorders (Paul, 2004, pp. 49–73, 187).

Here are brief descriptions of the five factors the NEO PI-R purports to measure. *Neuroticism* is the tendency toward experiencing or focusing on what would typically be considered negative emotions, such as anger, anxiety, self-consciousness, vulnerability to stress, or depression. *Extroversion* is the quality or intensity of an individual's relationships with others, and includes tendencies related to personal warmth, gregariousness or friendliness, assertiveness, thrill- or excitement-seeking, activity vs. passivity, and positive emotions toward others. *Openness* to experience includes fantasy life, aesthetics, feelings, ideas, actions, and values. *Agreeableness* has to do with such qualities as trust in others, a straightforward attitude, altruism, compliance, and modesty. And finally, *conscientiousness* considers such facets as competence, orderliness, dutifulness, striving toward achievement, self-discipline, and deliberation. These groups of qualities, or factors, are measured by answers to a five-point Likert scale, with responses ranging from strongly agree on the low end to strongly disagree on the high end. The NEO PI-R is one of the most heavily researched personality tests in history, with much empirical data to support its validity and accuracy (Erford, 2006, pp. 99–100). However, critics of the NEO PI-R, and tests like it, claim that the distinctions of the five factors are completely superficial and can be characterized as "a psychology of the stranger," where the categories articulated and sampled by the test give little if any actual insight into an individual's nature beyond what a stranger might assess with the most superficial of observations (Paul, 2004, p. 194).

The NEO PI-R is generally administered and interpreted by a mental healthcare professional such as licensed psychologists, who also provide the written report. The 16PF has less restrictions and may be administered by a trained counselor or life coach. Once you have taken the 16PF and/or the NEO PI-R yourself, you can judge whether

188

the insights provided by the test results add value to your process as an actor or not. When combined with the kind of self-evaluative work suggested in earlier chapters, it may well be that standardized testing models are an interesting variation on our self-knowledge theme. Whether this approach is more or less valuable than the others will of course be left to the actor's personal preference.

Madness, Insanity, and the Mental Illness Model

Madness and insanity are two words from a bygone age. They refer to extraordinary states of mind and dangerous behaviors far outside of the "normal" rules of society. Both of these words can also be used from the first-person perspective: "I feel like I'm going mad." "I must have been insane when I did that." However, in contemporary medical and psychiatric terminology, these types of words are no longer used. Medical terms such as *borderline personality disorder* or *bipolar disorder* are intended to render a diagnosis of disease and to impersonally classify the "patient" into a category representing a constellation of symptoms and behaviors that are represented by the label. Interestingly, this impersonal medicalized terminology is almost always used in the third-person context, never in the first-person. You don't say, "I think I'm going borderline personality disorder" or "I really got bipolar disorder last night at that party!" You say, "I must be crazy to believe him!" While mad, insane, and crazy all are labels that can be applied to others, they also can describe internal emotional or psychological states or altered forms of consciousness.

189

There has been a debate raging in modern psychology since its beginnings in the late 1800s. The debate is the same that we noted in Chapter 1 as being between Plato and Aristotle: the inner (experiential) and the outer (hard, empirical science). It is the same debate that led to the rise of both behaviorism (an outer, third-person view) and humanistic psychology (a belief in the dignity of the individual and a valuing of inner experience). It is also the debate that Wilber seeks to solve with his quadratic model, described in the previous chapter. And it is the same debate that has been going on in actor training and theory for almost as long: does one develop a character from the *inside out* (building the character's emotional experience utilizing the inner psychological depths of the actor) or *outside in* (the "technical approach" depending on outward physicalization and use of props to reveal character to an audience)?

In most of this book so far, we have explored psychological theories that deal with the inner world and emotional state or development of the subject. Even the more deterministic theories, such as Freud's, still postulated an inner experience subject to the effects of unconscious forces on mood and emotion. Only in the previous section on psychological testing have we ventured into the world of the hardcore third-person, wholly empirical viewpoint.

In looking at madness and other extreme states of mind that we might be asked to portray in some fashion, we have the same two choices of perspective and approach, the internal, experiential way the character might "feel" or perceive reality, and the external "diagnosis" of the clinical, empirical lens that describes a character's behavior in impersonal third-person terms. Both can be useful. However, as I mention above, to this point, I have favored the internal over the external. I don't have the space in the rest of this book for a detailed discussion of the internal "madness perspective," or what it feels like "on the inside" to be insane. That could, and perhaps should, be a book in itself. And so, I will reverse myself here and concentrate almost exclusively on the ways contemporary medicine categorizes those in mental states outside of society's accepted norms, those who were once called mad but now are diagnosed with mental illness.

Before I begin, however, I will point you toward two books that should be on every serious actor's bookshelves, which cover this subject matter, that of madness and insanity, in great detail from the inner, experiential dimension: *The Meaning of Madness* (Burton, 2010) and *Exploring Madness* (Fadiman & Kewman, 1979). Both of these excellent books will enrich your character-building toolkit and your basic imagination as an actor.

Modern medical vernacular about these subjects is defined by the *Diagnostic and Statistical Manual of Mental Disorders, 5th Edition* (APA, 2014) published by the American Psychiatric Association (APA). In its 991 pages, the DSM-5 attempts to categorize every known psychiatric disorder, reduces it to a diagnostic label, and recommends treatment practices for that illness or combination of illnesses.

Following are brief descriptions of several widely acknowledged psychological disorders, as defined by the National Institute of Mental Health (NIMH), which provides a website with categorization information very similar to the DSM-5:

Borderline personality disorder ("BPD") is a serious mental disorder marked by a pattern of ongoing instability in moods, behavior, self-image, and functioning. These experiences often result in impulsive actions and unstable relationships. A person with BPD may experience intense episodes of anger, depression, and anxiety that may last from only a few hours to days.

Some people with BPD also have high rates of co-occurring mental disorders, such as mood disorders, anxiety disorders, and eating disorders, along with substance abuse, self-harm, suicidal thinking and behaviors, and suicide.

While mental health experts now generally agree that the label "borderline personality disorder" is very misleading, a more accurate term does not exist yet.

People with borderline personality disorder may experience extreme mood swings and can display uncertainty about who they are. As a result, their interests and values can change rapidly.

Other symptoms include: frantic efforts to avoid real or imagined abandonment; a pattern of intense and unstable relationships with family, friends, and loved ones, often swinging from extreme closeness and love (idealization) to extreme dislike or anger (devaluation); distorted and unstable self-image or sense of self; impulsive and often dangerous behaviors, such as spending sprees, unsafe sex, substance abuse, reckless driving, and binge eating; recurring suicidal behaviors or threats or self-harming behavior, such as cutting; intense and highly changeable moods, with each episode lasting from a few hours to a few days; chronic feelings of emptiness; inappropriate, intense anger or problems controlling anger; having stress-related paranoid thoughts; having severe dissociative symptoms, such as feeling cut off from oneself, observing oneself from outside the body, or losing touch with reality.

191

Seemingly ordinary events may trigger symptoms. For example, people with borderline personality disorder may feel angry and distressed over minor separations—such as vacations, business trips, or sudden changes of plans—from people to whom they feel close. Studies show that people with this disorder may see anger in an emotionally neutral face and have a stronger reaction to words with negative meanings than people who do not have the disorder.

Some of these signs and symptoms may be experienced by people with other mental health problems—and even by people without mental illness—and do not necessarily mean that they have borderline personality disorder. It is important that a qualified and licensed mental health professional conduct a thorough assessment to determine whether a diagnosis of borderline personality disorder or other mental disorder is warranted, and to help guide treatment options when appropriate.

(NIMH, 2017b)

Depression (major depressive disorder or clinical depression) is a common but serious mood disorder. It causes severe symptoms that affect how you feel, think, and handle daily activities, such as sleeping, eating, or working. To be diagnosed with depression, the symptoms must be present for at least two weeks.

Some forms of depression are slightly different, or they may develop under unique circumstances, such as:

Persistent depressive disorder (also called dysthymia) is a depressed mood that lasts for at least two years. A person diagnosed with persistent depressive disorder may have episodes of major depression along with periods of less severe symptoms, but symptoms must last for two years to be considered persistent depressive disorder.

Perinatal depression is much more serious than the "baby blues" (relatively mild depressive and anxiety symptoms that typically clear within two weeks after delivery) that many women experience after giving birth. Women with perinatal depression experience full-blown major depression during pregnancy or after delivery (postpartum depression). The feelings of extreme sadness, anxiety, and exhaustion that accompany perinatal depression may make it difficult for these new mothers to complete daily care activities for themselves and/or for their babies.

192

Psychotic depression occurs when a person has severe depression plus some form of psychosis, such as having disturbing false fixed beliefs (delusions) or hearing or seeing upsetting things that others cannot hear or see (hallucinations). The psychotic symptoms typically have a depressive "theme," such as delusions of guilt, poverty, or illness.

Seasonal affective disorder is characterized by the onset of depression during the winter months, when there is less natural sunlight. This depression generally lifts during spring and summer. Winter depression, typically accompanied by social withdrawal, increased sleep, and weight gain, predictably returns every year in seasonal affective disorder.

Examples of other types of depressive disorders newly added to the diagnostic classification of DSM-5 include: *disruptive mood dysregulation disorder* (diagnosed in children and adolescents) and *premenstrual dysphoric disorder* (PMDD).

Signs and symptoms [include]: persistent sad, anxious, or "empty" mood; feelings of hopelessness, or pessimism; irritability; feelings of guilt, worthlessness, or helplessness; loss of interest or pleasure in hobbies and activities; decreased energy or fatigue . . . difficulty concentrating, remembering, or making decisions; difficulty sleeping, early-morning awakening, or oversleeping; appetite and/or weight changes; thoughts of death or suicide, or suicide attempts . . .

193

Not everyone who is depressed experiences every symptom. Some people experience only a few symptoms while others may experience many. Several persistent symptoms in addition to low mood are required for a diagnosis of major depression, but people with only a few—but distressing—symptoms may benefit from treatment of their "subsyndromal" depression. The severity and frequency of symptoms and how long they last will vary depending on the individual and his or her particular illness. Symptoms may also vary depending on the stage of the illness.

(NIMH, 2017c)

Bipolar disorder, also known as manic-depressive illness, is a brain disorder that causes unusual shifts in mood, energy, activity levels, and the ability to carry out day-to-day tasks.

There are four basic types of bipolar disorder; all of them involve clear changes in mood, energy, and activity levels. These moods range from periods of extremely "up," elated, and energized behavior (known as manic episodes) to very sad, "down," or hopeless periods (known as depressive episodes). Less severe manic periods are known as hypomanic episodes.

Bipolar I disorder—defined by manic episodes that last at least seven days, or by manic symptoms that are so severe that the person needs immediate hospital care. Usually, depressive episodes occur as well, typically lasting at least two weeks. Episodes of depression with mixed features (having depression and manic symptoms at the same time) are also possible.

194   *Bipolar II disorder*—defined by a pattern of depressive episodes and hypomanic episodes, but not the full-blown manic episodes described above.

Cyclothymic disorder (also called cyclothymia)—defined by numerous periods of hypomanic symptoms as well numerous periods of depressive symptoms lasting for at least two years (one year in children and adolescents). However, the symptoms do not meet the diagnostic requirements for a hypomanic episode and a depressive episode.

Other specified and unspecified bipolar and related disorders— defined by bipolar disorder symptoms that do not match the three categories listed above.

People with bipolar disorder experience periods of unusually intense emotion, changes in sleep patterns and activity levels, and unusual behaviors. These distinct periods are called "mood episodes." Mood episodes are drastically different from the moods and behaviors that are typical for the person. Extreme changes in energy, activity, and sleep go along with mood episodes.

People having a manic episode may: feel very "up," "high," or elated; have a lot of energy; have increased activity levels; feel "jumpy" or "wired"; have trouble sleeping; become more active than usual; talk really fast about a lot of different things; be agitated, irritable, or "touchy"; feel like their thoughts are going very fast; think they can do a lot of things at once; do risky things, like spend a lot of money or have reckless sex.

People having a depressive episode may: feel very sad, down, empty, or hopeless; have very little energy; have decreased activity levels; have trouble sleeping, they may sleep too little or too much; feel like they can't enjoy anything; feel worried and empty; have trouble concentrating; forget things a lot; eat too much or too little; feel tired or "slowed down"; think about death or suicide.

Sometimes a mood episode includes symptoms of both manic and depressive symptoms. This is called an episode with mixed features. People experiencing an episode with mixed features may feel very sad, empty, or hopeless, while at the same time feeling extremely energized.

195

Bipolar disorder can be present even when mood swings are less extreme. For example, some people with bipolar disorder experience hypomania, a less severe form of mania. During a hypomanic episode, an individual may feel very good, be highly productive, and function well. The person may not feel that anything is wrong, but family and friends may recognize the mood swings and/or changes in activity levels as possible bipolar disorder. Without proper treatment, people with hypomania may develop severe mania or depression.

(NIMH, 2017a)

Obsessive-compulsive disorder ("OCD") is a common, chronic and long-lasting disorder in which a person has uncontrollable, reoccurring thoughts (obsessions) and behaviors (compulsions) that he or she feels the urge to repeat over and over.

People with OCD may have symptoms of obsessions, compulsions, or both. These symptoms can interfere with all aspects of life, such as work, school, and personal relationships.

Obsessions are repeated thoughts, urges, or mental images that cause anxiety. Common symptoms include: fear of germs or contamination; unwanted forbidden or taboo thoughts involving sex, religion, and harm; aggressive thoughts towards others or self; having things symmetrical or in a perfect order.

Compulsions are repetitive behaviors that a person with OCD feels the urge to do in response to an obsessive thought. Common compulsions include: excessive cleaning and/or handwashing; ordering and arranging things in a particular, precise way; repeatedly checking on things, such as repeatedly checking to see if the door is locked or that the oven is off; compulsive counting.

Not all rituals or habits are compulsions. Everyone double checks things sometimes. But a person with OCD generally can't control his or her thoughts or behaviors, even when those thoughts or behaviors are recognized as excessive; spends at least one hour a day on these thoughts or behaviors; doesn't get pleasure when performing the behaviors or rituals, but may feel brief relief from the anxiety the thoughts cause; experiences significant problems in their daily life due to these thoughts or behaviors.

Some individuals with OCD also have a tic disorder. Motor tics are sudden, brief, repetitive movements, such as eye blinking and other eye movements, facial grimacing, shoulder shrugging, and head or shoulder jerking. Common vocal tics include repetitive throat-clearing, sniffing, or grunting sounds.

Symptoms may come and go, ease over time, or worsen. People with OCD may try to help themselves by avoiding situations that trigger their obsessions, or they may use alcohol or drugs to calm themselves. Although most adults with OCD recognize that what they are doing doesn't make sense, some adults and most children may not realize that their behavior is out of the ordinary. Parents or teachers typically recognize OCD symptoms in children.

(NIMH, 2017d)

Schizophrenia is a chronic and severe mental disorder that affects how a person thinks, feels, and behaves. People with schizophrenia may seem like they have lost touch with reality. Although schizophrenia is not as common as other mental disorders, the symptoms can be very disabling.

Symptoms of schizophrenia usually start between ages 16 and 30. In rare cases, children have schizophrenia too. The symptoms of schizophrenia fall into three categories: positive, negative, and cognitive.

Positive symptoms: "Positive" symptoms are psychotic behaviors not generally seen in healthy people. People with positive symptoms may "lose touch" with some aspects of reality. Symptoms include: hallucinations; delusions; thought disorders (unusual or dysfunctional ways of thinking); movement disorders (agitated body movements).

Negative symptoms: "Negative" symptoms are associated with disruptions to normal emotions and behaviors. Symptoms include: "flat affect" (reduced expression of emotions via facial expression or voice tone); reduced feelings of pleasure in everyday life; difficulty beginning and sustaining activities; reduced speaking.

197

Cognitive symptoms: For some patients, the cognitive symptoms of schizophrenia are subtle, but for others, they are more severe, and patients may notice changes in their memory or other aspects of thinking. Symptoms include: poor "executive functioning" (the ability to understand information and use it to make decisions); trouble focusing or paying attention; problems with "working memory" (the ability to use information immediately after learning it).

There are several factors that contribute to the risk of developing schizophrenia.

Genes and environment: Scientists have long known that schizophrenia sometimes runs in families. However, there are many people who have schizophrenia who don't have a family member with the disorder and conversely, many people with one or more family members with the disorder who do not develop it themselves.

Scientists believe that many different genes may increase the risk of schizophrenia, but that no single gene causes the disorder by itself. It is not yet possible to use genetic information to predict who will develop schizophrenia.

Scientists also think that interactions between genes and aspects of the individual's environment are necessary for schizophrenia to develop. Environmental factors may involve: exposure to viruses; malnutrition before birth; problems during birth; psychosocial factors.

Different brain chemistry and structure: Scientists think that an imbalance in the complex, interrelated chemical reactions of the brain involving the neurotransmitters (substances that brain cells use to communicate with each other) dopamine and glutamate, and possibly others, plays a role in schizophrenia.

Some experts also think problems during brain development before birth may lead to faulty connections. The brain also undergoes major changes during puberty, and these changes could trigger psychotic symptoms in people who are vulnerable due to genetics or brain differences.

(NIMH, 2017e)

In looking at these various mental states through the lens of third-person medical diagnostic language, the actor, to some extent, must work in reverse. If, for instance, you felt a character had certain symptoms of obsessive-compulsive disorder, you could experiment with, and even construct, certain external behaviors that would align with that diagnosis. But you would also need to create some connection between that external behavior, say rubbing the hands together constantly, and the internal experience of the character doing the compulsive rubbing.

Nonetheless, as a way of entry into the world of the mad or mentally disturbed, the above clinical descriptions can be quite helpful. As an example, you might try exhibiting or acting out various symptoms

198

listed above and see how they make your body feel. Do they create tension in your body in ways that you are not used to? Do any of the symptoms spontaneously generate emotions or feelings? Perhaps you could play out a scene that you are familiar with as a schizophrenic with positive symptoms? Negative symptoms? How about a character who was clinically depressed (using the details of the symptoms described above)? Or say your character suffered from borderline personality disorder and kept bursting into angry inappropriate diatribes? How does the scene play differently with different diagnoses, labels, and symptoms?

Conclusions

If you have read this book through from the beginning and done the exercises to the best of your ability, you have probably noticed a few things. Almost all of the exercises I have provided have been aimed at the individual; very few propose group activities.

If you are a teacher or an instructor at the conservatory, you may find this frustrating. However, there is a reason for this. Psychological self-exploration is a very personal endeavor, requiring great bravery and honesty, the details of which should probably not be drawn into a classroom for open conversation. Second, if you have actually *done* the exercises suggested in this book, you probably have learned a few things about yourself and the way you fundamentally view and interact with the world. That is because psychology, or rather applied psychology in the format I have tried to present, stimulates development; when used as an *action*, psychology is a *growth technique* in addition to being a tool for character development.

My thesis is that an actor's basic job is to be self-aware, deeply self-aware. Self-awareness does not necessarily just happen; look at the number of people you know that seem to have no idea of who they are or why they act in life the ways they do. But self-awareness can be cultivated; it can essentially be trained, and in order to do that effectively the individual requires maps of the territory they presume to traverse during that training. Every bodybuilder understands the basic muscle groups and location in the body, as well as how to exercise them to greatest effect. That is what I have tried to provide in this book, a diverse set of maps (like an anatomy chart) of the inner terrain that an actor must explore in order to become deeply self-aware, and thus more expressive and effective in their communications with others through the art of performance. More than likely, your relative success (or frustration) with the ideas (maps) and tools (models) presented in this book is in direct proportion to how fully you committed to applying what you learned through action, even if that action was basically silent introspection on your own feelings and experiences. As with the bodybuilding analogy above, muscle is built in direct proportion to the effort applied.

It is my hope that by updating and expanding the types of psychological lenses that can be applied to the actor's craft to include perspectives introduced after the great Stanislavsky and other early acting theorists formulated their ideas, we can create a new kind of actor: one who starts from a deeper understanding of the self, and is able to approach their work of communicating profoundly with their audiences from a multiplicity of perspectives, some of which may not often have been available in the past.

I will add one other tool to this process that I did not cover in the body of this book, but which remains one of the most powerful paths toward expanded self-awareness available in the postmodern era. *Meditation*, in its various forms (which includes the popular "mindfulness"), has become one of the fastest-growing and widely used techniques for self-development in the Western world. I have written an entire book on the subject of applying meditation to actor training, *Advanced Consciousness Training for Actors* (2018), which may be a useful addition to your self-development toolkit. It is my belief that a rigorous program of self-directed training that includes a regular meditation practice and a deep psychological self-exploration, as proposed in this book, is as critical to the professional actor's ultimate success as ongoing vocal training or bodywork. In order to be the "complete package," it is impossible for the actor to ignore the development of their own consciousness.

Acting, more than being just a career, is a way of *being in the world*, and to the extent that actors can be in the world more fully, more authentically, and with a deeper self-understanding than perhaps others are willing to dare, they can communicate and reflect important aspects of being human that have the power to transform and enlighten the audiences who come to marvel at their seeming magic. And if this is true, that acting can transform and enlighten others, then perhaps acting remains an elevated art, as it was in the days of the Greeks, and even before with the shaman and the medicine people of prehistory, where acting and performance originally came into being (Bartow, 2006; Roach, 1993).

The ancient Greek aphorism "know thyself" was a maxim inscribed in the Temple of Apollo at Delphi and later expounded upon by the philosopher Socrates, who taught that "the unexamined life is not worth living." But I say that the actor's life *is* worth living, and the modern tools for enacting a quest for self-knowledge are most readily accessible through the study and application of psychology. May you know yourself well and transform your audiences for the better.

References

APA (2014). *Diagnostic and Statistical Manual of Mental Disorders, 5th Edition: DSM-5*. New Delhi: CBS Publishers & Distributors.

Bartow, A. (2006). *Training of the American Actor*. New York: Theatre Communications Group.

Burton, N. L. (2010). *The Meaning of Madness*. Pune: Mehta Publishing House.

Erford, B. T. (2006). *Counselor's Guide to Clinical, Personality, and Behavioral Assessment*. Boston, MA: Houghton Mifflin Co.

Fadiman, J., & Kewman, D. (1979). *Exploring Madness: Experience, Theory, and Research* (2nd ed.). Monterey, CA: Brooks/Cole Publishing.

NIMH (2017a). *Bipolar Disorder*. Retrieved from www.nimh.nih.gov/health/topics/bipolar-disorder/index.shtml.

NIMH (2017b) *Borderline Personality Disorder*. Retrieved from www.nimh.nih.gov/health/topics/borderline-personality-disorder/index.shtml.

NIMH (2017c). *Depression*. Retrieved from www.nimh.nih.gov/health/topics/depression/index.shtml.

NIMH (2017d). *Obsessive-Compulsive Disorder*. Retrieved from www.nimh.nih.gov/health/topics/obsessive-compulsive-disorder-ocd/index.shtml.

NIMH (2017e). *Schizophrenia*. Retrieved from www.nimh.nih.gov/health/topics/schizophrenia/index.shtml.

MBTI Online (2017). *Official Myers Briggs Test & Personality Assessment*. Retrieved from www.mbtionline.com.

Page, K. (2018). *Advanced Consciousness Training for Actors: Meditation Techniques for the Performing Artist.* New York: Routledge.

Paul, A. M. (2004). *The Cult of Personality: How Personality Tests Are Leading Us to Miseducate Our Children, Mismanage Our Companies, and Misunderstand Ourselves.* New York: Free Press.

Roach, J. R. (1993). *The Player's Passion: Studies in the Science of Acting.* Ann Arbor, MI: University of Michigan Press.

Urbina, S. (2014). *Essentials of Psychological Testing* (2nd ed.). Hoboken, NJ: Wiley.

202

Index

absorption 158
acting 1–4; Adlerian psychology
112–118; autonomy 140;
concentration 158; cultural
context 7–8; Erikson's psychology
144–150; Freudian psychology
65–75; Horney's psychology
126–132; Jungian psychology
79, 82–83, 84, 85, 86, 87,
88–103; Maslow's psychology
154, 161–166; multi-perspectival
orientation 12–13; neurotics
122; personality tests 184;
"post-dramatic" approach 10;
postmodernism 8–9, 47; self-
awareness and self-knowledge
199–201; Wilber's psychology
172–181; *see also* characters
active imagination 28, 29, 77, 87–88,
100–103
Addams, Jane 156–157
Adler, Alfred 105–119, 156; activities
for actors 112–118; AQAL
approach 170; cooperation 111;
early childhood recollections
108–109, 114–115; influence on
Maslow 150, 151, 154; life goals
and lifestyle 107–108, 115; social
context 111, 112; will to power
106–107
adolescence 130, 141–142, 143
affective memory 2
aggression 54, 65, 69, 85, 107, 123
agreeableness 188
Allport, Gordon 37, 186–187
American Method 3, 56, 154
American Psychiatric Association 190
American Psychological Association
(APA) 20, 33, 35, 47–48
anal stage 57, 66–67, 68, 69, 139
anima/animus 28, 84
anxiety 64, 193; basic 121–122; Freud
58–59; obsessive-compulsive
disorder 196
AQAL approach 169–172, 177
archetypes 78–79, 82, 83–84, 86,
89–90
Aristotle 189
arrogant-vindictiveness 124
Association for Analytical Psychology 29

auditions 4, 176, 177
autonomy 139–140, 145, 147–150, 157

Bandura, Albert 45–46
Barzun, Jacques 37
basic anxiety 121–122
Beck, Aaron T. 46
behaviorism 5, 26, 45, 189; Diderot
as forefather to 2; historical
developments 30–34, 35;
humanistic critique of 37;
Maslow 151, 152, 154; models 6;
rejection of 44
beliefs 5, 123; fictional 107–108, 113
Benedict, Ruth 151, 155
"Big Five" personality factors 186–189
bipolar disorder 194–195
birth order 109–111, 118
Blumenfeld, Robert 11, 69
body 103
bodywork 39, 40
borderline personality disorder (BPD)
190–192, 199
brain 19, 33, 44, 198
Brentano, Franz 18, 25
Breuer, Josef 21, 22
Briggs, Katharine 185
Brücke, Ernest 21
Buddha 15–16
Buddhism 43, 170
Bugental, James 35, 37
Bühler, Charlotte 35, 37

care 143
Carnicke, Sharon 2–3
Cartesian split 17
Cattell, Raymond B. 186, 187
characters: active imagination 103;
Adler inventory 114; archetypes
89–90; cooperation 111;
coping strategies 128; defenses
72; developmental lines 180;
developmental stages 146;
dominance/power relationships
117–118; dreamwork 100;
early childhood recollections
115; emotional self-study
132; expectations 108; free
association 74–75; hierarchy of
needs 161–163; inside out or

outside in approaches 189; life goals and lifestyle 116; mental illness 198–199; motivation 1; neurotics 122; Oedipus complex 59–60; persona 95; postmodern perspective 47; self-actualization 160, 163–165; self-image 129, 131; shadow 85, 96; stages of psychosexual development 66–68; type analysis 90–91, 93; *see also* acting
Charcot, Jean-Martin 21, 22
childhood memories 108–109, 114–115, 130
China 16
Christianity 17
cognitive behavioral therapy (CBT) 46
cognitive development 177–178
cognitive neuroscience 5, 48
"cognitive turn" 44–46
collective unconscious 28, 78–79, 82, 86
community feelings 111
compensation 106
competence 141, 145
competitiveness 4, 126
compliance 123
compulsions 195, 196
computer model of cognition 44
concentration 158
conditioning 33–34
Confucius 16
conscience 55, 67, 140
conscientiousness 188
consciousness: behaviorist critique 31, 32; cognitive psychology 44, 45; Eastern philosophies 15–16; Freud 23, 27, 54; Jung 82, 84; Maslow 35; spectrum of 167, 170–171; states of 168–169; stream of 20; Titchener 20; Wundt 18; *see also* the unconscious
continuity 135
cooperation 111, 112, 118
coping strategies 122–125, 127–128
Costa, Paul Jr. 187–188
culture 7–8, 27, 122, 126, 144, 157
cyclothymic disorder 194

Darwin, Charles 20, 33, 107, 156
defenses: active imagination 102; basic anxiety 121–122; Freud 25, 58, 59, 61–64, 70–72; Maslow 159
deficiency needs 153–154
Democritus 16
denial 25, 62, 64, 71
depression 143, 192–193; borderline personality disorder 191; manic 194–195; "self-help" 46

depth psychology 37, 105, 154
Descartes, René 17, 45
despair 143
detachment 124–125
development: Erikson 134–135, 136–144, 145–150; Freud's stages of psychosexual development 56–60, 61, 64–65, 66–69, 136, 139, 140, 178; Horney 122; Piaget's model of cognitive development 177–178; "pillars" of psychology 48; self-development 159, 164; Wilber 168, 170–172
developmental lines 64–65, 168, 170–171, 177–180
Dewey, John 152
Diagnostic and Statistical Manual of Mental Disorders (DSM-5) 190–191, 193
Diderot, Denis 2, 8, 56
displacement 25
doubt 139–140, 145
dramaturgy 9, 86, 90
dreams 23, 60–61, 85–87, 96–100, 103
drives 24, 27, 54–55, 58, 68, 85, 140
dualism 17
Dubos, Rene 37

early childhood recollections 108–109, 114–115, 130
Eastern philosophies 15–16, 43, 160, 167, 170–171
ego 24, 25, 55–56, 88, 140; ego defenses 59, 61–62, 63, 72, 159; ego-development stages 134; ego integrity 143; fixed nature of personality 77; Jung 82–83; stages of psychosexual development 57, 58, 67, 69
ego psychology 61, 105
Einstein, Albert 156–157
Electra complex 67
embodied cognition 45
emotions 5; dreamwork 99; hysteria 22; Jung 88; schizophrenia 197; studying your 131–132; Watson 32
enactment 45
encounter groups 38, 39
enlightenment 160, 169, 170
Erhard Seminars Training (EST) 38, 39
Erikson, Erik 134–150, 172; activities for actors 144–150; AQAL approach 170; developmental stages 136–144, 145–150
Esalen Institute 38, 39
evolutionary theory 20, 107, 111, 156

204

existential psychology 38
expectations 108, 124, 126
extroversion 79–80, 91–93, 184, 185,
        187–188

Fadiman, James 44, 55–56, 64
faith 139
false memories 23, 62
family structures 109–111
fantasies: Jung 28, 29, 87–88;
        neurotics 108
feeling 80, 185
Feldenkrais, Moshe 40
femininity 84
feminism 59, 84, 120, 144
fictional beliefs 107–108, 113
film set protocols 176, 177
Fischer, Kurt 178
Fitzmaurice, Catherine 40
Fliess, Wilhelm 23
"flow state" 165
Frager, Robert 44, 55–56, 64
Frankl, Viktor 38
free association 60, 61–62, 72–75,
        98–99
Freud, Anna 61–65, 134, 168, 171
Freud, Sigmund 3, 6, 8, 31, 54–76, 112,
        156; activities for actors 65–75;
        Adler and 105; AQAL approach
        170; Brentano's influence on
        18; defenses 62, 63, 64, 70–72;
        developmental lines 171; dreams
        60–61, 85; Erikson and 134, 136,
        141, 144; free association 60,
        72–75, 98; Freudian text analysis
        68–69; history of psychology
        21–26; humanistic psychology
        contrasted with 37–38; id, ego
        and superego 55–56; inner
        experience 190; Jung and 26–28,
        30, 77–78; Maslow and 151,
        154; neo-Freudians 120; stages
        of psychosexual development
        56–60, 64–65, 66–69, 136, 139,
        140; see also psychoanalysis
Fromm, Erich 151
functionalism 20, 26, 31, 152

Gardner, Howard 178
generativity 143, 172
genetics 197–198
genital stage 58, 67–68
Gestalt psychology 151, 152, 154
Gilligan, Carol 178
goals: Adler 107–108, 109, 110, 113,
        115–117; Horney 128–129;
        Maslow 155

Goldstein, Kurt 151
Greeks, ancient 16–17, 45, 200, 201
group therapy 38, 39
growth 199; Adler 113; humanistic
        psychology 37; Jung 81; Maslow
        153, 154, 158; Wilber 168
guilt 140, 145
Gurung, R. A. R. 48

Hall, G. Stanley 20, 24
Hamlet 68–69
Harlow, Harry 36
hierarchy of needs 36, 38, 152–154,
        156, 161–163
Hinduism 43, 170
Hippocrates 16, 183
holism 152
honesty 158
hope 138–139, 145
Horney, Karen 120–133, 156; activities
        for actors 126–132; AQAL
        approach 170; basic anxiety
        121–122; coping strategies
        122–125, 127–128;
        developmental lines 171;
        idealized image 125; influence
        on Maslow 150, 151, 154;
        tyranny of the shoulds 125–126
Hulton, P. 9–10
human potential movement 40
humanistic psychology 35–41, 43, 45,
        189; see also Maslow
humors 16, 183
Hunt, Morton 17, 22
Husserl, Edmund 18
Huxley, Aldous 156–157
hypnosis 21, 22
hypomania 195
hysteria 21–22

"I" perspective 173–174
id 25, 55–56, 57, 58, 77
idealized image 125
identity 135–136, 141–142, 145, 146;
        see also self
identity confusion 141–142, 145, 146
identity crisis 135, 142
imagination 103; see also active
        imagination
imitation 45
India 15–16
individual psychology 105–106
individualism 111
individuation 30, 78, 83, 85, 154
industry 140–141, 145
inferiority 106, 109, 110, 111, 117,
        140–141, 145

205

208

Made in the USA
Columbia, SC
09 February 2022

55776001R10120